The Martyred City

The Martyred City

Death and Rebirth in the Andes

Anthony Oliver-Smith

University of New Mexico Press
Albuquerque

Library of Congress Cataloging-in-Publication Data

Oliver-Smith, Anthony.
The martyred city.

Bibliography: p.
Includes index.
1. Yungay (Ancash, Peru)—History.   2. Earthquakes—
Peru—Yungay (Ancash)   I. Title.
F3611.Y86044   1986   985'.21   85–20974
ISBN 0-8263-0864-3
ISBN 0-8263-0865-1 (pbk.)

Contents

v

Preface and Acknowledgments

In one sense, all ages are catastrophic, in that they all have their calamities and disasters that punctuate the daily lives of people and societies. Some ages, however, seem particularly plagued by suffering and tragedy, and it can be argued that such periods mark the epochal changes in human history. Certainly, the fourteenth century, with its plagues and wars, so grippingly described by Barbara Tuchman in *A Distant Mirror,* comes to mind. Our experience of our own time is equally shadowed not only by our many wars and disasters, but by the possibility of ultimate catastrophe—nuclear holocaust. Ours is indeed a catastrophic age, and this is increasingly reflected in much of our culture.

Many of the disasters that plague our era are much the same as those that have afflicted humankind since our beginnings. Earthquakes, avalanches, droughts, floods, volcanic eruptions, typhoons, hurricanes, and other natural forces have been punishing human society with unhappy consistency throughout our existence. However, incalculable human suffering and destruction have also issued from our inabilities to control our own technology and social relations. In many cases, our technology has allowed us to make vast improvements in our lives, but increasingly, we find that in solving one problem, we create others, often of more difficult and serious consequence than the original.

It might be argued that technosocial disasters are inadvertent, and yet, despite our greater understanding, the despoiling of our life-supporting environments continues relatively unabated in much of the world. Many would claim that the wars which have afflicted this and other centuries have been equally inadvertent. This might be true insofar as we seem only marginally capable of controlling our social interactions on a national or international scale. Our one-sided emphasis on devel-

vii

oping technological solutions for these difficulties without regard for the impact of these solutions has not only created disaster in the natural world, but has turned us into colossally efficient killers of our own species as well. The crowning achievement of our technological perspective, harnessing the atom, has brought us to the edge of the ultimate disaster, the extinction of the planet. In a way, the threat of nuclear war has made us all victims, all homeless, if home is a place where one is safe. In that symbolic sense, disaster threatens to become the mind-set for the planet. We have all been cut off and set adrift from certain traditional forms of security by modern life, but the threat of nuclear war has compounded this by making us all vulnerable to a seemingly blind and impersonal mass destruction. In that sense, then, in our century, as in no other, disaster has become a model for interpreting life. Everyone, not only the millions of disaster victims and war refugees, is now bonded in a catastrophic vision by the threat of nuclear war. The lament of many a disaster victim, "It seemed like the end of the world," has become a real possibility and a universal fear.

Notwithstanding our catastrophic preoccupations, one of the more enduring assumptions in current belief seems to be that disasters are freak occurrences, rare, one in a million, long-shot events in what is otherwise uneventful normality. Actually, the occurrence of disasters is rather more the rule than the exception on a world scale. The second half of the twentieth century seems to have been particularly buffeted by these events, which, if anything, appear to be increasing in both area and severity of impact.

Certainly one point which is immediately observable from disaster statistics of the last half century is the major difference in loss of life between the Western industrialized nations and the developing nations of the Third World. In the last forty years, natural disasters have accounted for approximately two million deaths around the world. Some 85 percent of these deaths occurred in non-Western, nonindustrialized nations. In a sense, those most vulnerable to economic forces are also by circumstances of nature most vulnerable to destruction by disaster. Underdevelopment has compounded both the risk and the destruction of disasters for these people.

This book is about one of those disasters and the tragedy and recovery of such vulnerable people. Although I have described the event itself, my greater concern is to examine those processes of reconstruction of material, social, and psychological life which enable people to recover from major losses of family, community, and culture. It is the story of a small town in the Peruvian Andes which was obliterated by an enormous avalanche on a bright Sunday in May of 1970. Some 300 to 500 people out of a population of 4,500 survived the destruction and burial of the town. The story of these people and their dramatic struggle to survive and rebuild their lives and their community is important, for what it tells us not only about them as a specific group, but also about ourselves as a species and our capacities to deal with the overwhelming circumstances of catastrophe and tragic loss. Their story is a clear and wonderful demonstration of the human capacity to survive. We are not merely the passive pawns of powerful forces, whether they are natural or historical, submitting unquestioningly to conditions beyond our control. While we may not be able to control those forces, we adapt, we alter, struggle, and, often, to use Faulkner's word, prevail. The lessons of this little Peruvian town are then, ultimately, not only how to survive materially and socially, but also how to restore meaning and significance to one's self and one's fellows. This is much more than surviving; it is prevailing. It is a lesson we need desperately to keep in mind in a world which seems increasingly affected by forces that have gone beyond the control of ordinary human beings.

It is through the lives of individuals that much of this story will be told. The names of all these individuals have been changed to safeguard their privacy as much as possible. These people are human beings who have survived the worst that nature or life can throw at anyone. They have known pain in such a way that their lives have been unalterably changed. They have not been necessarily purified or ennobled by the experience, but they have been given a kind of knowledge which tends to put the other problems of life in different perspective. Dickens's words "It was the best of times. It was the worst of times." have often been used to describe disasters. Extreme experiences seem to evoke the extremes of human behavior. There are acts of incredible nobility and heroism, and there are acts of meanness and cowardice. Indeed, if disaster demonstrates anything about human behavior, it is that it brings out both the best and the worst in people, sometimes even in the same person. Yungaínos know this better than most of us. For the most part, the lives of survivors as they struggled to reconstruct display a kind of quiet, dogged courage in meeting the daily challenges and overcoming obstacles made larger by tragedy and deprivation. I do not agree with Somerset Maugham that "suffering for the most part, makes men petty and vindictive." The lives of the survivors of Yungay, in all their humanity, stand as active proof that human beings do not prevail through vindictiveness, but through persistence, understanding, and courage.

To tell this story I have had the help and support of many people, both in the United States and in Peru. The late Anne Bailey came to work with me in Yungay during my first year of fieldwork. She collected a significant portion of the data on which this book is based and mere mention of her here is scant repayment for her help and friendship during that time. Her recent tragic death is a loss to me, to Yungaínos, and to anthropology. A great debt is also owed Barbara Bode, whose own work in the same time and region of Peru as well as our long discussions have contributed much to my understanding of what was taking place in Yungay (Bode 1977). I also owe a great deal to Lynda Kapsch, R.N., whose sensitivity and understanding of the crucial ethical dimensions of relationships between health-care professionals and patients helped me immeasurably in understanding the ethical problems in working with people under stress. The long-term support, guidance, and friendship of Paul Doughty also deserve much more than mere recognition in these pages. Put simply, since my first course in anthropology he has generously guided and nourished my efforts. Any insights in this book on the importance of ritual and symbol in human adaptation to change have issued largely from my lengthy conversations with Dennis Owen, who has my profound gratitude and friendship. I am also deeply grateful to Carol Bates for the insight and understanding that my research on the reconstructive spirit in human affairs does not end with Yungay. Pamela Richards and Rona Mazur read this book in early draft forms, and their helpful comments are truly appreciated. And finally my profound thanks to Faith and the late Richard Martin, who once again opened their home to me for the completion of this book.

This book, and the research on which it is based, could not have been undertaken without the support of the Midwestern Universities Consortium for International Activities for the fieldwork in 1970–71. My fieldwork in 1974 was supported by the University of Florida. The Society for Health and Human Values generously provided funding for a field trip in 1975. The University of Florida again sponsored a short research trip in 1978, and the Center for Latin American Studies at the

University of Florida funded a final field session in 1980. None of my work could have been carried out without the support of these institutions, and they have my sincere gratitude.

In Peru the number of people who contributed greatly to this book is impossible to calculate. Virtually everybody I encountered, from colleagues in Lima and officials in department and provincial capitals, to disaster assistance workers supported and encouraged the project. In particular I would like to thank Lucio Rodomiro Vasquez Giraldo for his continuing help throughout the years of this study. Similarly, the help and support of Luis Rafael Briceño and Betty Hidalgo Rosas made both my life and my study immeasurably more pleasant and easier. Our friendship now goes back twenty years. Research assistance in Yungay was provided by Antógenes Salinas and the fifth-year students (Class of 1971) of the Colegio Santa Inés de Yungay. Their help was invaluable and profoundly appreciated. I thank Isaias Zabaleta Figueroa, Walter Arteaga Losza, and Ricardo Losza Méndez for their generosity with their own materials.

The list of persons to whom I am deeply indebted in Yungay must include nearly the entire community, from its rebirth almost fifteen years ago to the present. In Yungay everybody helped. In a sense, as I think most anthropological studies ultimately are, it has been a collaborative effort. However, more than that, nothing can repay the kindness, hospitality, and cooperation with which the Yungaínos welcomed and sustained me in the midst of their own misery and loss. For all that, such thanks as are offered here are vastly inadequate. Perhaps this book, for which they have been patiently waiting since I first explained to them my presence in Yungay back in October of 1970, will serve as the smallest compensations for what I owe them. They invested a great deal in this project. They all helped me, out of friendship and because they wanted their story to be told. They were all there that Sunday in May fifteen years ago.

Chapter 1
The Death of a City

 May 31, 1970, was clear and warm. Although there had been unusually heavy rains late in the season, the sky on this Sunday was cloudless. The twin snow peaks of Mt. Huascarán overlooking the town of Yungay glistened in the sun against the vibrant blue of the Andean sky. The streets were crowded with Indian peasants going to market: women in black skirts and brilliantly colored blouses, men in black homespun uniforms. Large numbers of outsiders and tourists were in town also. At that moment there were Czechoslovakian and Japanese teams of mountain climbers attempting to scale the north peak of Huascarán.

Sunday in Yungay has always been a day of both activity and rest. The day begins early with masses in the church and the arrival of peasants coming down from their hillside hamlets to church and market. The trucks arrive early from the coast and the larger mountain cities with manufactured goods to sell in the market. The market is a colorful hive of activity from 7:30 in the morning until about 1:00 or 2:00 in the afternoon. Vendors from the coast, bringing everything from long bolts of brightly colored cloth to magical and folk medicinal cures, hawked their wares enthusiastically to townsman and peasant alike. The sound of highland music blared from dozens of tiny transistor radios to compete with the cackle of chickens, the din of barking dogs, the laughter of children, and the general bustle of people engaged in the ultimately social act of marketing. Food cooked over open kerosene stoves and the smell of frying trout from Andean lakes pervaded the market, giving the place an atmosphere of a very busy and crowded outdoor kitchen.

Sunday was also a day when people came from outlying districts and other provinces to visit relatives, and town residents took daytrips into the country. On this particular Sunday Yungay was enjoying all the

1

normal bustle of its market and church and the influx of camera-wielding tourists. Three couples had been married by Father Claudio Lopez that morning between masses. There was an air of expectancy among the children and younger people of the town because after lunch the Verolina Circus would be giving a performance in the walled soccer field on the outskirts of the city. Many of the adults were grateful for the rest from the children that the circus would provide, since a great many of them had been partying until the early hours of May 31 at a dance given by the *Centro Social Yungay* as a reception for the ladies in their membership. In addition, many people planned to listen to the world cup soccer matches which would be broadcast on the radio later in the afternoon from Mexico City.

As the afternoon wore on, the town became quiet. With the children already enjoying the circus in the stadium, adults were relaxing at home or sitting in the sun or in the palm-shaded main plaza. In the plaza a group of tourists were taking pictures of Huascarán, chattering excitedly about the magnificent view which Yungay enjoyed of Peru's highest mountain.

Rosa Martínez was just finishing lunch at home with her sons, Samuel and Juan. Rosa's home was on Galvez Street, up the slope of Shacsha Hill above the main part of the city. From the front door of her five-room adobe house, she had a splendid view of Huascarán, which seemed almost to rise right out of the ridge of Shacsha Hill. The quiet murmur of Santa Rosa Creek which passed next to her house completed a scene of natural beauty and tranquility. As Rosa and Juan finished washing up the last of the lunch dishes in their traditional outdoor kitchen they talked about the possibiity of selling some of the piglets that they were raising in the corral area out behind her restaurant in town. Rosa always had one project or another in the fire. She had started with almost nothing and by sheer determination and energy had carved a niche for herself and her children in Yungay society. Her restaurant did fairly well, and she had been steadily improving her house over the years. From very modest beginnings, her home now had cement floors, electricity, and a single tap for water. The house still lacked an indoor bathroom and a real living room, but they would come in time. While Rosa was not satisfied, she was nonetheless pleased with what she had achieved so far.

Roberto Falcón was chatting by the pumps of his service station with

Dr. Fausto Gutierrez, a Yungaínos lawyer working in the departmental capital of Huaráz, who visited his hometown whenever he could. With his busy legal schedule, Dr. Gutierrez relished escaping Huaráz to spend his Sunday quietly with friends in the lovely surroundings of his birthplace. The drive up the callejón from Huaráz was always pleasant, and there was no better time to visit Yungay than a sunlit Sunday in May. Roberto and Dr. Gutierrez were leisurely discussing the potential of the offer of an automobile dealership which had been proposed to Roberto for Yungay by a major distributor in Lima. Considering the number of cars recently purchased by those enjoying a wave of economic improvements, Roberto was feeling optimistic about the venture. Since Dr. Gutierrez had stopped only for gas for his return trip to Huaráz, Roberto would soon close up to return home for a quiet Sunday afternoon with his wife and young children.

Miguel Mejía, the hatter, had just arrived at his in-laws' house in the outlying hamlet of Pampac with his seven children in tow. The previous Friday, Mrs. Mejía, almost nine months pregnant, had gone to her parents' home for a short visit. Within minutes of her late afternoon arrival in Pampac, her pains had started, and a healthy little girl had been born shortly after midnight. On Sunday, Miguel had struggled through the tasks of getting all seven children fed, to and from mass, and out to Pampac to see their mother and new little sister. Mrs. Mejía's labor had been fairly easy, and she was rapidly regaining strength. A family conference had decided that the new daughter would be named Beatriz. A new child would certainly add to the already great responsibilities that Miguel barely managed to meet, but while his family was one of his greatest worries, it was also one of his greatest joys. The sight of his seven healthy children gathered around their mother with their new daughter at her breast made him very happy.

Alfredo Vasquez, a driver for the interprovincial bus line, Expreso Serrano, was listening to records in a shop with a group of friends. Alfredo was not from Yungay, but he enjoyed taking his days off there because, as he said, "I have friends here, and it's such a nice place." After the fifteen-to-twenty-hour drive up the steep and narrow dirt roads over the Andes, most of it driven by night, Alfredo enjoyed resting in Yungay and visiting his friends in the city before returning to Lima and his family. Asunción Montoya and his wife were relaxing after a Sunday lunch with his parents in the neighboring village of Acobamba just north of the city. Asunción, known to his friends by the Quechua diminutive of "Ashuco," was a primary schoolteacher in Yungay and the chief organizer, and one of the best players, of the province's excellent soccer league. The sounds of the crowd of children at the circus filtered up to the little cottage where Ashuco and his wife and parents relaxed contentedly after a good meal. They chatted quietly as they sat in the warmth of the afternoon sun in the patio.

At 3:23 P.M. the entire north-central area of Peru shuddred under the impact of a massive earthquake. Survivors report that it began with a few seconds of a gentle swaying motion, typical of the kind of tremor that occurs throughout Peru many times a year. The swaying motion was then followed by a violent shaking, which lasted for an estimated forty-five seconds. The shaking had a side-to-side movement making it difficult to walk or run. The adobe buildings of Yungay began to crumble after about fifteen seconds of the heavy tremors. The red roof tiles rained dangerously to the ground as the whitewashed walls of Yungay's houses shook violently in the quake, some of them falling into the streets, some falling inward upon their residents. People were quickly enveloped in debris and clouds of dust thrown up by the shaking earth and the falling buildings. The quake then began a vertical motion and the rain of debris increased. Alfredo Vásquez and his friends raced out of the record shop into the street and were narrowly missed by a collapsing wall. When it became impossible to stand, Vásquez and his three friends knelt, embraced in the street amidst the hail of debris, and awaited death. Roberto Falcón, with Dr. Gutierrez, could barely stand at the service station as the gasoline pumps heaved crazily up and down with the shuddering impact of the quake. Rosa Martínez clasped her sons to her as the walls of her home collapsed around them. On their knees in the chaos of the quake they began to pray. "This is the day of final judgment," she told her sons. As the roof tiles sailed dangerously around them, they crawled into the open space of their patio.

The three Tamaríz brothers and their parents, all close to their home in the village of Yanama Chico high above Yungay, were thrown to the ground by the violent heaving of the earthquake. The air was filled with a great roaring sound. Realizing that Huascarán "was coming," they struggled to their feet and began running up the hillside to higher ground. A ferocious blast of wind toppled them again, and they were pelted by a hail of mud. The wind blew so violently that it stripped the

4

leaves, branches, and even the papery bark from the eucalyptus trees near their house, leaving them standing denuded, "like telephone poles." The Tamaríz family huddled together on the hillside as the world darkened and the avalanche, "roaring like a wild bull," tore down the canyon. It swept high up first one slope and then another as it followed the canyon's broad contours. One wave careened along the slope just below the Tamaríz family and obliterated half of Yanama Chico. The avalanche passed them, sweeping away people, animals, houses, and the green patchwork of fields, leaving behind a pale grey wake of mud. The thundering diminished to a low guttural roar as the avalanche reached the valley floor eight kilometers distant.

Asunción Montoya was on his way home with his wife when the earthquake struck:

When I heard the landslide, I resigned myself to death, but it by-passed Acobamba and hit only part of the stadium. For a moment a sepulchral silence hung over Yungay. It took five or ten minutes before people began to react. For a while everything was visible and then it darkened. We grouped together in a field on Runtu Hill and began to collect food and blankets from the houses in Acobamba within a half an hour. We made a circular shelter in a corn field and there we spent a terrible night. There were continuous strong tremors, and the women began to cry and wail and commend themselves to God. In those moments even the most unbelieving among us set about thinking of a Divine Being.

Many people in Yungay sought shelter in the church, the largest building in town. Others ran from their collapsing houses to the main plaza, hoping to avoid the rain of tiles from the high roofs of the center of town. Still others, all too few, sensed a further danger after the end of the quake and began to run. The tremors had barely ceased when Alfredo Vasquez picked himself up and started running toward the plaza to see if his bus was damaged. Before he had gone very far, he collided with an old man who screamed at him that a landslide was coming and ran toward the cemetery hill, the only high ground close to the center of town. Vasquez heeded the warning and, losing all thought of his vehicle, set out at full speed for the cemetery hill. He said he ran as fast as he had ever run in his life. He had no thoughts; he simply ran, ignoring the screams and moans of the trapped and injured people in the ruins of the city. From behind him he felt a blast of air and a roar, and the sky began raining small stones as he ascended the hill. Although he was not to discover it until much later, his right ear was severed by a flying stone. He could see at the top of the cemetery the gigantic statue of Christ with his arms outstretched to the town below and the mountain above. The walk up the steps was filled with people struggling over the rubble of broken masonry and shattered coffins to gain the uppermost tier of the cemetery under the outstretched arms of the statue of Christ. The remains of the long dead lay strewn grotesquely among the broken coffin planks and destroyed niches. Vásquez was enveloped to his waist in the icy mud of the huge avalanche which had swept away the town behind him before he was able to struggle to safety at the feet of the statue. He was pulled out of the mud by someone he did not know and never saw again. Nor did he ever see again the old man who had warned him of the avalanche in town.

Juan Beltrán, the mayor of Yungay, was at home in the suburban area of Aura just south of the city limits when the tragedy struck. Five of his six children were walking through Yungay on the way to the circus. They never arrived. After the quake, he and his wife ran from the house into the street.

Then I remembered the servant girl. . . . She was feeding the ducks in the garden. I ran to the garden and worked open the door and the wall which had fallen and we got her out. It took us a minute. Then we began running to town for my children and . . . down came the avalanche . . . it sounded like thousands of airplanes. We came upon a father and son embraced. They said that they saw the avalanche coming and waited for death together. It passed ten meters away from them, and they were unharmed. If we had not stopped to help our servant, we would have reached Yungay and been killed by the landslide.

Antonio "Mala Noche" was not so detained. He remembered all too well the horror of the Ranrahirca avalanche of 1962. Since Aura was much closer to the old avalanche path of Ranrahirca, he reasoned that Yungay would be safer. Even before the quake had ceased its shuddering, he was making his way to what he thought was the safety of Yungay. As the avalanche roared down upon Shacsha Hill, it split into two lobes, one over Yungay and one over Ranrahirca, sparing Aura in between. "Mala Noche" had left Aura and reached Yungay just as it was buried.

Miguel Mejía, surrounded by his entire family in Pampac, could only stand in awe and terror as he watched the city of Yungay being devoured in a matter of seconds. The avalanche, preceded by its guttural roar and the hail of stones, rose suddenly to a tremendous height, writhing like a thing alive, as it appeared over Yungay's protective Shacsha Hill and then crashed down upon the city, its grey mass spreading out fanlike as it destroyed the city, ravaging ever more as its borders widened.

Antonio Flores, who had been at the Club Social Yungay when the earthquake hit, actually saw the enormous block of ice break away from the north peak of Huascarán and fall a full mile before crashing into the glacier below and jarring loose more millions of tons of ice and rock. The awesome sight of that plummeting mass filled him with terror. As soon as the quake had stopped and he was able to run, he set off toward the hills north of the city. Others, like Alfredo Vásquez, but still all too few, began racing toward the cemetery hill. Antonio's way was blocked by the mountains of rubble of fallen buildings. Antonio ran, mute and deaf to the cries of the trapped and injured within the vast ruins of the city. "Impelled by the instinct of survial, I forgot in that moment all human sentiments of compassion," he said. He never looked back (Zavaleta Figueroa 1970:13). His flight took him toward Cochahuaín. As he ran, the earth shuddered with the impact of the avalanche, and "a sound like the roaring of thousands of wild bulls" filled his ears. A howling wind created by the air displacement of the avalanche hurled millions of tiny pieces of broken stone ahead of it which sparked and flashed as they hit in the city suddenly darkened by clouds of grey dust. When he reached Cochahuaín he turned to look behind him. Yungay was gone and in its place was an expanse of grey viscous mud. He could see four palm trees where the main plaza had been, the mud lapping around their trunks, as though still hungry for the last morsel.

Roberto Falcón and Dr. Gutierrez also saw the landslide fall from the glacier of Huascarán. Roberto relates:

Dr. Gutierrez said, "We've got to escape." I began to run to my house. My wife and children were there. I had to save them. Before going far, I met Julio Vasquez and Enrique Figueroa. They shouted to me that there was no salvation for my wife and my children or for anyone, that everything was over for us. I turned to run back to the station. Enrique and Julio died on the way to the cemetery. As I made my way back, Dr. Gutierrez saw me and picked me up in his car and we began to drive out of town. In that instant, Señora Ofelia de Giraldo, who had escaped the collapse of her house, begged me to help. I grabbed her and her two children and threw them into the car. As we started out again, Felipe Navarro, the schoolteacher, ran alongside of the car and dived in the window. He grabbed Sra. de Giraldo's kids and we held onto him. As we reached the outskirts of town, I could see the mud coming and the road was blocked by fallen houses. The mud kept coming but through the dust we could see that a big truck [which had come up to market from Chimbote] was slamming its way through the debris. The truck opened the way, and we followed it through to safety here in Pashulpampa.

When Roberto Falcón, Dr. Gutierrez, Felipe Navarro, Sra. de Giraldo, and her children reached the area known as Pashulpampa, just north of the city in the protection of 4,000-meter Atma Hill, they abandoned their car and began to climb the slopes. When they were halfway up the hill, they heard the roar of the avalanche as it coursed down the river toward Caraz and Huallanca, the towns immediately north of Yungay. Roberto and Dr. Gutierrez took some other people to Pashul-pama and, after leaving them in the safety of the high ground, they began walking back along the hill toward Yungay. Roberto relates:

The dust of the earthquake had been [momentarily] cleared away by the landslide and we could see. The doctor did not look. Dr. Gutierrez asked me what I saw and I said, "Doctor, Yungay has disappeared and all you can see are four palm trees, and Yungay has forty-eight, and this cannot be because my wife and four children are there. . . ." Dr. Gutierrez then looked and said, "You are right . . . there is the cemetery, but its shape has been changed." Then we began to walk toward Yungay, thinking how many brothers needed our help.We had gone 400 meters but then the dust came up and everything darkened, and we were afraid. We fought against our fear but lost. We went back to the people we had left in the pampa. We began building huts out of corn stalks, in which to pass the night. Up to this point, at six o'clock, I had not cried. We made three huts for 15 people. There were people in shock. The owner of the field where we were, Julio Figueroa—he had been trapped in the mud with a broken spine—he told us to take all that we needed.

As soon as the shaking ceased, Rosa and her two sons heard a sound from the east like a dynamite explosion. They struggled through the rubble of their house to the street and began running up the hill toward Aura. They had just crossed the bridge over the Santa Rosa Creek when they met Dr. Dueñas, fleeing toward Yungay from Aura. "Don't go, the danger is there! Come along here!" he screamed. They hesitated briefly, undecided what to do. But it was already too late. As they began to return toward Yungay, they were hurled to the ground by a tremendous blast of wind, and the air was filled with a deafening roar. Rosa struggled to her feet and turning toward Juan, who had two-year-old Samuel in his arms, screamed at him to follow her. That moment was the last she ever saw them. The avalanche buried Samuel and Juan forever. When the avalanche careened over her, Rosa felt a sudden crushing weight on her chest, and then she blacked out. Somewhat later she came to briefly, struggling to breathe against the horrible pressure surrounding her body. She was completely buried except for the lower part of her face in the frigid mud. She felt the cold seep into her body, even to her heart. "This must be death," she thought. Not realizing that she had been swept more than a mile by the avalanche, she felt that her sons were somewhere nearby. She thought she was still near her house on Shacsha Hill. The entire right side of her body was numb, but her left arm was bleeding and in great pain. Still enveloped in darkness and struggling to breathe, she coughed to clear her mouth and throat of the foul mud. As though from the depths of a dream or from a long distance, she heard two voices. "This one moves. Clean her mouth." Two men began to clean the mud from her head and shoulders. She felt them tie a rope around her waist. When they pulled her half-naked body from the icy mud, the agonies caused by the movement caused her to pass out again. She awoke again when they began to bathe the mud from her body at the edge of the avalanche. The pain became so intense she begged them to let her die. She lost and regained consciousness many times. During the night she remembers a man building a small fire of brush near her to keep her warm, his seated figure only dimly perceived in the shadows thrown by the fire as he kept vigil for her through the cold Andean night (Zavaleta Figueroa 1970:40).

Chapter 2
Disaster:
Event and Experience

 On that afternoon of May 31, 1970, a massive earthquake struck Peru, killing thousands of people and devastating an area larger than Belgium and Holland combined. The focus of this natural holocaust was the city of Yungay, a small provincial capital in a high valley of the north-central Andes. The earthquake that struck Peru on that Sunday afternoon has been recorded as the worst natural disaster in the history of the Western Hemisphere and among the worst natural disasters in the world. It registered 7.7 on the Richter scale and affected an area of about 83,000 square kilometers. It claimed approximately 70,000 lives, injured 140,000 people, and destroyed or damaged more than 160,000 buildings, roughly 80 percent of the buildings in the area. Over 500,000 people were left homeless, and the lives of approximately three million others were affected. Economic losses surpassed half a billion dollars. In addition to homes, industries, public buildings, roads, railroads, bridges, and schools, electrical, water, sanitary, and communications facilities were also destroyed or seriously damaged. Forty-five seconds of the earthquake obliterated many of the slow, tortuous steps taken toward economic development in both highland and coastal areas. One hundred and fifty-two provincial cities and towns and over 1,500 peasant villages were seriously damaged or destroyed.

In Yungay the earthquake shook loose a slab of ice and rock about 800 meters wide and 1.2 kilometers long from the sheer northwest face of Huascarán, Peru's highest mountain. This mass, with a volume of a million cubic meters, fell on Glacier 511 where it picked up more material, growing perhaps to twenty-five million cubic meters of material. This immense mass of ice, mud, and rock careened down the mountainside at a velocity varying between 217 and 435 kilometers per hour. As it moved, it picked up huge masses of morainal material and hurled thousands of boulders, some weighing thousands of tons, down into the valley. Heat generated by the friction of the swiftly moving avalanche melted glacial ice, creating a gigantic, churning flow of mud and rock. The momentum of the slide carried it the sixteen kilometers from its origins on Huascarán to the valley floor in four minutes. The avalanche developed three separate lobes as it extended itself over the lower parts of the valley and into the river. These lobes spread across an area of about twenty square kilometers, including Yungay and many other smaller communities in the general vicinity, as well as the powerlines for the valley and several miles of highway. It was owing primarily to the extreme velocity of the avalanche that Yungay was buried. The smaller lobe of the avalanche over the city was formed when the mass of ice, rock, and mud hurtled over the ridge, some 200 meters high, that separated Yungay from the main lobe of the landslide. Eyewitnesses report seeing a "wall of debris as high as a ten-story building" rushing down on the town. All that remained of Yungay some four minutes after the earthquake had ceased its tremors were four palm trees where the main plaza had been, a few tiny groups of survivors huddled in various protected locations in the high ground close to the city, and an immense expanse of grey, viscous mud, punctuated by huge boulders which appeared to grow in size as the mud settled around them in the days that followed. The thickness of the mud in Yungay about a month after the tragedy was estimated at five meters. The total volume of ice, mud, rock, and water which descended that day from Huascarán upon Yungay, Ranrahirca, and the Santa River is estimated to be approximately fifty million cubic meters (Erickson, Plafker, and Fernandez Concha 1970:1–12).

This book is about the destruction of Yungay and the survivors' efforts to rebuild their lives in a refugee camp not far from their original homes. It is both story and study of human survival. The story is meant to convey a sense of what life was like for those who worked to reconstruct their community, while the study documents and analyzes the sociocultural processes that people use to adapt to overwhelming forces of destruction and change.

Although the horror and suffering of the Yungay disaster took place in a specific time and place under specific historical conditions, it must be understood within the broader context of rapid and potentially dislocating social change. In the last two centuries we have witnessed the disruption and destruction of numerous societies with consequent social dislocation and appalling human suffering. Most of these changes are not the result of natural disaster, but regardless of the source of rapid social change, the process involves common elements and problems for those whose lives are disrupted. The Yungay survivors' attempts to forge a new, meaningful existence in the face of almost total destruction of their town may tell us a great deal about how people cope with and adapt successfully to massive social change.

Earthquakes, avalanches, floods, volcanic eruptions, plagues, famines, droughts, typhoons, hurricanes, and other natural disasters have afflicted human society with unhappy consistency throughout history. In the last thirty years alone there have been over 800 major disasters, and the number of high mortality disasters has increased in the last decade, in part due to larger concentrations of population (Dworkin n.d.:2).

But what is a disaster? The word itself has many connotations that admit little definitional precision. A common dictionary definition states that a disaster is "a calamitous event, esp. one occurring suddenly and causing great damage or hardships" (Urdang 1968:377). However, even when the term has a specific reference, disaster may have a variety of meanings, referring alternately to the "agent" (the earthquake, fire, hurricane, etc.), the impact inflicted by the agent, or the evaluation of the impact (for example, "conditions in the postimpact situation are disastrous"). The agent itself is not enough to define a disaster. A hurricane at sea is not seen as a disaster unless there are ships and human lives involved. A disaster involves two elements: a natural (or man-made) phenomenon and a human population. What really constitutes a disaster, then, is the combination of a destructive agent and a group of human beings; all demographic, biological, social, cultural, infrastructural, and ecological aspects are affected.

Disaster, therefore, concerns us with a situation or set of conditions in which a population finds itself. Because of the nature of their environment some populations are at greater risk than others. Some societies, whose traditional hazard management techniques have been adequate, have been placed at greater risk by political economic factors beyond their control. The recent drought and famine in the Sahelian region of Africa illustrates how external political economic forces undermined the internal capacities of drought management and were as responsible as the natural forces for the catastrophic famine and permanent environmental destruction that occurred (Glantz 1976).

Consequently, a disaster occurs when a natural phenomenon brings damage or loss to the major social, organizational, and physical facilities of a community to the degree that the essential functions of the society are interrupted or destroyed, resulting in individual stress and social disorganization of varying severity. In disasters, therefore, we are dealing with a novel set of conditions for which the community is relatively unprepared; and the relative balance between individual and social needs and their satisfactions is lost. Since the disaster damages or destroys the society's ability to provide for the needs of its members, new arrangements or adjustments have to be formulated for the society to continue functioning as an entity. Therefore, any discussion of a disaster and its effects on a community must consider the issues of adaptation and change as well as the drama of impact.

The Yungay disaster was not only a massively destructive force, leaving death and human agony in its wake, but the cause of overwhelming change for the surviving population as well. The idea of massive, rapid change may at least partially explain the human fascination with the catastrophic, or ultimately the apocalyptic, vision. For example, revolution overturning power structures, sweeping away the old, reorganizing human relationships in a new order, grips our imaginations intensely. Despite our fascination with catastrophic change, and no matter how overwhelming the forces for that change may be, the human capacity for major change requires time and develops slowly. Indeed, even a far-reaching revolution is often the final event of processes which have been at work for decades, or even centuries. While important people may fall from power rapidly and new laws are promulgated by instant decree, the modes of life, the social relations, norms, and values, the rules of the game—the foundation of individual and social life—are not as easily nor as rapidly changed. The traditional means of ordering existence— the regulation of social and economic interaction, the family, the relationship between human and cosmos—generally alter much more slowly than we imagine. Thus, we must tread cautiously in our attempts to understand and analyze the effects of a force as cataclysmic as the Yungay avalanche, which altered irrevocably the physical and social realities of a community in a few scant minutes. If the goal of any scientific endeavor is to reveal the underlying structures of reality, then it is necessary to grasp that the time dimensions of social change are much slower and its processes far more complex than our fascination with the apocalyptic vision has led us to believe (Bell 1979:8).

Why this is so is an issue that lies at the very core of human existence. I use as a point of departure the premise that human beings act out their lives in terms of a perceptual framework that tells them both how the world is (the nature of reality) and how the world ought to be. Anthropologists label this framework the "culture" of a group, and one anthropologist, Anthony F. C. Wallace, has coined the term *mazeways* to describe variation in the ways a culture is understood by its individual members (Wallace 1956a:266). Our perceptual frameworks are dynamic syntheses of the material conditions of existence and our understandings of them. Each of these elements builds upon the other through a complex dialectical process. This means that material conditions and events are partly a function of the way we understand them. Our understandings guide the action that we take in response to material wants, and these actions produce new realities (material events) and ways of understanding that, in turn, guide our next action. Synthesis produces consistent but constantly evolving perceptual frameworks (cultures). In the dynamics of its relationship to objective reality, culture carries the human potential for creating, molding, and resisting change. Human adaptation, then, is a dialectic between materiality and the meanings we assign to it (Handwerker 1980:1).

Human existence reflects the ability to reason, to use the knowledge gained from past experience to act on the present, and to predict and respond to the demands of the future. Life unfolds through time and is never a precise repetition of the past. Nevertheless, it involves a "normal" cycle of events, a certain patterned consistency of problems faced and solutions implemented. The mundane tasks of living are usually predictable, and the mundane solutions to familiar problems are used over and over again because they are time-tested. It is this predictability that allows us not only to act but also to understand, to make sense of reality, to see a logic through our own sets of categories and thereby both understand and shape experience for our future and continued understanding. In essence, we need our past. We are dependent upon it for understanding our present and for molding and adapting to our future, whatever uncertainties it may hold.

Thus, our past allows us to adapt and change, but the change takes a form based on the known, repetitive pattern of events of our basic social institutions, which Paul Bohannan has called "event systems" (1963:360). These event systems are cyclical in the sense that we face variations of similar and recurring problems and respond with adjustments of known solutions. We alter our solutions to respond to the presentation of variation in similar problems. Our past reveals to us patterns of problems and of solutions; these patterns constitute the basis of "normal" or processual social change.

Never is this past so necessary as when the normal cycle of events is interrupted. When historical events disrupt our patterns of predictable, institutionalized events, we either adjust our social processes to the new conditions or we do not survive. We can see an important distinction here between normal social processes of change and history. In Bohannan's schema, history is a noncyclical lineal sequence of nonrecurring events, each event affecting the development of subsequent events. The distinction between recurrent and nonrecurrent events is, in part, the essence of change. Many disasters, which are the events of history rather than process, are unpredictable and potentially disruptive to society and its characteristic event systems. Historical events may change the cycle of the event system, leading to new adjustments, which, in turn, lead to new repetitive event systems (Bohannan 1963:360). The point here is that disaster is rarely part of process. It is history, and the aftermath of disaster is social process, based on past knowledge, coming to grips with history. Consequently, when people are struck by a disaster, their responses are founded on understandings from the past, not exclusively on the new and unique conditions of an afflicted present.

The study of rapid, massive change resulting from the events and processes of history rather than event systems focuses not on the event as much as on the relationship between the old and new event structures and the passage which people must negotiate between the two. Our responses to change are always innovative but are set within the parameters specified by our perceptual frameworks, and these are a function of our pasts. This dependence on past understanding gives traditional ways of acting their power. It is hardly surprising that when people are faced with catastrophic change, many of their actions appear to be attempts to reconstitute the social patterns and institutions of the past. But this "traditionalism" does not necessarily mean that people inten-

16

tionally or unintentionally resist change out of some stubborn refusal to participate in a new world or a transformed social order.

I do not mean to suggest that human beings faced with change must by nature resist and can be dragged only reluctantly into new circumstances. Instead, the event structure, the repetitive pattern of institutionalized social events must be predictable to actors if they are to undertake planned, rational action. This predictability comes only from the understandings that are structured from the past. People will embrace change if they have a sense of understanding it or a degree of control over it. In situations of massive change, people will attempt to gain understanding of or control over changed conditions by structuring them in terms of familiar concepts and working out new solutions to new problems with tested understandings from the past.

I think it is important to recognize that such a process is both difficult and fraught with ambivalence because it may involve not only a venture into uncharted waters, but also the loss of familiar meanings and symbols as well as the acquisition of new ones. Successful adaptation to change then requires innovative behavior and reformulation and reinterpretation of past knowledge to render present contexts meaningful. Meaning becomes as essential a concept as adaptive success in change. A continuity of meaning, tying what may be a lost or disappearing past and a confusing, bewildering present to a frighteningly uncertain future, becomes the basic element in the successful adaptation to changed circumstances. In this context, the human propensity to defend the predictability of life, or what Peter Marris has termed "the conservative impulse" is crucial to any adaptation to change (Marris 1975). Without this continuity of meaning, the thread that ties past, present, and future into a comprehensible whole, we are unable to interpret what events mean to us or to explore new kinds of experience, new modes of being and acting, which enable us to survive in our altered environment with any degree of confidence. The past is a necessary element in the present, necessary for our efforts to impose a structure of logic on altered circumstances. It is crucial for creating and coping with change.

The people of Yungay, then, must be seen as involved in a struggle to link their destroyed past to their present misery and insecure future. Yungay is the real name of a real place. It would be pointless to employ a fictitious name for a town which a little more than a decade ago appeared on the front pages of the world's major magazines and newspapers. The surviving Yungaínos want their story to be told; they would protest vigorously if I were to employ a fabricated name for their community. They are acutely aware of the sense of tragedy and drama in their history and the unique role which they and their community played in the worst natural disaster in the history of the Western Hemisphere. They are proud of having survived nature's onslaughts and the subsequent efforts to move them from their homeland. Their struggle to survive as a community has become a deeply felt aspect of Yungaíno identity. For them, their town, its destruction, and its subsequent rebirth have come to symbolize their sense of continuity through history and their own personal refusal to surrender. In Yungay, a phrase heard often was "I am a survivor! An authentic Yungaíno!" The determination of the survivors to found and maintain a new Yungay, albeit one of vastly different appearance, near the avalanche which buried their old community, constitutes a refusal to allow part of their identity and their culture to die. Theirs is a history and culture of survival and persistence in the face of natural and social threat. They struggled to preserve the existence and the identity of their community because it was a real and tangible part of individual identity on a personal as well as a collective basis.

I have been writing about this disaster-stricken community for several years now, but the task has had more than its share of false starts. The difficulty lies in the fact that Yungay is a compelling human story as well as an important context for the study of human adaptation and social change. In academic disciplines, scientific treatises are normally written quickly, and experiential accounts come later when one is in a more contemplative frame of mind. In my case, this tactic ended in frustration. I could not divorce the analytic from the experiential without doing violence to both. This is the case more frequently in anthropology than many would care to admit. What I experienced at Yungay in the aftermath of the avalanche is inextricably bound up with my own understanding of the survivors' reactions and responses. My description of the flow of events and our actions constitutes a narrative. It is only out of this personal narrative and my interpretation of the Yungaínos' experience that an analysis of human adaptation and social change can be constructed.

I first came to know Yungay in the summer of 1966 as a student in the Cornell-Peru field school in the Callejón de Huaylas, the valley where the city was located. The valley lies between two massive chains of the Andes which run through the heart of Peru. On the west are the rugged mountains of the Cordillera Negra (black range) and on the east the magnificent Cordillera Blanca (white range), whose ragged and sharply angled peaks are perpetually snowcapped. The whole valley, some eighty miles long, is dominated by the twin summits of Huascarán, Peru's highest mountain at 22,190 feet. The city of Yungay was located at the base of Huascarán. It was here that I began my first real field experience in anthropology researching local folklore. I spent the summer traveling around the valley in trucks, climbing up to the more remote peasant villages by foot, and interviewing (and frightening) people all over the valley with incessant and not terribly subtle questions about the *pishtaco*. The *pishtaco* is a figure in Indian folklore, a night-prowling marauder who murders Indian peasants for profit. He is the classic ogre, a large man, white or mestizo, who wears a leather jacket, boots, and a broad-brimmed hat. All in all, I came fairly close to fitting the description. My research topic nearly got me stoned out of one peasant community so distant that few outsiders had ever ventured there, and my questions evoked unbridled hilarity among sophisticated townfolk. They would literally double up with laughter at the thought of this green gringo, who certainly looked like a *pishtaco,* sauntering into Indian peasant villages to ask them questions about *pishtacos.* In short, it was an active and adventure-filled first field experience. At the end of the summer I was determined to return and study some other aspect of the area.

In the summer of 1969, I was ready to begin dissertation research on the Yungay market as a mechanism of ethnically differentiated social mobility. A series of circumstances forced a change of plans, and I postponed the research for a year. Had I not reluctantly decided to postpone my research, both my wife and myself would have been in Yungay the day the city was obliterated. We did not receive the news about Yungay immediately. Late in the evening of May 31, the news of the earthquake began arriving in the United States, but it was not until June 4 that I heard what had happened in Yungay. The news hit me hard, not only because the tragedy was so immense. I knew that I had lost many friends. Although I could no longer carry out my original research plans, I decided to return as soon as possible to the Yungay area, or to what was left of it. This time my topic would be the study of disaster and social change.

At the time I had little idea what this research would entail. A quick reading of the sociological and geographical literature revealed mostly short-term, "in-and-out" studies emphasizing individual, group, and organizational behavior during impact and the immediate aftermath of disaster. Almost all the studies were done either in Europe or North America. At that time very few anthropologists had analyzed the sociocultural aspects of natural disasters, although Anthony F. C. Wallace's work on cultural crises laid the groundwork for a productive theory of the effects of sociocultural disintegration (Wallace 1956a, 1956b, 1957). Apart from an early study of the long-term social effects of a munitions ship explosion (Prince 1920), a hurricane (Bates et al. 1963), and a volcanic eruption (Schwimmer 1969), there was little relevant material for my research on reconstruction and social change after disaster. Certainly nothing within my own experience prepared me for life in a disaster zone.

By the time I arrived in Yungay in October of 1970, the rehabilitative system which the Yungaínos came to consider such a fiasco was well under way. Transportation facilities had been restored, and aid, commerce, and people had resumed the normal flow of movement between highlands and coast. Consequently, it was no major problem for me to get to Yungay to begin work. After a short stay in Lima to tend to bureaucratic requirements for fieldwork in Peru, I threw my gear together in a pack and boarded a late afternoon bus for the Callejón de Huaylas. Since the Lima area had suffered relatively little in the quake, the first leg of the all-night journey to the callejón did not reveal much of the devastation. As night fell, the cramped interior of the green and orange Expreso Serrano bus and the jolting ride over hastily repaired mountain dirt roads convinced me that sleep would be impossible. During the trip I learned a great deal about the effect of the earthquake from the driver and my fellow passengers. Even four months after the disaster it was almost the sole topic of conversation among the highland residents returning to their devastated valley. We reached the remains of the city of Huaráz at the southern end of the valley at dawn, and the full impact of the destructive force of the earthquake became immediately apparent. The morning was cold and clear, and the immense piles of dust-colored rubble of what had once been a city of 40,000 people dominated one's vision. Fully half of Huaráz's population had perished in the earthquake, crushed by the falling walls of the traditional adobe buildings. Bodies were still being found amidst the rubble, and the stench of rotting flesh was still faintly in the air.

We stopped only briefly in Huaráz before heading up the valley to Yungay and points north. In Huaráz we had picked up Don Epifanio Bellido, a part-owner of the bus company and a resident of old Yungay. After being introduced to Don "Epicho" by the driver whom I had talked with much of the night, I questioned him about the present state of the Yungaíno survivor camp located in the place called Pashulpampa. Don Epicho politely but firmly corrected me, stating emphatically that the camp was no longer called Pashulpampa, but Yungay. He went on to insist that the new city and capital of Yungay would remain in the camp located next to the avalanche which had buried the old city. He told me vehemently that a town meeting in the camp had just recently been forcefully disbanded by the police because the people had been protesting the rumor that the provincial capital was to be removed to Tingua, some fifteen kilometers to the south. Don Epicho was howling mad about this and went to great efforts to explain the injustice, the bad economics, and the general lack of logic in the government's plans. "We have everything. Tingua has nothing. We have all the resources that old Yungay had. We have land. We have water. We have over fifty peasant communities surrounding the camp. Just think of that as 'human capital!' Tingua has none of this!"

Nothing that Don Epicho said, however, prepared me for the sight of the avalanche. The road to Yungay followed a winding course up and down many hills through the eastern slopes of the valley and through many villages and towns, each one displaying the grievous scars of the earthquake. Houses that had not succumbed immediately to the violent quaking were shot through with cracks and fissures and were dangerously unstable and uninhabitable. The countryside was dotted with the colors of tents of all descriptions, where most people had been living for the four months since the disaster. Immediately before reaching Yungay the road passes through the adjoining suburban community of Aura. Yungay cannot be seen except from the hill at the end of Aura's main street. The immensity of the tragedy strikes with the impact of a sudden blast of cold wind in the face, as one's gaze sweeps across the moonscape of the avalanche scar. The immense expanse of grey-crusted mud extends

21

over twenty-two square kilometers, completely covering the slope where the town was located. The surface was rough, pock-marked, and cratered where the mud had sunk into the hollows of the terrain. There was the impression of motion conveyed by the sweep and flow of the slide over the slope. The vastness of the scar was interrupted here and there by huge boulders, weighing many tons and some standing over twenty feet high, and the four lone palm trees next to the ruins of the church tower were the only visible remains of the city. The trunks of the palm trees were muddied much higher up than the level of the ground, indicating how much the mud had sunk since the disaster.

As I crested that hill in Aura, confronting for the first time the enormity of the devastation, I saw clustered in the distance near the palm trees a group of thirty to forty people. By chance I had arrived on October 28, the anniversary of the political foundation of the province of Yungay. The people had gathered by the palm trees in the avalanche to listen to a number of speeches by local leaders. As I got off the bus and moved toward the group, I was to hear for the first time a phrase which would be repeated over and over during my time in Yungay. "No nos han dado nada!" (They have given us nothing!) This allegation was always stated with a bitterness which hid none of the alienation and disdain the people held for the reconstruction authorities of the dev- astated zone. The phrase reveals a problem which plagues and exacerbates the relations between victims and aiders in every disaster, that of different perceptions of need and loss.

The road across the avalanche scar then climbed still another low rise behind which was located the refugee camp of the survivors of Yungay. The camp is only about 700 meters north of the site of the buried city. My first impression of the camp was of a disordered collection of bright green and yellow tents, straw mat shacks, and lean-tos strewn about the gentle slope of a hill called Atma which then abruptly rises to a height of over 4,000 meters. The area was considered safe from further landslides. The camp was nestled in a triangle created by the alluvial fans of the peaks of Huascarán on the south and Huandoy on the north. Atma Hill effectively blocks Huascarán from view, but Huan- doy's beautiful and imposing presence peers over the northern slope of Atma.

After this quick view of the camp, I decided to return to Mancos to look up Lucio Vasquez, a close friend of many anthropologists in the callejón for many years. I was hoping to stay with Lucio until I could find a place to live in Yungay. Lucio's house in Mancos had been seriously damaged, and he and his mother and daughter were living in the garden where there were a couple of the ever-present green and yellow tents and the camper cabin of his pick-up truck, in which Lucio slept. The Vasquez family, like virtually everybody I met in the devastated area, welcomed me warmly and offered me the hospitality of their home, apologizing profusely for the conditions in which the disaster had left them.

While staying with Lucio in Mancos, I managed to visit a number of the communities of the Yungay area. A few days after my arrival I traveled some fifteen kilometers north to visit the city of Caraz where the reconstruction authorities had set up an office. I had a rather lengthy interview with the regional supervisor. It was late in the afternoon with a rainstorm threatening ominously over the clouded peaks of the Cordillera Blanca when I finally set out to hitch a ride back to Mancos. Traffic in the callejón, particularly in those days so soon after the disaster, ebbed rapidly after five o'clock in the afternoon, and I had some trouble getting a ride. Finally a Peace Corps truck picked me up just as the rain began to fall in great wind-swept sheets across the valley floor. By the time we reached Yungay, night had fallen and the rain had made driving almost impossible. We passed through Yungay and up over the avalanche with difficulty. The rain continued to fall in torrents as we made our way through Aura and out onto the Ranrahirca lobe of the avalanche, to cross the hastily erected Bailey Bridge over the Ranrahirca River into Mancos.

The roar of the wind and the pounding of the rain on the truck's cabin effectively muffled any sounds we might have heard, but when we arrived at the bridge, we found only the end posts and twisted girders illuminated in the dim shafts of our headlights. An avalanche had followed the river's course and had taken out the bridge, probably moments before our arrival. There was nothing to do but turn back. The Peace Corps volunteer who drove suggested that I stay in Cochahuaín with an Irish volunteer worker named Bill O'Neill, who was organizing an aid program in the area for the many children orphaned by the disaster. Cochahuaín was the suburb immediately to the north of Yungay. The avalanche had arrived literally at the back walls of the southernmost houses of the community but had not damaged them

23

severely. The earthquake, however, had seriously weakened most of the houses, and the community was now totally abandoned. Bill was living in a large house which had been abandoned by its owners because the avalanche had pushed in the wall of its backyard.

We slowly negotiated our way down the muddy roads to Cochahuaín and the one house showing the dim light of a candle through the rain. Once there Bill welcomed me and offered a cot, a blanket, and a kerosene lantern in one of the back rooms of the house. The rain continued to pour down as I settled myself for the night, plagued by misgivings about the storm, the destroyed bridge, the house, the avalanche, and the murderous mountain lurking high in the clouds beyond that battered back wall. The misgivings rapidly became outright fear as I lay there in the dim light of the kerosene lamp, listening to the rain. My great fear was that the torrential rains would swell the glacial lakes between Huascarán and Huandoy and create a flash flood or another avalanche. The rain persisted, and my anxiety grew more acute as the hours passed. Sleep was impossible. Finally, sometime around 3:00 in the morning, the rain stopped and I breathed a sigh of relief and muttered something to myself about getting some sleep after all. I could not have been far from dropping off when a dull crunching sound issued from the mountain. I lay there in the velvety darkness, my heart pounding in my temples, now completely awake again. It had been a *derrumbe,* the detachment of a piece of the glacier from its matrix and its short and essentially inconsequential fall down the glacier's face. I did not know that then.

In the remaining hours of the night, I heard five more *derrumbes* from Huascarán. I slept very little that night. I arose haggard and drawn at about seven to find Bill, ever the cheerful Irishman, bright and refreshed from a good night's sleep, making tea for us both. I queried him about the noises from the mountain and expressed my total astonishment that he could contemplate living in such a location. He explained that the *derrumbes* were frequent occurrences and did not seem to be of major concern. I was not convinced. After my cup of tea and a bit more cheery conversation from this incurable optimist, who, by this time, I was convinced was totally out of his mind, I set off on foot across the avalanche to return to Mancos.

The morning was cool and clear with only a trace of clouds drifting about the face of Huascarán. The sun still could not be seen behind the towering mountains, but it etched a golden border on the snow peaks. The avalanche and the valley as a whole seemed to glow in the gentle irridescence of dawn. As I crossed the Yungay lobe of the avalanche slowly, uneasily taking in my surroundings, I began to have serious doubts about whether I was psychologically equipped to handle research in such an environment. I had not even spoken to the victims of the tragedy and already my mind was filled with the terrifying images of death and destruction in that beautiful environment. Picking my way over the crusty surface of the avalanche, I realized that it was littered with light debris, newspapers, articles of clothing, a medicine bottle, chunks of wood, a mattress corner, its ticking spilling from a tear, poked up through the surface of the encrusted mud. These tattered remnants were the evidence of the life that had perished that day in Yungay.

By the time I had returned to Lucio's house, I had recovered a bit of my spirits and had decided that I would grit my teeth and stick it out in the callejón. I had no idea of what awaited me in this "valley of death," as the callejón was being called in those days, but nobody had ever done this kind of disaster research in anthropology before, particularly with the predisaster experience that I had.

Later in the day, Lucio and I crossed the avalanche again to Pashulpampa. The camp was bustling that day, filled with people moving about the market area of shacks and lean-tos and among the tents, which extended up the hill beyond the road. The restaurants strung out along the road were filled with people eating and drinking, and the straw shack market was alive with the colorful dress of the Indian peasants who had come to town for marketing. People stood in front of the shack stores or restaurants, leisurely conversing, while others strolled along the road marking the western edge of the camp. The whole atmosphere was strangely disconcerting. The only thing to indicate that these people were the survivors of one of the worst disasters in recorded history was the tents. I do not know what I really expected, but this impression was soon dispelled.

Lucio and I entered a restaurant made of lashed eucalyptus logs and woven straw mats to get some lunch. Several groups of people sat at bright blue tables, eating and drinking. We sat at an outside corner table so we could talk and watch the general activity of the town as well. After we had ordered food and beer, Lucio was recognized and greeted by several friends. One of these friends was a Yungaíno, a survivor of

25

the avalanche. He had been drinking at another table when he noticed us enter the restaurant. He was quite drunk, and when told that I was going to live in the camp, he insisted on buying us a beer and making a little welcoming speech. At some point in his discourse, he was struck by my name, Antonio, which was the name of the young son he had lost in the avalanche. The tears welled up in his eyes as he told us this, and soon a friend appeared at his side to take his arm and attempt to lead him away. He shook off his friend and continued to tell us about his little son, Antonio, the tears now streaming down his face and his voice choked with sobs. His friend again attempted to lead him back to his own table. Shaking him off again, he exploded in a torrent of vile insults, heaped upon his hapless companion. The abuse did not faze his friend, who persisted and eventually led away the now incoherently sobbing man. Thus began my residence in Yungay. This was a scene, which, like the phrase "They have given us nothing!," I was to see and experience countless times.

In October of 1970 with no little uneasiness, I began a study of social change and disaster in the refugee camp of Yungay, concentrating on the issues of structural change in the social, economic, and political institutions of the rapidly developing settlement. Given the tragedy of the situation, these were "safe" issues emotionally. My initial experiences in Yungay left me acutely aware of my own feelings of fear and vulnerability. If I focused on the development of social institutions, I would not have to deal, analytically at least, with such personally threatening themes as loss and grief, pain and death, or fear and hate. But no community, much less one in Yungay's condition, permits the luxury of such compartmentalization.

When I initially entered the community of Yungay, I attempted to maintain a position of scientific objectivity. Objectivity is a value instilled in many social scientists-in-training as scientifically crucial and professionally obligatory. But immediately, I began to feel the conflict between what I hoped was scientific objectivity and my identification with and sympathy for the people of the community. I found that it was impossible to maintain distanced objectivity in the face of their suffering. Most field anthropologists and sociologists have undoubtedly wrestled with the same dilemma to one degree or another. Anthropological fieldwork is founded on personal relationships with people, and total objectivity in the best of circumstances is difficult to sustain, but when the people are suffering and needy, it becomes even more difficult. Disasters like Yungay create conditions which go beyond the limits of deprivation and poverty; the physical and psychological trauma of loss and change can be devastating.

In the wake of the disaster, tragedy set the psychological tone of daily life in Yungay. Tragedy was a condition, not a situation, not merely episodic. Even when people are abysmally poor, tragic situations usually only punctuate the pain of everyday reality. Poverty may be an on-going, abiding condition. Tragedy, however frequent, is not normally a continual state. But in Yungay, particularly in the year following the disaster, people spoke of the disaster as *la tragedia*. The term was used as if it were an abiding condition of their lives, much the same as their experience with poverty. This was the condition of tragedy, a condition in which profound personal anguish and grief were, in fact, the reality of existence. The fact that suffering has now been tempered by time does not lessen its significance in the lives of Yungaínos. All time has been divided into two periods: before and after *la tragedia*. Thus, to avoid the substance and experience of the tragedy would be to distort the reality of Yungay.

Much of what transpired in Yungay is amenable to quantitative analytical techniques, but the sense of event, of place, of tragedy can be communicated only through the admittedly subjective eye of the viewer. Statistics on the tonnage of mud and rock, the numbers of dead, of wounded, of survivors, of immigrants, market revenues, births, deaths, marriages, and meetings tell only part of the story of Yungay. Yungay also demands the personal approach in anthropology, which John Honigmann has called the core methodology of the discipline (1976). Much of this book must be narrative, describing what I saw in Yungay during the time I was there. Like any anthropologist in the field I kept field notes and journals, administered questionnaires, and recorded data as faithfully as possible. But this book is not created from questionnaires or field notes alone. It is also drawn from the vivid experiences of life in a disaster zone—the moods, feelings, colors, and smells that still live in my memory.

I found that as a researcher, my responses to the tragedy of Yungay were complex, and only a few were conscious and well rationalized at the time. My initial attempts to achieve scientific distance reflected not only training, but probably also psychological need to escape from the continual daily assault of sorrow and pain which characterized life in

27

the camp in that first year after the quake. My adherence to a "scientistic" position in the survivor camp seems to have been a combination of "objectification" (Bettleheim 1960) and "psychic numbing" (Lifton 1967), designed to preserve a semblance of emotional stability in chaotic circumstances. At first, I was psychically numbed by all the pain and sorrow surrounding me in the camp, rendered unable to empathize and share with people the difficulties they were experiencing. Efforts to objectify, to get outside myself and consider situations as one might observe them in a laboratory enabled me to achieve a certain scientific distance, but my adherence to my scientific role seems now to me a psychological device that kept me from being overwhelmed by the daily horrors of Yungay life.

But I could not maintain these defenses for very long, as I came to know and care for people in the camp. I responded to the stresses of life in the survivor camp by unconsciously sharing the grief of many friends and acquaintances. Although it certainly became important to the research, my participation in many of the mourning rituals, including the occasional heavy drinking, helped me deal with my misgivings that I was engaged in a ghoulish study of vulnerable people under great stress and pain. Some years later I was to find that these activities served a positive function not only for myself, but in a minor way for the Yungaínos as well. When I returned for further research after an absence of several years, I was introduced to newcomers to the community simply as, "This is Antonio. He was with us." The sharing of the experience of the difficult first year had been meaningful for them as well as for me.

Finally, I abandoned my position as a nonintervening, objective observer in what was probably the most conscious of my responses to life in Yungay. The camp was a community in dire need at all levels. Yet, the impermanent status of the camp made large-scale aid risky and possibly inefficient. No one knew from one day to the next when the order might come to move the entire population to another place. As an outsider from North America, I was taken to be a powerful and influential person (which in a relative sense I was). Quite often people in the community would seek me out for advice or leadership in dealings with government aid agencies, and I was forced to confront the issue of direct intervention. The distinction between participant observation and nonintervention in individual and community affairs is always blurry, and the resultant problems are difficult for field researchers to resolve. My solution to the dilemma did not follow any precise rule of thumb.

When I first decided to return to Yungay, the Peru Earthquake Relief Committee asked me to be their volunteer representative in the valley. The PERC had been formed in the early days after the quake by North American and Peruvian anthropologists, ex-Peace Corps volunteers, students, and other people who had worked in the Callejón de Huaylas. Donations were sought from private individuals who had lived or worked in the valley and from philanthropic institutions to fund small-scale projects of disaster relief and reconstruction. As PERC representative I was in a position to channel some of the aid into the Yungay refugee camp. Because the camp was considered temporary, reconstruction aid there ran the risk of being misplaced. I consciously tried to obtain aid that would be both effective and transferable should we receive the order to relocate. I was relatively successful in keeping my role in the acquisition of even these small quantities of aid somewhat out of the realm of common knowledge in the community. I felt that if word got around that I had access to any form of aid some people would tailor their information to what they thought I would like to hear in order to get further assistance.

But this sort of quasi-official action was not the only type of intervention asked of me. Frequently, people would approach me with individual problems, and I was forced to deal with them in light of what I thought their effects might be on the community or the individual, and in terms of my own capabilities. For example, if I were asked to intercede for a woman whose government-built module dwelling had been usurped by another person of greater social or political power, I would try. When friends asked me how to approach the authorities on housing or food needs, I replied to the best of my knowledge and experience. However, when queried about arguing the case against relocation to reconstruction authorities, I would decline on the basis that I had no more knowledge about the situation than they did. I could not decide for them whether to choose a location for greater geologic safety or for the maintenance of traditional culture and society. In other words, I was often called upon to perform tasks which I had neither the right nor the ability to carry out. My variable response to these dilemmas was probably far from ideal, but it was still preferable to the essential sterility of a position of pseudo-detachment.

Chapter 2

Human diversity and survival are the core values of the science of anthropology; it is not value free. The experience of research in the tragedy of natural disaster deepened my understanding of this value in a direct and personal sense. Therefore, I must inform the reader of my bias in my observation of human behavior in the Yungay disaster. Actually, my residence and experience in Yungay has left me with both a bias and an obligation. My bias is in favor of the survival of Yungay, even though its tradition has many elements with which I am not in accord. Things can change. My obligation is to tell the story of the survival of Yungay. Survivors are bearers of testimony. Yungaínos are witnesses for each other in the reconstruction and strengthening of their community and culture. My role, as both they and I see it, is to be their witness beyond the borders of the valley, to tell the story of their survival.

To tell the story that I encountered in those chaotic days of October 1970, I felt I had to gain a clear vision of the community of old Yungay. The effects of a disaster can never be fully understood without a thorough understanding of the preimpact context. Consequently, armed with my neophyte field notes from four summers before, the few publications of historians and anthropologists, and the memories of survivors, I set about attempting to "reconstruct" the lost city of Yungay.

Chapter 3
Yungay *Hermosura:*
Place and People

The Valley

The Callejón de Huaylas, the intermontane valley in which Yungay was located, possesses a pastoral beauty which impresses even Peruvians, who are rather accustomed to the grand vistas of Andean scenery. The callejón (corridor), nick-named the "Peruvian Switzerland" for its alpine beauty, is in effect the valley of the Santa River which bisects it on its northward course before turning sharply west to the sea. The western slopes of the valley rise rather abruptly, permitting only limited agriculture, to the arid heights of the Cordillera Negra, a chain of rugged, blunt peaked mountains reaching as high as 16,500 feet. The eastern banks of the river rise more gradually, through greener foothills patchworked by the miniscule plots of peasant agriculture and dotted by groves of eucalyptus. In the lower parts of the valley to the north, there are lush orange groves in sight of the glaciated peaks of the Cordillera Blanca on the east. Although the grade is more gradual, the green foothills on the eastern slopes eventually give way to much steeper inclines which culminate in the perpetually snow-capped Cordillera Blanca peaks. The entire range is dominated by Huascarán, a twin-peaked colossus whose northern summit reaches 21,860 feet and whose southern peak attains 22,190 feet, both of which overlooked the city of Yungay, as did the peaks of Huandoy immediately to the north. Legend has it that Huascarán and Huandoy are the lovers Huascar and Huandi, an Inca general and a local princess who ran away together against her father's wishes. They were soon caught and turned into the neighboring peaks, condemned forever to be within sight of each other but never able to touch. The water from

31

melting glaciers which fills the Llanganuco lagoons between the two peaks is said to be the tears of the anguished lovers.

Many of the other peaks in the Cordillera Blanca are over 18,000 feet high, and virtually the entire 125-mile range is snow- and ice-capped. In addition to being one of the more seismically active regions in the world, the Cordillera Blanca peaks are very sharply angled, ranging from 45° to nearly 90°, and many of them are dangerously unstable. The north peak of Huascarán is probably the most unstable ice-capped zone of the entire range. The northwest face of Huascarán was the source of the avalanches which destroyed the village of Ranrahirca in 1962 and the city of Yungay in 1970.

The Cordillera Blanca range is frequently notched by glacier-carved U-shaped gorges and canyons which drain numerous streams into the Santa River thereby providing the more abundant agriculture with water during the six-month dry season from May to October. A number of these spectacular gorges, such as Llanganuco above Yungay and Paron above Caraz, just to the north of Yungay, are capped by vast lakes fed by the clear icy waters of melting glaciers. In post-Pleistocene times, the glaciers of the Cordillera Blanca have been in retreat, and huge lakes have been formed by their melting ice flowing into the deep furrows gouged in the terrain by their previous forward advance. Some of the lakes nestle serenely, surrounded by clumps of quenual and quisuar trees in high-altitude plains of the Cordillera Blanca. Other lagoons glisten in the clear Andean sunlight like sapphires embedded in stark, boulder-strewn moonscapes. The staggering beauty of these lakes, always a source of pride to the people of the callejón, scarcely disguises a threat as ominous as the spectacular snowpeaks. Four of the five provincial capitals of the region are located on or near rivers which flow from these lakes. Early in the morning of December 13, 1941, an immense chunk of glacial ice plummeted into the lake at the head of the Quebrada Cojup above the departmental capital of Huaráz at the southern end of the callejón. The wave of water created by the icefall destroyed the natural dam, unleashing a vast torrent of water and debris that careened wildly down the canyon toward Huaráz. Residents of the northern end of the city awoke to hear a roar like that of an approaching locomotive. Moments later, Centenario, the northernmost barrio of Huaráz, was enveloped in the roaring mass of rock and mud. Almost 5,000 people lost their lives. Beauty and danger go hand and hand in the callejón.

Yungay in History

The geologic instability of the region has been a major theme of life in the callejón. Outcroppings of huge granidiorite boulders all over the valley are undeniable evidence of avalanches in the prehistoric era. Despite the risk, people have been living in the valley for millennia. Nomadic and seminomadic cave-dwelling hunters and gatherers inhabited the region around Yungay as early as 10,000 B.C. The first major record of higher density human population in the callejón appears with the spread of Chavin, the first pan-Andean cultural tradition, around 800 B.C. There are many Chavin-style ruins in the callejón, one of the most notable being the temple mound upon which the cemetery of Yungay was constructed. The Chavin era was followed by a series of other cultural influences from both coastal and highland regions. Sometime between 1463 and 1471 the Inca Pachacutec conquered the entire Callejón de Huaylas and placed it under the domination of the Inca empire. Less than seventy years years later, the Inca empire fell to the invading Spaniards, who entered the callejón from the north in January of 1533. With the coming of the Spaniards, the name of Yungay appears more and more frequently in the historical record. Since the Callejón de Huaylas was one of the principal mountain routes of communication and travel, Yungay, among other towns, was visited fairly frequently and was the site for encampments and meetings during the conquest and its subsequent struggles, including the civil war between Pizarro, who had claimed a large part of the callejón for his own encomienda, and his rival Almagro.

The coming of the Spaniards also signals the beginning of another major characteristic of life in the Callejón de Huaylas and in Peru in general. The separation of society into social and ethnic groups was certainly an important aspect of Inca society, but such a system was elaborated with the purpose of integrating the disparate cultural groups which made up pre-Columbian Peru into all but the very highest stratum of the Inca empire. Inca social organization, however stratified it may have been in terms of social classes, did not result in the alienation of major groups of population from the means of production or the mechanisms of distribution. After the conquest, however, the Spanish instituted a series of political and socioeconomic measures which increasingly deprived the Indian population of control and access to land. The most

Peru and the Department of Ancash

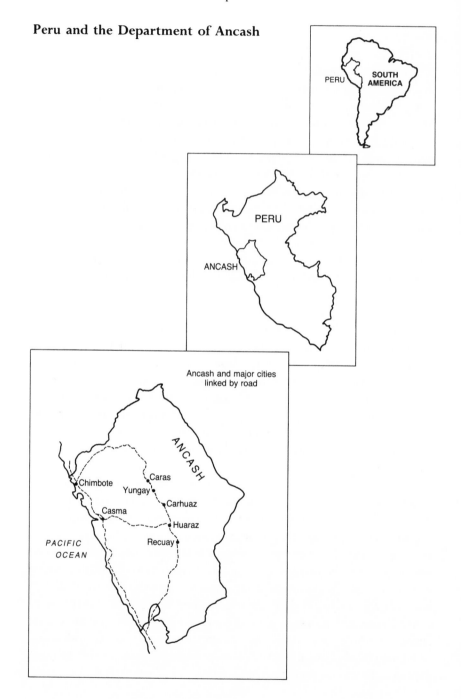

important of these institutions were the repartimiento, the encomienda and the reducción, all designed to control and exploit the Indian population. The repartimiento refers to the Indian labor which was granted to a Spaniard under the encomienda system. The encomienda was a royal grant of rights to collect tribute from the Indian population on a specific land area. The Indians were to pay tribute through work in the mines and in the textile mills (*obrajes*), which were being founded in the new settlements called reducciónes where the Indians were forced to live. The ultimate result of such policies and later measures taken under the republic was the marginalization of the Indian population to the poorer lands on the valley slopes, while the large landholders, of mostly Spanish or mixed descent, laid claim to the better lands on the valley bottom. As well as banishing the Indian to marginal lands, the Spanish conquest through disease and various other abuses also reduced the population of the callejón from its preconquest level of 164,000 people to 30,000 Indians and 20,000 mestizos (people of mixed ancestry) by 1750 (Walton 1974:23).

The Callejón de Huaylas was divided into two repartimientos, one of them, known as the Repartimiento de Huaylas, claimed by Francisco Pizarro himself. Pizarro took an Indian princess, the daughter of the Inca Huayna Capac and a Huaylina, as his mistress. She bore him two children, one of whom was given the encomienda of Huaylas. In 1540 the encomienda of Huaylas had 4,800 Indian families as tributaries and included all of the area encompassed by the present provinces of Carhauz, Yungay, Huaylas, Corongo, Sihaus, and Pallasca. Around 1550 a number of textile mills were founded in various locations throughout the valley, including Yungay. These mills produced such fine materials that they were exported to Europe. During the 1570s, the program of reducciónes began in earnest in the callejón, forcing Indians living in dispersed outlying settlements to congregate in more compact villages and towns, where they could be more efficiently administered to in matters religious and economic. This policy of town planning, including the Spanish grid pattern, cast a decidedly Hispanic appearance on all the settlements in the area.

The date and circumstances of the actual founding of the city of Yungay, however, are subject to considerable debate. One interpretation maintains that the city was founded on August 4, 1540, with the name *la senorial noble y heroica villa de Yungay* (Carrasco et al. 1962:11). We do know for certain that in 1571, Alonso de Santiago de Valverde, the representative of the Viceroy Toledo, founded a city called Yungay for the Dominican order who established a convent there. In 1579 the convent was elevated to a priory and with its four members endeavored to serve the religious needs of an immense territory, comprising more than 5,000 square kilometers and literally hundreds of towns, villages, and hamlets, not to mention the natural obstacles of both the Cordillera Blanca and the Cordillera Negra. Apparently, Yungay was used as a base from which priests and brothers traveled to the distant parts of their jurisdiction in their efforts to bring Christianity to the Indian population (Gridilla 1937:284). By the end of the sixteenth century, the head priest of the Yungay priory was administering eight haciendas, and the town had a population of 3,253 people (Walton 1974:27). There were two textile factories which were supplied by several thousand head of sheep owned by the local Confraternity of the Rosary and the hospital.

After the conquest and the initial evangelizing of the Spanish, the area of Yungay seems to have settled into relative obscurity during the sixteenth and seventeenth centuries. However, the patterns for later developments had been set. While the Indians had been gathered into more compact settlement forms, they were being increasingly relegated to the higher slopes for agricultural exploitation. With the founding of the Spanish priory there, the urban settlement of Yungay was also becoming a center of white, elite residences and institutions.

In the eighteenth century the first of a series of historic natural disasters occurred which have so influenced life in the province and the entire valley up to the present. On January 6, 1725, the town of Ancash, some two kilometers to the north of Yungay, was destroyed by an avalanche from the glacier of Huandoy, the peak immediately to the north of Huascarán. Ancash, located at the base of a canyon of the same name, was a small but apparently prosperous settlement of 1,500 people. The landslide which buried the town is said to have been caused by a seismic tremor which dislodged a block of glacial ice, sending an immense mass of mud, ice, and rock down onto the town, which was in the midst of the fiesta of the Epiphany (Walton 1974:22). Those few who survived the cataclysm of Ancash never attempted to rebuild their homes and moved to Yungay.

The eighteenth century witnessed not only the first of the historic geologic catastrophes which were soon to become a characteristic of life in the callejón, but also the beginning of another series of events which were to become typical as well—Indian uprisings and rebellions. In the latter part of the eighteenth century, the colonial regime added a customs tax to the tributes already being paid, producing in 1776 a violent protest all over the continent (Dobyns and Doughty 1976:132). In Yungay the protest took the form of a violent demonstration over still another tax which the Corregidor of Huaylas chose to impose on the local populace in place of the normal payment in kind. The tax collector is said to have barely escaped with his life from towns in Yungay district (Carrasco, Ramírez, and León 1962:12).

While Yungay is said to have contributed arms, men, and supplies to the struggle for independence from Spain, it was never the scene of nor was it intimately involved in any events of great importance to the war for independence. After independence was won, the callejón was the scene of another struggle between those who wished to unite Bolivia with Peru and forces opposing the confederation. In 1839, fourteen years after independence, the decisive battle in that conflict took place in Yungay district. The battle was fought in Ancash Canyon, near a hill called the Sugar Loaf, not far from the site of the destroyed town of Ancash. The forces of General Santa Cruz were defeated, and the Peruvian-Bolivian Confederation was disbanded. In celebration of the victory, the Peruvians changed the name of the department from Huaylas to Ancash, unconcerned that the name was also that of the avalanche-destroyed town and would bear a tragic precedent for life in the new department.

Perhaps the most important consequence of the years of struggle and national boundary consolidation was the new definition of the Indian as landowner. In 1824, the liberator Simon Bolivar declared that Indians were citizens and as such had rights of private ownership of the land they occupied. The immediate effect of this declaration was the distribution to private individuals of the lands held communally, which had been granted to Indian communities by the Spanish colonial authorities. The 1828 constitution confirmed Bolivar's decrees with laws stating that landless Indians were to be awarded lands from "surplus" (i.e., communal) holdings of the Indian communities. Superficially these actions can be seen as beneficial, but their ultimate effect on the Indian population was very damaging. In the first place, the laws were a direct assault on the Indian community, which provided at least a modicum of protection from outside forces. The internal practice of distributing lands to community members according to need was in effect destroyed by the legislation. In addition to dealing a mortal blow to the protective communal aspects of the Indian community, the new laws also made previously inalienable land now available for sale (Dobyns and Doughty 1976:165–66).

In effect, the laws gave a free hand to the dominant literate classes, all too willing and able to falsify titles, bills of sale, and other documents to usurp the new lands of illiterate and essentially defenseless Indians (Orlove 1977:162). The ultimate effect of the new legislation was a massive transfer of Indian lands to the dominant elite. The Indians were dispossessed of the best lands and were forced to move higher up the slopes of the intermontane valleys to less desirable and less productive terrains. The resulting pattern of elite residence and ownership of more productive valley bottomlands and Indian residence and exploitation of the upper reaches of valley slopes, creating the well-known latifundia-minifundia patterns, still prevailed in the callejón at the time of the disaster.

Indian impoverishment and urban elite exploitation continued to characterize life in the Callejón de Huaylas during the nineteenth century. In this context, perhaps the most important historic event of republican Yungay took place in 1885 during still another Indian rebellion. The rebellion of the Indian chieftain Pedro Pablo Atusparia presents a complex of events which have singular importance because the response of the citizens of Yungay demonstrates the kind of social attitudes that existed in the late nineteenth century, attitudes which, at the demise of the city, in 1970, almost a century later, had undergone little substantial change.

In the latter part of the nineteenth century Yungay enjoyed its "golden age." The city had advanced well beyond the stage of being a simple priory town. Although it was located slightly north of the geographic midpoint of the valley, it had become an important central place for the region. In the late 1860s, the Italian geographer Antonio Raimondi had made extensive visits to study the entire callejón, and, as tradition has it, gave nicknames to all the towns he visited. The nickname he chose for Yungay was "Hermosura," beauty. Located in the verdant foothills overlooking the Santa River with the spectacular view of Huascarán at its back, the growing city was a lovely place.

The city's status as the home of the regional elite in the midst of the Indian masses had become a fact. Its upper class consisted of a relatively small but extremely powerful group of large landowners who resided in elegance in the city itself, while administrators and "straw bosses" looked after their rural hacienda properties and their Indian peasant serfs. Residing in the city as well were a small commercial class and some professionals, a doctor, and several teachers, most of whom were related closely to the landowning elite. The rest of the city's population consisted mainly of lower-class mestizo artisans and Indian laborers and servants, who were often brought down from upland haciendas to serve in the houses of their lords.

This traditional, almost feudal, life-style was maintained in the late nineteenth and early twentieth centuries by an upper class which had not yet departed for the more luxurious and comfortable life of Lima. In addition, a number of English and German colonists had immigrated to the area and, through the common factors of race, education, and class, had rapidly become assimilated into the upper strata of society. The names Terry, Pohl, Phillips, and Hudson were still common in the upper classes of Yungay society before the disaster. The members of this upper class owned large amounts of land and capital and enjoyed the benefits of the traditional servitude of the Indian peasants. The elite constructed elegant houses in and around the main plaza of the city and filled them with furniture and decorations imported from Paris and transported to roadless Yungay by burros. These homes, built in the traditional Spanish style around columned internal patios adorned with statuary, were the scene of sumptuous social gatherings for all the provincial elites of the valley, which were becoming increasingly interconnected, primarily through marriage. According to the oft-recounted traditions, the Yungay caballeros of that epoch were dashing, swash-buckling types who seemed to have spent most of their time galloping off to nearby Caraz, alternately romancing the ladies and terrorizing the men. Thus, it was a Yungay steeped in provincial elegance and privilege which was suddenly faced with a region-wide Indian rebellion in 1885.

The rebellion grew out of a nonviolent protest in the departmental capital of Huaráz over still another tax to be levied on the Indian population. The Indian spokesman, Pedro Pablo Atusparia, the mayor of the village of Marián, was imprisoned, beaten, and humiliated publicly by having his braids cut off. The braids were a symbol of Indian nobility and descendence from the pre-Columbian Inca empire. This ultimate insult brought the Indian population down in fury upon Huaráz, which fell to them almost immediately. After their relatively easy victory, the Indians freed Atusparia and named him their leader. He immediately undertook the direction of the now full-scale rebellion which was to spread rapidly throughout the valley.

When news of the rebellion reached Yungay, the mayor, Don Manuel Rosas Villon, organized the "Urban Guard," a group of approximately thirty upper-class individuals (often referred to as "white" by Yungay authors) armed with rifles, knives, and clubs to repel an army whose advance force was estimated at 8,000 Indian "soldiers." This force, now only a few short kilometers south of Yungay, made one tentative sortie which resulted in one dead Yungaíno and the capture of an Indian. The Yungaínos decided to execute the Indian in reprisal for the death of their comrade. When informed of his fate, the Indian asked his captors for a priest to hear his confession. He was told "Dogs don't confess" and summarily shot (Angeles 1963:111).

Atusparia, still attempting to avoid a full-scale battle, sent another emissary to the city with an offer to the Yungaínos to surrender their city in exchange for their lives and the safety of their property. The reply was, "We prefer to be exterminated before surrendering to Indian dogs" (Angeles 1963:111). With the rejection of their surrender offer, Atusparia ultimately launched his entire army of 20,000 men upon Yungay. The Indians singled out and killed those members of the urban guard who had not yet fled with their families, dismembered their corpses, and exhibited their heads on lances as they sacked the abandoned houses and commercial establishments of the city. Atusparia, however, prevailed over his more sanguinary cohorts, and a general massacre of the population was avoided. Although it ultimately fell to the Indians, Yungay was the only provincial capital of the valley to resist the Indian advance. Atusparia controlled the entire Callejón de Huaylas for several months before the federal government in Lima sent a large contingent of well-armed troops, which defeated the Indian forces and quelled the rebellion. Yungay was proud to be the only town in the entire department of Ancash to resist the rebellion of Atusparia, even though it is now conceded, even by Yungaínos, that his cause was just. A symbol of that pride, in the form of an obelisk mausoleum containing the remains of four of the urban guard, was erected in the Yungay cemetery in 1920

(Angeles 1963:106–22). The image of Yungay as an essentially middle-
and upper-class white citadel of culture and civilization in the midst of
and in opposition to the despised and deprecated Indian masses was to
persist in legend, if not in fact, up to its ultimate destruction in 1970.

Yungay and Its Province

At the time of the avalanche, Yungay was the capital of one of sixteen
provinces of the Department of Ancash. A department is an administrative and governmental unit roughly equivalent to an American state.
The province of Yungay was further divided into eight districts, acquired
through annexation from other provinces and subdivision of existing
districts since the province's foundation in 1904. Of all the provinces
in Ancash, Yungay is one of the most varied and difficult administrative
units to maintain. Its political jurisdiction extends from the warmer
valleys of Conchucos Canyon on the Cordillera Blanca's eastern slopes
into the Callejón de Huaylas and over into the arid regions of the
western slopes and high plain of the Cordillera Negra. Only three of
the eight districts could be reached by road at the time of the disaster.

Before the disaster Yungay province contained approximately seventy-
six formally defined communities, half of which were located in Yungay
district. There are other hamlets, small groups of homesteads, and other
forms of settlements which are not formally recognized scattered among
the official communities. Population figures for the province reflect the
centrality of the capital district, which represented 43 percent of the
total population. The city of Yungay contained 10 percent of the province's populace. Mancos, the next largest city, well known to be Yungay's
only interprovincial rival, represented barely one-fifth of the capital city's
population.

The historical background of settlement patterns in the Callejón de
Huaylas in general is somewhat clouded, and this situation in Yungay is
especially aggravated by the continuing devastation of many urban areas
by unsettled geologic conditions. In Yungay, all the major tributary
systems of the Santa River from the Cordillera Blanca had at one time
both a large village network on the descending slopes and a town or
city at the point of confluence with the Santa. In 1725 an avalanche
from Mt. Huandoy wiped out the town of Ancash and most of its 1,500
people. The town was never rebuilt, and its indigenous hinterland was

41

integrated into the village system of the neighboring city of Yungay, becoming one of the major segments of the network. In 1962 another major avalanche from Huascarán obliterated the town of Ranrahirca at the confluence of the Llanganuco and Santa rivers. Although some attempts to rebuild the city were made, it was never to regain its former prominence. The hinterland of Ranrahirca also turned toward Yungay, which earlier in the century had become the capital of the province. When Yungay and the reconstructed Ranrahirca were destroyed in 1970, the massive hinterland, which at one time had corresponded to three separate central places, was without a focus for its economic, religious, educational, and administrative life.

Prior to its destruction, then, Yungay had become the central place for a region, partially through geologic accident. However, Ancash's demise in 1725 does not fully explain the preeminence of Yungay in the nineteenth and twentieth centuries. Two other competing towns still remained. In 1904 Yungay had been named the capital of its newly created province. Why Yungay had been able to achieve such a status is not entirely clear, and there is little information on the matter. Yungay may have achieved dominance because it was the only town in the north end of the valley inhabited by Spaniards during the colonial era. The three other cities of what eventually became Yungay province, Ancash, Ranrahirca and Mancos, may have been predominantly Indian settlements, perhaps administered to by the Spaniards in Yungay. It is immediately apparent, however, that one cannot trace Yungay's importance to geographical and demographic factors alone, since all four towns in the area of the present province, and many others in the entire region, had very similar attributes. Sociopolitical forces were clearly instrumental in Yungay's centrality. The city became a power cluster of administrative, religious, educational, political, and economic services for the region encompassing all three cities (and many other towns) and the vast peasant hinterlands. The other cities remained lower-order central places, important only for their own hinterlands.

As the capital, the city of Yungay was the seat of the vast majority of the province's institutions. Political organization was based on two systems of authority: the formal system of provincial and district authority and the traditional politico-religious authority system of the network of peasant villages, which was separate but dependent on the formal system. The formal system of provincial and district authority

42

derived its power ultimately from the national government and could call on the nationally organized police (Civil Guard) to impose its will if necessary. On the provincial level the resident authority in Yungay was the subprefect. At the local or city level, the authority was the mayor. Both the subprefect and the mayor formally appointed two representatives in the numerous communities of the district and province.

The traditional system existed in part as an arm of the formal government, but also had functions which were essentially independent of the formal political system. The district of Yungay was divided into two separate barrios (sections), each of which had an *alcalde pedaneo* (Indian or "petty" mayor) appointed by the mayor of Yungay. The Indian mayors were the key figures in the important ceremonial activities of the Catholic religious calendar and were largely responsible for the recruitment of the unpaid labor gangs from Indian communities which worked on provincial and district projects. However, all power, whether through formal or informal channels, flowed from Yungay. The *autoridades* were there.

The population of every tiny hamlet, as well as every district capital, was dependent on the capital city for administrative services. Every birth certificate, marriage license, death certificate, transfer of title, tax receipt, movement of all but the smallest lots of bulked merchandise, and many other documental and legal services had to pass through the hands of Yungay's three lawyers, three notaries, eight judges of varying categories, and innumerable clerks, secretaries, and accountants employed in the various public offices. Yungay not only had provincial, district, and local government offices, but the offices of voter registration, the public beneficent society, the police and the military, banks and tax collection, and the courts.

Perhaps even more important than its political and administrative centrality were Yungay's economic functions. The city provided a large and prospering market for the entrance and distribution of manufactured products from the industrialized coast into the rural areas as well as an outlet for the marketing of food from rural areas to Yungay and other urban centers of the highlands and the coast. The market was a node of economic and social articulation for provincial rural and urban areas and for highland and coastal regions of the nation.

Yungay also had a large complement of retail stores, selling such

43

diverse products as building materials, tools, clothing and footwear, patent and prescription medicines, electrical appliances, jewelry, books and stationery supplies, and sporting goods. In fact there was very little in the way of modern commercial goods, short of cars and televisions, which could not be purchased in Yungay's stores. Occasionally, what the stores did not stock was supplied by the itinerant vendor, who brought "the latest" in smaller dry goods and novelties from Lima.

The Yungay market also provided food for the city's population. The countryside around the city offered a wide variety of ecological niches because of the extremes in altitude. The lower lands were extremely fertile and, with the temperate climate of the valley floor, provided ideal conditions for all types of garden vegetables. Farther up the sides of the mountains in cooler climes, crops such as wheat, potatoes, corn, mashua, olluco, hops, and barley were grown. On the highest and coldest levels, up to about 13,000 feet, only potatoes and occasionally corn and wheat were grown. There were few large herds of cattle, pigs, or sheep in Yungay's part of the valley, although many peasant families had small numbers of these animals, which grazed at all levels. Thus, within about five hours' walk of the city, an immense variety of products were produced to feed the city.

Daily peasant women in large numbers marketed extremely small amounts of crops left over from subsistence needs to generate enough cash to purchase manufactured necessities in town. Even though the money they made was minimal, often no more than forty or fifty cents a day, the high number of sellers provided a substantial flow of food into the city each day. This source was supplemented by largely rural women "brokers" who both wholesaled and retailed local and nonlocal agricultural products. These women often maintained contracts with peasant producers and at harvest time bought crops from them for resale in the Yungay market. These women, working on a scale too small for large agriculturalists to bother with, assured, along with peasant sellers, a steady flow of food into the city.

Yungay also served as the educational center of the province. Yungay province had forty-eight primary schools, three secondary schools, and a normal school. Two of the three secondary schools and twenty-two of the forty-eight primary schools were located in Yungay district. The normal school was located in Tingua at the southern border of the province in the district of Mancos. Most families in the smaller communities of Yungay and other districts sent their children to high school in Yungay.

With the presence of so many educational institutions in the city and district, education was very much a cultural tradition in Yungay. Both of the eulogistic volumes produced by Yungaínos about their province (Angeles 1963; Carrión Vergara 1962) devote a great deal of space to teachers and schools. The educator was the personification of the *hombre culto* (cultured man) concept so admired in European and Latin American cultures. In addition, being an educator could be very important if one had political or economic ambitions. With the higher education necessary to become a teacher so close in Tingua, the socioeconomic elite and aspirants to that class in Yungay did not have to undergo much economic hardship to achieve such a status.

Finally, religious institutions bestowed an important form of centrality on Yungay. While almost 80 percent of the highland villages had their own little chapels, only two Catholic parishes in the province had priests—Yungay and Mancos. Church attendance in Yungay was considerably greater than in Mancos, due largely to the greater number of peasant communities in the district. The indigenous fiesta systems of Santo Domingo, Yungay's patron saint, and Santa Rosa of Lima were central events of the religious calendar. In addition to the church, there were nine religiously oriented organizations for both men and women, charged with various functions such as care of certain images and altars within the church as well as charitable works.

Much to the consternation of the parish priest, Yungay also had five small Protestant denominations of fundamentalist persuasion. Appealing primarily to the humbler rural people, especially those who had left their peasant communities to struggle in poverty for a better life in Yungay, the Protestants foreswore smoking, drinking, and dancing for nightly hymn singing and Bible reading. They considered urban Catholic Yungaínos to be arch sinners because they manifestly enjoyed smoking, drinking, dancing, and other sinful activities. Protestants considered the especially devout rural peasants to be benighted, misled, and exploited by the church, which because of its concern with saints, ritual fiestas, and money, they viewed as both pagan and worldly. The local Catholic priest ranted and raved in the pulpit that the Protestants were emissaries of the Devil and at one point papered the walls of Yungay's buildings with posters warning his flock against the new satanic doctrines invading the province. Yungaínos in general considered Protestants to be strange folk, undeniably honest and hardworking, but annoying, especially when they sang their hymns until all hours of the night.

On the Eve of Destruction

Yungay was always a beautiful place, but in May 1970 it was especially lovely. The early months of the year had brought heavy rains which would keep the valley much greener into the dry months of June, July, and August. With its whitewashed houses and red-tiled roofs, the city was nestled amidst the vibrant green cradle of Shacsha Hill with the gleaming white of Huascarán to its back and the brilliant blue Andean sky overhead. One entered Yungay from the south through Aura, crossing the Calicanto Bridge over the Santa Rosa Creek and onto the main artery of the Second of May Street. This street, more often known as Calle Comercio, was narrow and cobble-stoned, permitting two-way traffic only if the vehicles encroached upon the proportionately narrow sidewalks. On any busy day cars, trucks, buses, bicycles, pushcarts, and people competed good naturedly with each other for both street and sidewalk. The narrowness of the street, along with the small overhanging balconies of the second floors of the buildings, the slightly leaning street lamps, and the tangled web of electric lines overhead, conveyed the effect of a corridor of constant and intense movement. From the walls of this corridor projected a profusion of small signs advertising the Banco de Credito del Peru, Bata Shoes, the Bar Welcome, the Bazar Mendoza, and other establishments in the three blocks between the bridge and the town's main square.

The square, the plaza de armas, was the pride and joy of the city. At the turn of the century, the plaza of Yungay had been a large open area which served as an Indian market ordinarily, and occasionally as a bullring on festive days. The houses surrounding this open area on three sides were elegant two-story buildings with balconies. The local cemetery had occupied the fourth side, which sloped upward toward the hills. The modern plaza, which was begun in 1904, was more than a hundred yards long and ninety yards wide. Yungay's church, whose towers were never completed, replaced the old cemetery on the eastern side. The plaza was rimmed by roads, and its central area was divided by cement walkways into eight trapezoidal gardens of roses and geraniums; the narrow ends pointing to the center where a large ornamental fountain was surrounded by another circular garden and wrought-iron fencing. More than thirty tall palm trees added to the decorative beauty of the plaza. In the evening people strolled in the plaza, which was lit by large globes atop gaily painted red and white lampposts.

The fountain, purchased from England in 1904, was the inspiration of one of the city's wealthy landowners, who donated one year's income from one farm for the project. The town council raised the rest of the money for the project by organizing bullfights, raffles, and other community activities. When the fountain arrived in crates from England to the port of Casma a caravan of three to four hundred Indians was sent to bring the heavy wooden crates of unassembled parts overland to Yungay. As the caravan crested the Cordillera Negra to the west of the city, the aristocratic gentlemen, "forgetting their noble heritage and their social prejudices," sallied out enthusiastically to take the crates from the Indians and march triumphantly into the city, where rich and poor alike celebrated the event with an unforgettable fiesta (Carrión Vergara 1962:102). The actual construction of the fountain was only slightly delayed by the fact that the assembly instructions were in English, an obstacle that was eventually overcome through the efforts of five educated gentlemen and a priest.

The modern city still had the Spanish grid plan imposed shortly after conquest, with streets running north and south, east and west. With the growth of the city in recent years, many of the streets had been lengthened considerably and the outlying areas of the city had lost much of the strict rectangular order of the older neighborhoods close to the central square. Most of the houses in Yungay were one-story adobe-brick structures with interior courtyards and red tile roofs. The houses around the plaza and the main street had two stories and balconies. Many of these buildings had been the homes of Yungay's traditional, landowning upper class but in recent years had been donated or sold to the city for use as public buildings. The city hall, located on the plaza de armas, was one such building noted for its ornate balconies and interior rooms of dark, wood-paneled elegance. The city had also developed a number of rather well-to-do suburbs during the sixties. The mayor of the city actually resided in the suburb of Aura, and the subprefect of the province and many wealthier citizens had moved to the elegant suburban complex of pastel-colored two-story houses called Cochahuaín, just northwest of the old city.

The cemetery on the western edge of the city was another source of civic pride. On the top of a hill called Huansakuy, the cemetery is constructed over the walls of a pre-Inca temple. During construction, the laborers excavated a massive stone wall, which encircled the entire hill, as well as a wide variety of pre-Columbian ceramics and domestic articles near the cemetery's entrance. The entire cemetery of six tiers, each with four rows of burial niches, is surrounded by its own high wall, and its entrance consists of a series of imposing stone pillars and an archway through which passed the broad ascending stone steps to the six levels of burial niches. A brilliant white stone image of Christ, arms outstretched, stands some five meters high atop the cemetery looking out over the city to Atma Hill and beyond that to Huascarán. Written in large white letters on the hillside was the word *Hermosura*. The cemetery of Yungay was considered so beautiful that many people from other cities asked to be buried there (Patch 1970:5).

The relationship between the living and the dead is given great importance in Yungay and in Latin America in general. With its above-ground niches, the cemetery was often visited by relatives of the deceased on Sunday afternoons. Funerals, their anniversaries, All Souls' Day, and other similar events were elaborately celebrated in Yungay at the cemetery. John Gillin notes that in Latin America "the living tend to dote upon inevitable death with a certain sweet sadness (tristeza). This is connected with the importance of the soul, whose essence outlives the body" (Gillin 1965:515). The cemetery of Yungay was considered to be one of the most important ritual centers and beautiful attractions of the city. In fact, many of the brochures and descriptions of Yungay include pictures of the cemetery, with its imposing statue of Christ gazing over the town in the shadow of Huascarán.

Although many of its political and economic elites had moved from the center of town, life in Yungay still focused around the main plaza. The church, whose exterior facade was still incomplete, faced the plaza from the east and the town hall from the north. The market, all the stores and artisans' workshops, the daily outdoor market, and the city's one movie theater were located either on or within a stone's throw of the plaza. The great majority of the city's population including many elite families still resided in the older portion of town as well. The plaza and its surrounding institutions were the hub of much of the daily activities of life in Yungay. Since the city's major functions were either administrative or economic, most people worked in the area of the plaza. After work, if a man wanted to see his friends outside the home, the small bars and restaurants, the local pool hall, and the "Club Social Yungay" were clustered in the general area of the plaza and provided a friendly context for socializing. The plaza itself was a favorite place for Yungaínos at almost any time of day, but late afternoon or early evening seemed to be the time when social life in the city would begin. As the sun dipped behind the steep ridges of the western Cordillera Negra, its light still bathing the towering ice of Huascarán in an orange glow, the plaza lights would illuminate the center of Yungay in the gentle dusk, and people, some wrapped in traditional reddish brown ponchos against the evening's growing chill, would begin their evening paseo around the plaza. Older couples would greet each other in passing or stop for short conversation. Young men and women could stop and sit on the benches around the fountain and converse in full view of the community without fear of scandal, but perhaps a bit of matchmaking gossip.

While not all social groups interacted with complete freedom there, the plaza was the one place in Yungay where everyone in the province, from the wealthiest landowner to his hacienda serf or the local water carrier, could be seen at one time or another. Social relations among all Yungaínos were oriented in large part by elements of class and ethnicity, basic factors common to social differentiation in most plural societies. Biological race was less important, although uninformed concepts of race were often called upon to justify social attitudes. At the time of the conquest and during the colonial period, racial characteristics were crucial in defining social status and legal rights in the Andean region. The basic differentiation was between Indians and whites, and racial identities in large part determined economic functions. Whites supervised and Indians labored. However, with rapid miscegenation among all segments of the colonial Peruvian population, strictly defined biological race soon lost importance in the evaluation of status, and the terms *blanco* (white), *mestizo* (mixed), *Indio* (Indian), and the numerous other terms developed to categorize the various admixtures became sociocultural labels rather than biological ones. Most people in Yungay were biological mestizos to one degree or another. Skin color ranged among all groups from a copper brown to a relatively light tan. While

Indians tended to be darker than mestizos, this was probably due as much to exposure to the sun as it was to genetics. Hair color ranged generally between medium brown to jet black; while baldness was generally more common among mestizos and whites it was also seen among the Indian male population. Almost everybody in Yungay had brown eyes, but blue eyes are very common among all groups in the nearby valley of Conchucos, just to the east. On the whole, the wide range of general racially similar characteristics among all the different socially defined groups in Yungay created an atmosphere with relatively little biological racial consciousness.

Race, however, tends to be defined often in social rather than in biological terms. There was considerable class and ethnic consciousness among all groups in Yungay province. People in Yungay, and in the Andean area in general, consider both class characteristics and ethnic identity important in organizing their social relationships and activities. The decisions individuals make about people they treat as social equals or friends, people they employ or work for, people they live near or interact with in all the other kinds of social interaction are all based on a complex blend of ethnic and class criteria with personal requirements.

As in much of Latin America, in Yungay a relatively rigid class hierarchy was a dominant feature of social organization. Class definition according to the nature of relations to the means of production and sources of power was fairly clear-cut. Wealth and power in Yungay resided in the hands of specific classes and was based largely on land ownership, large-scale commercial enterprise, professional skills, and administrative position. However, those members of the elite segments of Yungay society involved in commerce, administration, or professional activities were invariably linked in some fashion, usually kinship, to some form of land ownership. There was a small middle sector composed primarily of people providing specialized services in bureaucracy, retail commerce, artisanry, and technical skills to the city and province in general. The lower sectors of the socioeconomic ladder were composed of small groups of urban laborers and vendors and a vast peasant majority, which was indigenous for the most part. Peasant agricultural labor in its various forms provided the base on which the whole system ultimately rested.

While groups can be fairly easily isolated on a gross socioeconomic scale, they are somewhat more elusive when considered ethnically. Ethnic groups include people who biologically reproduce themselves and share the same fundamental cultural values. The shared cultural values provide the substance of common fields of communication and interaction. Ethnic groups also identify themselves and are identified by nonmembers as categorically different from other groups of the same system (Barth 1969:9–10). In Yungay, as in all of Peru, people recognized themselves and perceived others as being ethnically distinct, and yet strictly defined ethnic identities were possible only among the highest level of the upper sectors and the most traditional segments of the indigenous population (Van den Berghe and Primov 1978). Even though society was highly stratified along the lines of differential control of assets valued by every-body in the system, and ethnic categories generally conformed to the pattern of socioeconomic stratification, ethnicity in Yungay was char-acterized by a fluidity, producing an ethnic continuum rather than a ladder of bounded ethnic strata or castes. Cultural elements between the two extremes of Indian and elite culture simply graded into each other, often conforming to and sometimes differing from socioeconomic factors, as one ascended the ladder of social stratification. In Yungay it was easy to say who was an Indian on the basis of certain relatively agreed upon cultural characteristics as well as economic criteria. It was also easy to state who were the members of the traditional upper class for the same reasons. While socioeconomic functions largely determined the location of those in between, the fluidity of ethnic characteristics more often did not permit a facile ethnic identification of much of the population. Indeed, some indigenous cultural characteristics were shared by the entire population as simply part of highland life, as were parts of elite culture. This situation did not permit the possibility of a social organization of ethnic groups, but ethnicity was an important factor in the social organization and interaction of the province nonetheless. This fluidity and its encumbent mobility make all but the broadest catego-rizations of groups very difficult.

The fluidity of ethnic characteristics was undoubtedly a contributing factor to the period of transition which Yungay had been experiencing both socially and demographically during much of this century. In recent years Yungay had seen considerable social mobility into all but the uppermost ranks of society. This period of change had altered the traditional Yungay social structure from one of the relatively clear-cut distinctions of class and ethnicity to one characterized by greater mobility and less sharply defined categories, at least in the urban context. Since the early twentieth century, the province of Yungay, and much of highland Peru, had been experiencing a general movement "down," in the sense that the urban elite had been moving down from the Andean valleys to the coastal cities, the urban poor had been moving down to coastal urban slums, and the rural poor had been moving down into the city of Yungay itself as well as to coastal agricultural enterprises. With the coming of the Chimbote-Huallanca railroad in 1927, the vehicular road in 1940, and twice-weekly DC-3 air service from the Caraz airstrip to Lima in 1947, all sectors of the Yungay population had increased their geographic mobility greatly. The highest rungs on the Yungay social ladder, known locally as *los notables, los nobles, los blancos,* or simply *la crema* (the cream), maintained residences in the city, on their landholdings, and almost invariably in the national capital of Lima. In fact, the greater portion of the white, wealthy traditional upper class which had characterized Yungay society in its "golden age" had begun opting for the more comfortable and cosmopolitan life of Lima as early as the turn of the century, even before the railroad was built. Yungay names, such as Cisneros, Vinatea, Fernandez Coello, Angeles, Valle León, Bambarén, and many others are now among the wealthy and powerful classes of Lima. Very few traditional upper-class people resided in Yungay in the immediate predisaster period. Their elegant residences in many cases had fallen into disuse or had been rented out. In one case, the Villón mansion had been converted into the local high school, the Gran Unidad Escolar Santa Inés de Yungay. The upper class still maintained control over large tracts of land and derived income through rents or from the products and labor of the Indians who occupied the property as serfs.

Although most of the traditional upper class of Yungay resided full time in Lima, many maintained strong emotional ties with their birthplace or the birthplace of their parents.* Geographical origin is an important element in one's definition of self in many cultures. In the United States, the phrase *God's country* is often applied to one's home or place of birth. In Spain, one refers to *la patria chica* (the little fatherland) as often as to one's Spanish nationality. In Peru one's birthplace is part of one's identity. Once a Yungaíno, always a Yungaíno, regardless of residence. This strong tie to one's provincial homeland links Lima mi-

---

*The organization and description of social groups in Yungay generally follows the approach developed by Mangin in his *Comunidades Alteñas de America Latina* (1967).

grants of all classes with distant cities and villages of the Peruvian highlands and stimulates a constant flow of human and material exchange beween coastal cities and the highlands. Many members of Yungay's traditional upper class, now quite at home in the business, professional, or political circles of the national capital, frequently visited the site of their sierra origins to escape, they often said, the frantic Lima pace and its generally unpleasant climate. Many had, but many had not, forgotten the Quechua language which virtually everyone in the highlands speaks, regardless of class.

Maximo Carrillo Guevara, a well-known orthopedic surgeon, was a member of an old traditional upper-class family who returned regularly from Lima for visits to Yungay. Carrillo, a short, stocky man with a jovial disposition, loved to spend his visits in the city drinking a beer or two with old school chums who still lived in town and chatting congenially with other acquaintances of all social classes. Successful migrants to Lima were a source of genuine pride for Yungay, and Dr. Carrillo was highly esteemed by the citizens of Yungay. He was, as were many other Yungay migrants of the upper class, an enthusiastic booster for the city and its increased development. His name appeared frequently at the head of committees organized in Lima to raise money or support for Yungay's benefit. The Centro Union Yungay of Lima, composed of Yungaíno migrants of all social classes, but led by the traditional upper class, was an active organization on behalf of the development of the home province.

The fact that many of Yungay's traditional upper class had left their provincial home for the national capital did not mean that the city was without a resident elite group. A new provincial elite was very much in evidence in predisaster Yungay. Many of the resident provincial elite members were closely related to the traditional upper class through kin or ritual ties, and prior to the disaster attempted to spend at least part of their time in the departmental and national capitals. Many of the provincial elite had been educated on the coast and were sending their children there for higher education. However, virtually all of them maintained permanent residences and economic activities in Yungay. The provincial elite of Yungay engaged in a relatively wide range of activities and fields including agriculture, commerce, the professions, and politics.

The existence of considerable amounts of arable land, abundant water supplies, and a huge agriculturally based peasantry in Yungay always put a premium on the importance of land, its exploitation, its tenancy, and its ownership. Many provincial elites supported themselves almost entirely on agriculture, placing them in an exploitive relationship with the Indian peasants, the least powerful of Yungay's social sectors. Prior to the disaster, however, there was considerable concern among these agriculturally based elites. Rumors of the incipient arrival of a true agrarian reform by Peru's "revolutionary" military government had caused no little nervousness among Yungay landlords, both large and small. Yungay province contained 548 manor estates, haciendas, and other absentee holdings, 176 of these located in Yungay district. The size of these holdings ranged from over 5,000 hectares with hundreds of serfs to less than one hectare with a single tenant farmer. These haciendas existed along with a system of extreme minifundia of hundreds of tiny peasant-owned plots of land. Many landlords, fearing a true agrarian reform and total expropriation and loss of capital, had begun to sell off parcels of their land to the peasant serfs who worked on it. On one such hacienda, at 12,000 feet in the shadow of Huandoy, known as Timbrac with over 600 serfs, approximately half the land of the original estate had been sold to the resident peasants at the time of the disaster.

Timbrac was owned by the Morales family, and its chief administrator was the eldest brother and leader of the family, Alberto Morales. Morales's home in Yungay, despite his elite status, was not noted for its opulence. He lived the comfortable, if not luxurious, life of a working landowner and administrator. Instead of elegant statuary, the internal courtyards and patios of his large house were adorned with saddlery, agricultural tools, and sacks of grain and other crops. Some of his less land-oriented relatives occasionally referred jokingly to him as *chacragallo* (ranch rooster) for his devotion to agriculture and land. His life centered around the traditional exploitation of the vast landholdings, of which Timbrac was only a small part, which the Morales family and their affinal relatives, the Obregóns, owned all over the province. These estates were the economic base which had sent many family members into important positions in government, the church, and business on provincial, departmental, and even national levels.

Traditionally, Timbrac had been exploited under a *medianero* tenure system, in which seed, land, and fertilizer were provided by Alberto Morales, the labor and tools by the serfs of Timbrac, and the crops of wheat, hops, quinoa, and potatoes were divided between the two. The serfs of Timbrac numbered approximately 140 farmers and their families. Their ancestors had occupied the land for centuries. Every harvest season, Alberto Morales would ride up to his land on horseback to divide the crop. He usually stayed at least a week at Timbrac in the old manor house which had been forsaken for urban residence in Yungay years before. He supervised the harvest labors of the serfs, and the division of the crops and their transport to his storehouses in Yungay. The peasants treated him with deference and respect. On the whole, they considered Don Alberto to be a fair landlord, under the circumstances. In general he left them alone and treated them well when they performed household services in his home in Yungay. This tradition, known as *tapaco,* obligated the hacienda peasant community to provide domestic servants in the landlord's home. A serious, almost glum, individual, not known for his outgoing personality, Morales was paternalistic and firm, although not unfriendly, toward his serfs. On the whole he considered the Indians to be honest and hardworking, although somewhat simple and backward in their ways. The land and the peasants who worked it were the mainstay of Morales and Obregón economies, and in his profitable exploitation of these resources, Alberto Morales did not abuse them, provided they fulfilled their obligations. One of his peons once told me that Don Alberto was his best friend. Morales referred to the peon as "a good man, very *'servicial'* (diligent and respectful)."

Roberto Falcón, the eldest son of one of the wealthiest families in town, was an enthusiastic young man of thirty-two who taught math and physics in the local high school and had recently begun to take an important role in the economic development of the town. Yungay was the educational center of the province, and the status accorded to important people in educational institutions was high. As a university-educated secondary schoolteacher from a good family, Roberto enjoyed considerable prestige and respect for one relatively young. His relaxed, friendly manner and casual dress immediately put people at ease, making him very popular with his students as well as with the older people in town. Roberto was one of several educators among a particularly activist group of provincial elites who were generating a considerable amount of economic activity in the last few years of the city's existence. He had recently opened a service station in Yungay and had been approached by the Lima representatives of a major automobile manufacturer about the possibiity of opening a car and truck dealership for the northern end of the callejón. Life was good for Roberto and promised to get better. He enjoyed his teaching, his solid economic situation was getting even stronger, he enjoyed the respect and esteem of the community, and he loved his wife and four young children deeply.

Emilio Robles, although from humbler origins, was a good friend of Roberto Falcón. Roberto was a few years older than Emilio, but they had known each other in high school. Emilio was not originally from Yungay but from the district capital of Cascapara, where his family owned some land. His family had sent him to high school in Yungay and then to Lima, where he studied law. After graduation he returned to Yungay and set up a law practice. A young man of seemingly boundless energy, he had quickly involved himself in a wide variety of activities and was rapidly taking his place among the leaders of the community. He was active in politics, a frequent visitor at the Club Social Yungay, and an intense right wing on the Artesano Club soccer team of Yungay's thriving provincial league. His law practice was doing well, and he had been able to purchase a late model Dodge sedan, which widened even further his whirlwind sphere of activities.

Juan Antonio Mendez was considered the best doctor of the five that lived in Yungay. He was held in almost universal respect among both residents of the city and the rural peasant population, who appreciated the care and respect which he accorded them. He was a dark-skinned, sober man whose professional status placed him securely among the provincial elite of the city of Yungay, although he originally had been from Ranrahirca. He had lived in Ranrahirca with his family until it was destroyed in 1962. On that day in January, he had been driving through town on his way to Yungay when the avalanche descended upon the valley. Faced with the agonizing decision of whether to continue on and save himself or turn back for his family and almost certain death, he drove on to Yungay and escaped the landslide. Some in Yungay said that Dr. Mendez really never escaped the tragedy of Ranrahirca. The loss of his family in the avalanche or perhaps his inability to save them had imposed a subdued quality on his personality. People spoke of him with enormous respect and affection that was always tinged with a little sadness for the doctor's tragedy. Although Ranrahirca was partially rebuilt after the 1962 avalanche, Mendez chose to settle in Yungay and open a medical practice there. His skills as a surgeon were a source of great pride to Yungaínos, who boasted that if one lived in Yungay, it was no longer necessary to travel to Lima for proper medical care because Dr. Mendez was in residence.

Many of the province's resident elite were businessmen of one kind or another. Two of the city's most recent mayors had come from the commercial sector. Fausto Blanco had at one time worked as a male nurse in the Yungay hospital but lately had decided to buy and run a restaurant in Yungay called *Las Margaritas* (The Daisies). Mariano Mejía, mayor of Yungay in the late sixties, ran a thriving hardware store on Calle Comercio. The present mayor, Juan Beltrán, was the chief administrator for the nationally owned and operated guano fertilizer company. Beltrán, a burly, red-faced man with an outgoing personality, lived in the suburb of Aura next to his warehouse. Don Juan was kept very busy by his duties with the company. The vast majority of the farmers of the valley used guano fertilizer as it was considerably cheaper than the as yet unproven chemical fertilizers which had recently been introduced. Indian peasants, operating at near subsistence levels, understandably could not afford to risk greater sums of money on products that were still unproven to them in local conditions. He also administrated the labor recruitment of workers for the three- to six-month work sojourns on the guano islands. Despite the demands of his business, Don Juan had outlined an ambitious program for Yungay, including projects for paving all the streets, construction of a new market, completion of the water and sewage system, building a connecting bridge to a new road over the Cordillera Negra, and new efforts at promoting national and international tourism for Yungay. He also had begun taking special aim at what he termed "the food mafia," essentially other members of the provincial elite, who, through their own large-scale production or by wholesale purchasing, attempted to create artificially high prices for food in the local market of Yungay. He was waging a fairly open conflict with a few large agriculturalists and their urban allies for the establishment of controls on certain food exports such as milk from the province. Beltrán's position was that once provincial necessities had been taken care of, the surplus could be exported for the higher prices of the coastal urban markets, but that the local population should not be gouged.

The ruling elite of Yungay was completed by a group of official government functionaries, such as the subprefect, the maximum political authority of the province, the tax collector, the superior officer of the Civil Guard post, and any government project engineers or architects working in the area. Since Yungay had regional offices for over a dozen departmental and national government institutions, these professionals were rather numerous in Yungay. Although they shared in the power over local affairs, their allegiance to the city was tenuous at best. They tended on the whole to be a highly mobile group of people, although while in residence they interacted with the other elites. Occasionally, a government professional would marry among the elite and settle permanently in Yungay. Foreigners and minority group members who enjoyed equal or similar economic status interacted peripherally with the elite. Before the disaster Yungay counted exactly one Jewish family and one Lebanese family, both of which were accepted in elite circles of the city. American Peace Corps volunteers interacted with most of the social groups in the valley but tended to choose their closest friends from the top or middle groups. In one case, an American Peace Corps volunteer married into the family of the mayor of Yungay.

The middle sectors of Yungay society cut across what would normally be considered class lines, including people who were lower-echelon white-collar employees of the government, primary school system, banks, police, and army, as well as blue-collar workers, such as truck and bus drivers, and skilled workers and artisans such as mechanics or watch-makers. Economically there was some overlap between the lower-paid white-collar workers and the higher-paid blue-collar workers. Although normally some antagonism would have existed between white- and blue-collar workers, owing to the white-collar belief that any manual labor is demeaning, in Yungay this conflict seems to have been less apparent. Friendships in the middle sector, and occasionally between the elites and middle-sector people, were maintained despite the deeply ingrained belief in the inferiority of manual labor. Why this was so may be a function of Yungay's image of itself as an elite center in the midst of an Indian mass. Urban residence and middle-sector income generally conferred sufficient status for a broad acceptance as *decente,* a term applied to anyone who was not Indian, not servile, literate, and basically skilled at some specialization which provided a middle-class income. The *decente* status of one's parents was also significant. *Decente* status could be withheld from middle-income skilled laborers if their background was too clearly lower class, unskilled, or Indian. The opposing terms were *cholo* or *indio.*

Middle-sector white-collar workers also wore those collars open in the relaxed atmosphere of daily life in Yungay, indicating that the more distinct symbolic barrier of dress among males between classes was the necktie. Most middle-sector people, regardless of white-collar or blue-collar status, were literate, had attended the same schools, played for the same football clubs, and were involved in relatively similar sierra life-styles in the limited context of a small provincial capital. Middle-sector people did not enjoy the prestige of the upper class, but in many cases they did enjoy the friendship of the elite groups. Economically, the middle sectors did not possess the vast incomes of the elite groups, but even modest means in Yungay were sufficient to provide for a relatively comfortable life-style. Both food and labor were cheap, and it was not uncommon for members of even the poorer levels of the middle sector to have Indian servants. This relative comfort of the middle sectors coupled with the overarching links of urban highland culture in general provided numerous contexts for elite and middle-sector interaction.

The many governmental and educational institutions in the capital city assured Yungay of numerous middle- and lower-level white-collar workers. Antonio Flores worked as a teller in the Yungay office of the Bank of Credit of Peru. Although the job did not pay as well as he had hoped, it was a job with a future for a bright young man. Antonio had both energy and ambition and, despite the low pay, felt very positively about his future. He had recently become a member of the prestigious Club Social Yungay and often spent his free time there, enjoying the give-and-take banter of the other younger members or playing an occasional game of pool. While certainly not wealthy by anyone's standards, Antonio was definitely a member of the privileged classes of the city. He was not an aristocrat by any means, but neither was he a part of the common people. He was *gente decente* and therefore free to go and interact as he pleased in Yungay.

Although manufacturing on any scale was in a barely nascent stage when the disaster struck, Yungay was the center of operations for a busy passenger and cargo-trucking industry. Drivers and mechanics from the transport companies, technicians from the hydroelectric plant in Huallanca, hospital technicians, and other people in technically skilled jobs composed the blue-collar element of the middle sector of Yungay. Rodolfo Armendariz did not finish his last year of high school. He had quit to become a full-time assistant to an interprovincial truck driver. For years as a young boy he had been a *chulillo,* an apprentice, to a truck driver from Huaráz, helping to load the cargo, place the passengers, and collect fares in the large panel truck of his employer. Being a *chulillo* was a necessary step to becoming an assistant and then a driver. Sometimes on the long hauls over the Cordillera Negra to the callejón, the driver would let young Rodolfo take the wheel. In this manner, over the years he had learned not only to drive, but to drive the treacherous mountain dirt roads under all conditions. Although through his early teens he had worked, he was still able to complete all but the last year of high school before he decided definitely to work full time. An outgoing, gregarious person, Rodolfo made friends easily and kept them. His classmates in high school, almost entirely of the middle and upper classes, remained his friends even after he had left. His burly frame and rough-and-ready "cowboy on wheels" style were always welcome at the informal gatherings in the small bars around the plaza of Yungay.

While the middle and upper sectors of Yungay were predominantly urban in residence, the lower sectors were, on the whole, rural. The lower sectors of the province were composed of three groups, lower-class mestizos, cholos, and Indians, overlapping with each other as the major class divisions of Yungay society overlapped in the socioethnic continuum. Lower-class mestizos in Yungay were extremely economically varied, the most comfortable of them not far from the standards of middle-sector people, the poorest ranking with the Indian or the cholo. Most lower-class mestizos in rural areas farmed small plots and sold their crops in the various urban markets of the callejón. Urban members of the group included artisans and small store and restaurant owners. The major social characteristic of this group, particularly in their own eyes, was their non-Indian identity, their *decente* status, which was maintained at all cost. Much as poor whites in the rural American south strive to maintain distinct boundaries between themselves and rural blacks, lower-class mestizos will go to considerable lengths to distinguish themselves from the despised Indian masses.

Miguel Mejía was a hatter and a barber. He worked at both his trades in the same location just off Calle Comercio in the center of Yungay. A small, agile man, Miguel labored long and hard with his two skills to support his large and growing family—seven children under the age of thirteen and another on the way. Miguel did a good business in his hatter-barber shop, but it was not the kind of enterprise which could grow and avail him of the comforts of a middle-class existence. His children never went hungry and always had decent clothes, but largely because Miguel rarely stopped working. Many times late at night, the brilliant white light of his petromax lantern could be seen burning over Miguel's small figure hard at work blocking and cleaning hats for their owners to pick up the next morning. He was determined that his children, particularly his eldest son, Federico, would go further in school than he had with a primary school education and attain material success. To this end, Miguel had gone to considerable lengths to ally himself with *gente grande* (big people) through the institution of compadrazgo (co-parenthood). The godparents of his many children and his own godsibs represented in his eyes his buffer against catastrophe, and the help, the little step up, that each of his children would need to succeed in life that he himself could not supply. It was a source of great satisfaction to Miguel that he was a compadre (co-parent) of some of the most important people in Yungay.

Rosa Martínez also had many compadres in Yungay, but more often than not she was the godmother. Despite very humble origins, she had achieved a modest degree of success in Yungay. Rosa was the owner, cook, and head waitress of a small restaurant on Calle Comercio in the middle of town. She had to rent her restaurant, which due to its good location was not cheap, but nonetheless, she managed to support herself, her two sons, and a daughter in Lima. She had originally come to Yungay thirty years before from the eastern valley of Conchucos. She was nine years old when she made the four-day walk alone over the barren and frigid 16,000-foot passes through the Cordillera Blanca to seek work as a servant girl with one of the great families of Yungay. She had grown into a sturdy, attractive woman with broad, Indian cheekbones and brilliant black hair woven into long braids. The warmth of her personality and winning smile concealed a strength of will and determination which eventually enabled her to leave her servant job and run the modest little restaurant in central Yungay. She also had a small home near the eastern outskirts of the city. Rosa was my landlady in Yungay in 1966. She rented a room, which she eventually planned to turn into a small neighborhood store, to me and two other members of the field school. We also had "pension," a meal contract on a weekly basis at her little restaurant. Although Rosa had recently lost her husband and dressed in mourning, the atmosphere at her house and restaurant was always cheerful and warm. Rosa was a tireless worker and on her husband's death had decided that all her efforts from that time forward would be dedicated to the education of her two sons and her daughter, whom she wanted to send to Lima to learn dressmaking. Rosa herself had never learned to read and was just barely able to scratch out a shaky signature, and her Spanish still bore the traces of her Indian heritage.

Antonio Lino, known as Antonio Mala Noche (Bad Night) lived in the southern suburb of Aura. Mala Noche farmed for a living part of the time, but primarily he was a curer and, some said, a witch. He maintained that he was an herbalist and would discourse knowledgeably and at length on the wide variety of plants with medicinal properties in the Andes. Antonio said he had herbal remedies for everything from cancer to tuberculosis, from syphilis to pneumonia. He boasted that even the local doctors occasionally came to him on the sly, sometimes for their patients and sometimes for themselves. Although he grew some of his own plants and herbs, he found most of them in the varied callejón ecosystem which extended from glacial to subtropical. Mala Noche was widely respected by the people for his skills, and perhaps a little feared at times. His short, stocky figure, usually clad in khaki work pants and broad plaid shirts, was a familar sight in his Aura neighborhood, particularly whenever stories and folktales were being told.

Probably the most dynamic of all the social groups in highland society were the people characterized as being in transition between Indian identity and status as outsiders and full participation in Peruvian national society and culture. Mostly born of Indian parents in Indian communities, these people, often called cholos, but rarely by themselves, often spoke Quechua as a primary language and shared the Indian value of admiration for hard work, a definite asset when it comes to competition with middle-class and lower-class mestizos who may feel besmirched by any kind of manual labor. These people were upwardly mobile. Some were small farmers, others rural store owners, unskilled and skilled laborers, agricultural brokers, or truck drivers. Many were market people, involved in the various aspects of commercializing food products or manufactured goods imported from the coast. In fact, many of these energetic people would combine as many as three or four different occupations in order to succeed, not merely survive, economically.

The Tamaríz brothers, Raul, Joaquin, and Julio, all in their twenties, lived near their parents' home in Yanama Chico, a peasant village high above Yungay in the shadow of Huascarán's north peak. They worked small parcels of land near the village and helped their elderly parents with their holdings. Although their parents had never left the mountains, the three brothers had, since the age of twelve, often worked on the coast and in the guano islands as laborers. All three brothers had attended primary school for several years and had learned to read and write in a rudimentary fashion, speak Spanish well, and interact freely with non-Indian Peruvians during their sojourns on the coast. Although all three considered themselves farmers, the need for cash and the desire for more varied experience often prompted them to leave their village for work in the wider world. They felt, as so many others like them, that farming offered little chance of future progress or opportunity, but beyond the seasonal labor on large coastal farms or the guano islands, their opportunities to break away from rural sierra life were few.

Augusto Angeles was born in the peasant village of Pukapampa thirty-one years before and had always lived there. His father was a peasant farmer who had specialized in raising green vegetables for the Yungay market on approximtely one and a half hectares of land in the little village north of the city. Augusto was able to complete five years of primary school before going to work permanently at age thirteen. His first job was as a delivery boy for an uncle who was a baker in nearby Carhuaz for which he was paid the grand sum of four dollars a month. He soon picked up the rudiments of the baker's trade and three years later was working as his uncle's assistant for twenty-six dollars a month. Augusto's father died when he was sixteen, and he returned home to work the farm with his mother for the next six years. In the agricultural off seasons, Augusto signed on with the national fertilizer company for five- and six-month "campaigns" of work on the guano islands as a laborer until he was about twenty-two years old. During his stays at home on the farm, Augusto had met a young girl who worked in the market of Yungay. Although born in the city of Yungay, Mercedes Arroyo was also of rural background and spoke Spansh and Quechua with equal facility. Mercedes, known as Meche, and Augusto were married in 1962 and set up household on his father's farm. With Meche's marketing experience and Augusto's vegetable farm, the pair soon began to work not only as producers, but as exporters, carrying their own and other local producers' crops, primarily potatoes and green vegetables, to Chimbote and other coastal cities in rented trucks of friends. A truckload of corn, for example, costing them from seven to eight thousand soles with two to three thousand soles for transport usually brought a profit of two to three thousand soles in Chimbote, although occasionally in bad times they barely broke even. They planted green vegetables and took their own crops to Chimbote and raised two milk cows, three oxen, and a burro. They worked ten to twelve different pieces of land, either their own, or mortgaged or rented lands, which all together amounted to less than two hectares. It was a hard life, either working the fields or traveling to the coast to sell in the markets, but it was a life which provided an adequate living for them and their four children. Above all for both Augusto and Meche, it was a life with a sense of expectation, a sense of possibility. As they slowly increased the land under cultivation by renting more, they also expanded the volume of their trade, and their earnings, however slowly and painfully, also increased.

People like Augusto and Meche were learning fast. Although both of rustic background, they were rapidly acquiring a higher degree of economic and social sophistication than some in social categories above them, particularly when it involved rural-urban relationships which entailed cooperation rather than coercion. Although these *serranos* (highlanders) on the move often pleaded ignorance and naiveté in their dealings with coastal urbanites, those who dealt most with highlanders regarded them as astute and ambitious individuals. They were determinedly working their way out of rural lower-class and Indian poverty toward financial solvency and national Peruvian identity without denying their Indian or *serrano* origins.

Elena Olivera, who lived in the suburban village of Acobamba, like many mobile chola women, had worked in a variety of jobs in a variety of places. Twenty years before she had been a maid in Lima with a wealthy family for whom she retained considerable affection. Elena eventually returned to Yungay with her young son Rolando and, now in her forties, was a *negociante,* a small-scale importer of potatoes. She and a dozen or so other women like her were largely responsible for supplying the city with potatoes, an Andean staple, when they were not being harvested within the province. She traveled all over the callejón and down to the coast to buy potatoes for sale in Yungay. Despite her extensive traveling she could never accumulate sufficient amounts of capital to enlarge her operations, and her earnings remained discouragingly low. She was able, nevertheless, to maintain a decent home in

Acobamba and to support Rolando fully so that he could complete high school without having to work full time. Elena had never gone to school and could neither read nor write, but she believed fervently in education and had high hopes for Rolando.

Not far from Elena's permanent stall Juana Machco paid a daily charge for the right to sell green vegetables from a blanket spread out in the open plaza of the marketplace. Juana was a *rescatadora,* a rescuer, one of many chola women who made a marginal living selling small amounts (seventy-five cents' to one dollar's worth) of produce, which were bought from peasant farmers on a daily basis. For someone of Juana's scale, selling fresh vegetables at 15 to 18 percent profit on a tiny investment had another advantage; what she did not sell, she and her husband, who was an unskilled laborer, could eat. Both Juana and her husband, who lived just north of Yungay in Huantucán, were in their sixties and, although both had worked for many years in Yungay and were fluent in Spanish and Quechua, they were still living at the margin of bare necessities. Although the cholos as a group were upwardly mobile, the opportunities for real progress were few and the candidates were many. For people like Juana and her husband, the shift from rural labor to urban labor had brought few real improvements in their lives.

Indian peasant agriculturalists, the vast majority of the province's population, occupied the lowest rung on the Yungay social ladder. In many ways, like the other extreme of the social continuum, the traditional upper classes, the Indian peasants were more easily identifiable than the various ethnosocial gradations in between. Indians were rural, living in their own highland communities, characterized by local versions of a generalized indigenous culture. These communities in Yungay were on the whole rather small, with an average population of only a few hundred people. Indian peasant villages were organized in three forms in their relationship to land. The estancia was a community of peasant farmers who owned their own extremely small parcels of land which they worked independently. The Indigenous Community, now known as the Peasant Community, was organized around the communal ownership of lands with use granted to community members according to need. The hacienda, essentially a manor owned by an absentee landlord, was occupied and worked by Indian tenants in various servile and tenure relationships. On haciendas the Indian peasant had to contribute a number of days of work per week on hacienda lands in exchange for the right to live there and work a small parcel of land allotted to him. Other common tenure relationships are of the sharecropper variety such as *medianero* (halfer) or *partidario* (percentager), in which the landlord supplied land seed and fertilizer, the tenant supplied labor and tools, and they divided the crop according to an established percentage. The most important other forms include *arrendatario* (renter), *mejorero* (improver), and *aparcero* (one who pays the landowner in kind for use of the land).

Very often Indian peasant villages in Yungay combined elements of all three forms of community economic organization. Estancias and indigenous communities were often too land poor to support all their members, many of whom were ultimately forced to seek wage labor on haciendas. In turn, occasionally hacienda serfs owned a few small plots of land adjacent to or near the borders of the hacienda.

Whatever the land tenure relationship each community had, most peasant villages in Yungay had their own internal structure and organization and indigenous culture. The Indians in Yungay province participated in an internal local economy based on subsistence agriculture and small surpluses organized for distribution by kinship, mutual obligation, and reciprocity. The workings of the internal economy were closely linked to an internal prestige system and the local politico-religious informal authority structure. While most Indian communities were characterized by the continual struggle against poverty, the economic organization and the system did allow for a degree of internal inequality.

Despite the high degree of internal organization of peasant communities, they were all linked through lines of unequal power and dependency to the city of Yungay. Most of the major institutions of the Indian communities, while maintaining their particular forms of internal organization and expression, were tied in one form or another to the dominant society. The local economy is subjected to the demands of individuals or institutions of the dominant society in the form either of labor or payments in kind, cash, or labor for rights of usufruct of land. As well, the peasant mode of production, oriented toward subsistence and small surpluses of "petty commodities," was articulated with regional and national capitalism through peasant needs for cash and the demand by large enterprises for seasonal labor. Since peasant labor supported itself through subsistence agriculture, its wages could be substantially lower than those paid to full-time agricultural laborers. Indian peasants also participated in the national economy as small primary producers and commercializers of agricultural and folk products as well as consumers of a limited number of manufactured items sold in the Yungay market. The internal authority structure and its major institutionalized expressions, the labor contribution system and the fiesta system, were similarly linked to the formal political structure and parish of Yungay.

Arturo Cántaro, like the vast majority of Indian peasants, lived high above the rich valley bottomlands, on the Hacienda Timbrac of Don Alberto Morales in the *alturas* (heights) just below the towering glaciers of Huandoy. Arturo and his family labored long and hard to eke out a living on the hacienda. Arturo's brother, Epifanio, although living in a freeholding estancia not far away, was in similar straits, scratching a bare subsistence crop from some tiny holdings he had purchased and his wife had inherited. For both Arturo and Epifanio and their families, life was a fairly constant struggle against severe hardship. Land and capital scarcity in Epifanio's case and the obligation to give up one-half the product of his labors to Morales, in Arturo's case, for all intents and purposes condemned them to a life of poverty and continual hard labor with little growth or progress possible. Arturo and Epifanio, like most Indian peasants, had little access to adequate medical or educational facilities, although Morales had donated one room of the abandoned manor house for use as a school. They were deprived of justice in the courts, equality in the military draft, and participation in national institutions in general. Plagued by all the variables of institutionalized poverty, Indians like Arturo and Epifanio and their families were considered by most townspeople to be socially and biologically inferior. Whenever Arturo, who had occupied several community leadership positions, went into town, he had to force his rather straightforward and direct manner into a form of crawling obsequiousness before the citizens and authorities of Yungay. His somewhat ironic and mischievous sense of humor had to be completely suppressed. Although Indians enjoyed the social atmosphere of the Yungay market and were devout attendants at mass, most preferred to avoid contact with townspeople beyond that which was absolutely necessary. Interaction with townspeople generally demonstrated once again to the Indian his supposed inferiority. Mestizos were usually addressed as *señor, papá* (father), *mamá* (mother), or *papacito* and *mamita* (little father or mother). Townspeople

67

called Indians *hijo* or *hija* (son or daughter) or their diminutives, even if they were much older than those addressing them. When townspeople became angered with Indians, they referred to them as *indio* and *indio bruto* (brutish or loutish Indian). Indians always removed their hats when talking to townspeople and rarely maintained any steady gaze, usually staring alternately at the floor, their hands, or away into space, and only occasionally at the townsperson with whom they were talking.

The relationship between Yungay townspeople and the Indian peasants of the hinterland had its historical antecedents in conditions of oppression and deprivation as well as specific incidents of violence. Of late, although in neighboring provinces with similar conditions there had been a number of instances where mestizos had murdered Indians with impunity, Yungay recently had been relatively peaceful. As long as the Indian peasants maintained an unprotesting and respectful posture, the townspeople of Yungay tended to look rather benevolently on them, tempering their own authority with paternalism. Yungaínos often said that Indians were fairly content in their condition, preferring to live austerely and be satisfied with their life-style. The view that Indians were in fact like children, needing the authority and direction of townspeople, was commonly expressed in Yungay. However, the slightest altercation or perceived impudence or disobedience on the part of an Indian would release the utter disdain and contempt which most townspeople held for the Indian masses. Negative views, such as "the Indian is the closest animal to man," were common expressions of the contempt for the Indian. Indian sentiments toward townspeople whom they called *mishtis* (from mestizo) were articulated only in the security of their home village, and in some instances displayed only behind the mask of folklore. Indians consider townspeople and urban culture to be degenerate and sinful. Mestizos and whites are often portrayed in indigenous folklore as *pishtacos,* murderers who leach the fat from Indian bodies for sale as lubricants to industries.

While these hostilities did not go entirely unexpressed in appropriate contexts, recent times in Yungay were not characterized by any overt conflict between Indians and townspeople. Both groups, however, were becoming aware that new trends of change were beginning to seep into the province both socially and economically. The cases of peasant unionization and sporadic guerrilla activity in the southern Andes during the early and mid-sixties and the increasingly radical stance of the new military government did not go unperceived by privileged townspeople. While agrarian reform had floated in the air of Peruvian politics for generations, the statements of politicians had always been tempered by the placement of major hacendados on the committees of legal research in land reform. In the late sixties, statements of the military government began to be taken somewhat more seriously by townspeople and Indians alike. In Yungay the anxieties occasioned by agrarian reform rumors were being softened by increasing economic activity in the city.

Despite the bustle always seen in the morning on Calle Comercio and in the market, Yungay's people had always lived at the relatively leisurely pace of the Peruvian sierra. For middle- and upper-sector urbanites, most economic activities really took place in the mornings. By the early afternoon, most shoppers and sellers had abandoned the marketplace, and a long lunch and afternoon rest were enjoyed at home. Later in the afternoon shops would open again for a few hours to take advantage of the essentially social activity which brought people back into the center of town agan.

In the late sixties, this leisurely pace began to pick up. The city had recently acquired the efficient and full-time electric power of the hydroelectric plant at Huallanca to the north. Previously in Yungay electric power had been supplied by a rather decrepit generator on the eastern slope above the city, but this power had supplied electricity to the city only for a few hours in the evening. People from other neighboring cities with the hydroelectric power had chided Yungaínos for the rather faint orange glow which their light bulbs feebly emitted. The *naranjitas* (little oranges), as these lights were derisively called by other callejón residents, grated on the self-image of Yungaínos as citizens of a progressive city. In addition to its often intense commercial and administrative activity, the town was also in its final moments acquiring an atmosphere of intense social and economic activity. Industry was springing up in the form of a small-scale furniture factory and Guillermo Negrón's ice cream factory, which had already established subsidiary offices in five other sierra towns and one coastal city and had its own fleet of delivery trucks. The *Corporación Peruana del Santa,* a semiprivate development corporation, had bought land on which to build a tourist hotel, and the other four hotels in town had recently upgraded their facilities. César Oré's tourist agency maintained a certain amount of expertise in the much-practiced sport of mountain climbing for the

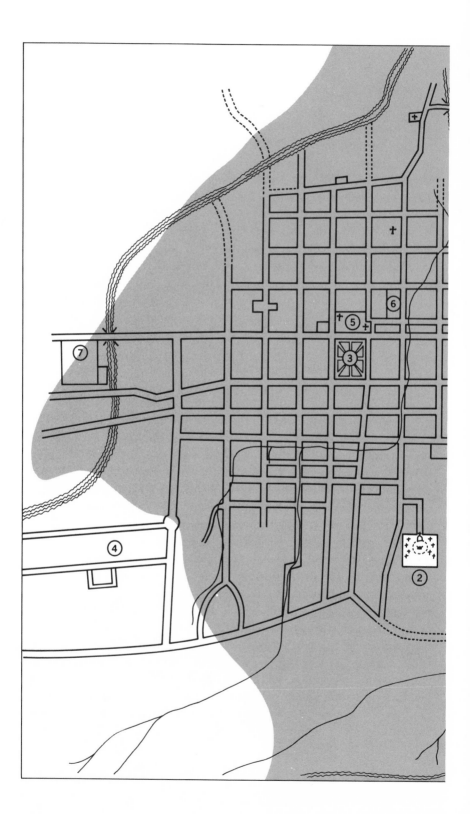

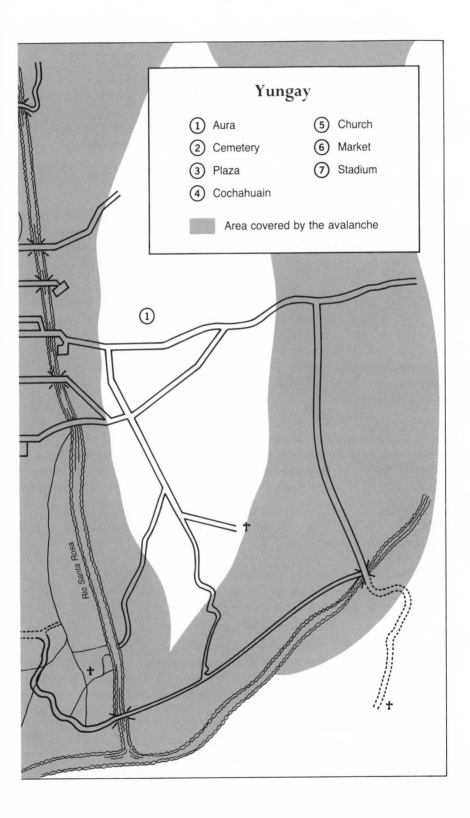

Yungay

1. Aura
2. Cemetery
3. Plaza
4. Cochahuain
5. Church
6. Market
7. Stadium

Area covered by the avalanche

Rio Santa Rosa

numerous climbers who visited Yungay in the summer months to ascend Huascarán, Huandoy, Chacraraju, and the other peaks in the area. The road into Yungay had been paved recently, and the city was in the process of financing the paving of all its streets. A potable water system was ready to be inaugurated shortly before the disaster. Designs for a new market and a new city hall had been approved and were awaiting financial planning.

The cause for this sudden impetus of social and economic development was, in the eyes of many surviving Yungaínos, the coming of full-time industrial power electricity and the final paving of the highway to Yungay. The electricity made industry on a mechanized scale now possible in the city, and the road facilitated more interaction between the cities of Mancos, Carhuaz, Caraz, and Yungay. Before the disaster the leadership of Yungay was a rather unlikely combination of the young and the old. The mayor, an older individual of extremely imaginative perspective, had combined forces with some of the younger professionals to promote the economic development of the city. When the hydroelectric power at Huallanca was used to light Huaráz, then nearby Caraz, then Carhuaz and then, bypassing Yungay, distant Trujillo on the coast, these younger Yungaíno professionals took matters into their own hands. They protested to the government that Yungay was the only provincial capital without light. They then informed the government that they had thirty days in which to hook the city up to the hydroelectric plant or the cable towers located in Yungay province which gave light and power to the entire southern half of the callejón would be blown up. The issue was solved when light was installed in Yungay shortly after the ultimatum was delivered.

With the light and power came the flowering of cottage and local industry into mechanized and regional industry. The city grew in size, extending many of its streets into hitherto unoccupied areas (see map 2). With the paving of the road came more commercial traffic and tourism and Roberto Falcón's fully equipped modern service station. Roberto was also beginning to consider seriously the offer to open an automobile dealership. In four years, according to Roberto, the number of cars, all purchased in Lima, had increased 100 percent. A Yungay-Lima taxi route was about to be established since there were so many people going back and forth for business and pleasure. Liberal young professionals, recently having completed their degrees on the coast, began to return to Yungay rather than stay on the coast as was the normal pattern. One of the five dentists originally from Yungay had installed a fully modern dental clinic. Dr. Juan Antonio Mendez had recently opened the only completely modern private clinic in the callejón. Four other physicians maintained private practices and worked in the hospital which had beds for sixty patients and modern operating facilities. There were also five well-stocked pharmacies.

With the influx of younger, more progressive professionals in leadership positions, certain hardened social attitudes, such as the prejudices against the Indians, appeared to be changing, particularly among the more educated sectors. The increased commercial and business activity also stimulated a more intense social life in the community. The *Club Social Yungay,* the bastion of traditional social power and influence in the city, was flourishing, but it had acquired a competitor in the *Centro Social Yungay* which had recently been formed by a number of younger professionals.

Both these clubs had full social schedules as well as programs of economic and social development. There were also seven sports clubs which fielded teams in soccer, basketball, and volleyball and sponsored parties, dances, and other social activities. One club, *Defensor Huascarán,* was in danger of establishing a sports dynasty, particularly in soccer, although the *Artesanos* were said to be the most prestigious economically and socially. The *Centro Union Yungay,* the city's regional club in Lima, also had a full schedule of social and cultural events dealing with Yungay and was involved in several projects for the benefit of their home province and city. Perhaps the tone of Yungay before May 31, 1970, can best be described in the words of Roberto Falcón, a man who was instrumental in the economic impetus that was emerging in Yungay:

All the attitudes were changing with the infusion of the young, progressive professionals. There was more commerce. The arrival of the electricity gave us a tremendous push. And the old? Old Yungay had a moment of lucidness before it went to die and in that moment it began to advance and progress.

Chapter 4
Aftermath and Aid

 The problem which the Peruvian government and people faced in the fading moments of that May afternoon was how to aid the victims of a disaster which had devastated an area larger than some entire nations. If we can imagine an area as large as Belgium, Holland, and parts of Denmark receiving a saturation bombing, we have an idea of the dimensions and the urgency of the task confronting the nation of Peru. The extent to which they succeeded in aiding the survivors on both a short- and long-term basis is a tribute to their efforts. The extent to which they failed is as much an indication of how little was actually known about disaster rehabilitation not only in Peru, but in the world, as it is a condemnation of that effort. That much was inefficient and poorly carried out is undeniable. There may also be some validity to the perennial disaster victim accusation of malfeasance and profiteering. However, a great deal was done on behalf of the victims. The successes and failures of Peru have served as examples for later aid efforts in other stricken areas. Indeed, the Peruvian earthquake, followed by the Nicaraguan (1972) and the Guatemalan (1975) earthquakes, stimulated a great deal of research on postdisaster reconstruction and rehabilitation in social and technological fields.

As May 31, 1970, came to a close, over 70,000 people lay dead, buried in the ruins of their homes and towns. The number of wounded would reach 140,000, and more than half a million people were left homeless after the quake had crumbled 80 percent of the buildings in the affected area. In the forty-five seconds of the earthquake, the lives of millions of people and the history of the nation of Peru had been tragically altered. All Peruvians remember where they were on the afternoon of May 31, 1970.

Chapter 4

For the miserable colony of Yungay survivors huddled in their make-shift shelters in the lee of Atma Hill and enshrouded in a huge cloud of dust rising thousands of feet above them, their apparent isolation within the tragedy was both frightening and demoralizing. Nevertheless, cooperation and community spirit for the most part prevailed amidst the desolation. Indian peasants contributed food to the survivor camp, and, with a few exceptions, owners of salvageable goods and available food surpluses donated them willingly for the common welfare. The wounded were cared for as well as possible, and the most frightened and traumatized were comforted by those whose emotional resources had not been exhausted at that point. Social distinctions and ethnic boundaries were largely ignored in those terrible moments of adversity when another's need or basic humanity seemed to be the only characteristic visible to his fellow human beings. Indian helped townsmen and, in turn, injured and homeless Indians were accepted into the makeshift encampment. The manifest need for human contact seemed to place other considerations, even the most deeply rooted prejudices and fears, in abeyance.

A sense of brotherhood, cutting across both class and ethnic lines, prevailed as Indian and townsman, lower and upper class, collaborated in the efforts to obtain immediate necessities. Both the subprefect and the mayor stated that in this initial period of two to three days there was a great respect for their offices and a heightened spirit of unity and common identity. A spirit of brotherhood prevailed during this time. People implicitly understood the need for the unity and cooperation of all people if they were to solve the immediate problems of survival. Concepts of private property were suspended, and goods were donated to the public welfare without thought of payment. The individual faced problems which could not be solved alone. Disaster seems to evoke this cooperative response in many cultures and societies around the world. The social solidarity and cooperation are often called the 'postdisaster utopia," although there is little that is utopian in the lives of disaster victims.

Since Aura was a suburb of the city of Yungay and itself an urban settlement of some size, much of the population abandoned it for the hills. The survivors passed the night on the hill of Aura overlooking the desolation on either side. People cried silently to themselves. The mayor of Yungay, Juan Beltrán, described the mental state of the survivors:

The trauma was reflected in a scorn for life. People spoke of another disaster happening in order to finish off life once and for all. Many were completely dejected, wanting neither to eat nor sleep; they had become completely detached from life, completely stupefied by the shock. Others still had not given up hope that their loved ones had somehow escaped. Still others denied the existence of God, saying that no God would let this happen to innocent people. I lost my faith. We did not pray. We did not hold mass. We did not have faith. God had sent us the disaster. We hated God. Many said that the disaster had been a punishment, but I disagree because my five little children had not done anything for which they should have been punished in such a way.

On the day after the disaster the survivors awoke from their makeshift shelters to face a new world and a changed life. In Aura, the mayor took charge immediately. "There was a spirit of union and a great respect for the office of mayor. I knew I had to take the reins. We all met at the house of Sra. de Soriano. I sought out people who were 'prepared,' principally policemen and teachers."

The first step taken was to boil water and put it into bottles. The mayor directed the stores in Aura not to sell anything to anybody without his permission. When they did sell, the store owners were not to raise prices. He ordered that all water was to be taken from the community fountains rather than scooped from the reservoir tank with buckets, which would have fouled the water.

On Runtu Hill, Asunción Montoya and his group of survivors, including the children from the half-destroyed soccer field, were afraid that the hill was going to collapse in the many aftershocks. Accordingly, since they had heard that the subprefect of the province and Dr. Ricardo Oliveros, one of the town's physicians, had fled to Pashulpampa where Roberto Falcón and Dr. Gutierrez were, the entire group left Runtu and went to the other location. At Pashulpampa there were five wounded people and further below, closer to the landslide, were many more, among them Rosa Martínez.

For three nights the survivors of Yungay and the surrounding area huddled together in Pashulpampa and Aura, protected from the elements only by their makeshift cornstalk shelters and whatever they could scavenge from the destroyed houses in the nearby peasant villages. During the days in the strange dust-filtered light of a hidden sun, more and more mutilated and dismembered bodies were found, corpses without heads or limbs, just batterd torsos, naked and disemboweled by the crushing fury of the avalanche. Overhead, above the choking shroud of dust, they could hear the sound of planes and helicopters, but could neither see nor be seen by them. The portable radio of a rural merchant told of the horror of the destruction of Huaráz to the south, but nothing was said of Yungay. They strained their eyes through the stinging dust to catch a glimpse of a passing aircraft. They maintained an anxious vigil next to the failing radio, waiting for news of aid for Yungay. The radio was filled with a continuous flow of news and information on the disaster, the destruction, and aid for the stricken area, but nothing about Yungay. An increasing feeling of abandonment began to pervade the camp, although the Indian peasants from the high country, among them Arturo Cantaro, whose own home was in ruins, came down with offerings of food from their meager surpluses. Up to this point the food from the Indians had been the only aid for the survivors. "We lived like people without civilization," said Asunción Montoya.

However much it might have seemed that way to Señor Montoya, the truth was quite the contrary. Although many people were benumbed with shock, many of the actions described by the survivors immediately after the earthquake indicate that within half an hour after the disaster had struck, manifestations of highly organized behavior began to appear. On the day following the tragedy, long before any aid arrived and, indeed, even before the fate of the valley or the town was known to the outside world, the survivors had already begun to reconstruct their lives. This is not uncommon behavior among disaster victims. Leaders either rise to the occasion or are rapidly replaced by those who feel capable of dealing with the situation. Although conflict and inefficiency may be present if disaster-stricken populations are left to fend for themselves, many of the immediate tasks of rescue and relief are undertaken by the victims themselves before outside assistance arrives. Human beings and groups do not completely dissolve or disintegrate when struck by disaster, but rather turn to the tasks of rescue and relief almost immediately (Fritz 1968:205).

In Pashulpampa, all the responsibility was given to the subprefect. A number of committees were formed among the able-bodied survivors, including committees for the acquisition of meat, the acquisition of vegetables, the construction of shelter, and aid to the wounded. The subprefect ordered all the animals in the area divided into two groups: those with surviving owners and those without owners. The peasants then told the city survivors whom the animals belonged to, and those whose owners had died in the disaster were designated to be used for food. A system of *ollas comunes* (communal pots) was organized to feed the growing camp. Water was a problem. Many people had no appetite but were very thirsty. All the streams and drainage ditches had been damaged by the earthquake and the water was muddied. At first, they tried to strain the water with women's stockings, but eventually they resigned themselves to eating corn and drinking muddy water until the food committees were able to acquire supplies. When the water was too muddy to drink, they strained the juice from pumpkins to slake their thirst. Food was collected from the schools in the nearby communities and, the day after the tragedy, a cow was killed to provide meat. Soon it became necessary to slaughter more and more animals because the population of the camp at Pashulpampa began to grow. Other pockets of survivors, from Acobamba, Ichicpuna, and Huiscurcoto, heard that the subprefect and the doctor were located in Pashulpampa and began to gravitate toward that encampment. Among the first to arrive were ninty-two people who had escaped death in the cemetery. They had spent the first night huddled at the feet of Christ in lamentations and terror in the many strong aftershocks which rocked the valley. Some of the people in the cemetery had been dragged out of the mud, stripped naked by the force of impact. They had wrapped themselves in the vestments of the dead to survive the frigid temperatures of the night. The following day they crossed the viscous, sucking surface of the avalanche on a walkway of coffin boards, laid down as they advanced, a macabre and pathetic procession leaving the place of the dead which had become a sanctuary for the living in the awful moments of impact.

The people who had been left homeless by the landslide or the earthquake in the peasant villages surrounding the buried city also began to arrive, as well as the circus people who had fled the stadium to Acobamba. At the time of the arrival of the first outside assistance, more than three hundred people had gathered in the area known as Pashulpampa under the organization of the subprefect. With such a large number of people, the leaders of the makeshift camp began to identify and classify each individual. A list was made of all the survivors of the city. There was no way of knowing specifically who had perished in the disaster. The people in Pashulpampa could only know who had survived, and it was assumed and hoped that their numbers would grow. For many people the search for family members went on for months, most often fruitlessly. All three couples who had been married on the morning of May 31 perished. However, scattered individuals, saved by quirks of fate and circumstances, began appearing over the following weeks. Luis Alvarez, known as El Pillo (the rascal), who ten minutes before the earthquake had driven over to Mancos for a beer party, appeared suddenly one day to great rejoicing of his friends. His family, parents, wife, and only child, were gone. Isaias Villa and Inez Puente also appeared. They had snuck away on a lovers' picnic into the countryside and had witnessed horror-stricken the destruction of their home from their trysting place on Atma Hill. Meche Angeles had gone to Chimbote alone on the day of the disaster as she often did when there was only a small amount of produce to sell, and Augusto was taking care of the farm and the animals. Both thought that the other had perished in the disaster. Two of their four children had died in the city, but Augusto and the other two were unharmed in the open area of their farm. Meche had also escaped death in Chimbote and almost immediately had set out on foot for Yungay. She walked for three days over the Cordillera Negra from Chimbote and had found Augusto and two of her children safe among the survivors in Cruzpunta.

For the majority of the people sheltered at Pashulpampa there was no such good news. With the shattered survivors filtering into the Pashulpampa camp came news of people who had certainly perished in the holocaust. Roberto Falcón relates:

The day after the avalanche around ten in the morning we went towards Yungay again. On our way we met a seventeen-year-old nephew of mine with his eleven-month-old sister in his arms. They had spent the night alone in the fields. He told me that my mother had died because she had arrived in Yungay from Mancos ten minutes before the avalanche. I had hoped that she lived, but she, and twelve other people of my family, had died. Until then I had not cried, but at this moment I began to weep.

The list of survivors began to grow as more people appeared from the shelters they had sought in the moment of impact. In addition to survivors from the city were all peasants whose homes and villages had been destroyed by the avalanche as it careened its way down the mountain toward Yungay and Ranrahirca. Thus, in Pashulpampa everyone acquired a disaster identity, and victims of the avalanche, *sobrevivientes* were differentiated from *damnificados* (refugees), victims of the earthquake only. This differentiation was to take on increasing importance in the social life of the survivor society after the emergency period had passed.

Over in Aura, Juan Beltrán assumed the responsibility of obtaining adequate water and food supplies for his stricken community. In addition to conserving, boiling, and bottling water, and prohibiting sales and price hikes in the few stores in the area, the mayor organized seven committees of four persons each who were in charge of the communal cooking in five different neighborhoods of the community. Each of these committees was given the responsibility of obtaining and cooking food in common pots for everyone in their particular zone of the town. The mayor also sought out the son of a wealthy man who had been killed in the disaster for his cooperation in feeding the population. The young man donated large amounts of vegetables from his father's fields and six cattle to be slaughtered for meat for the survivors. The next organized step taken by the survivors was to bury the dead of Aura. Everyone was fully aware of the dangers of epidemic disease if the corpses were left to rot, or to be eaten by dogs. No attempt was made at that time to bury the dead in the rubble of Ranrahirca or Yungay. The mud of the landslide began to sink in the days which followed the earthquake, giving forth a grisly harvest of mutilated and dismembered corpses.

As in Pashulpampa, the leaders in Aura also undertook to make a list of the survivors to assist the authorities when aid came. The first contact with the outside world did not come until Wednesday, June 3, so that during these four days the fate of the entire Callejón de Huaylas, and Yungay in particular, was unknown to the outside world. Some of the survivors left Pashulpampa as soon as they could on foot to find help for the stricken area, walking without food for four days over the rugged Cordillera Negra, since all the roads in the valley had been destroyed by the quake or buried under numerous small landslides. The survivors in Aura and Pashulpampa spent the days seeking food, caring for the wounded, and waiting for aid. When aid did not arrive on the first two days of the week, an attitude of resentment and bitterness began to form toward the authorities and the central government. Moreover, conflicts broke out among the survivors over the distribution of the slight resources at hand. One particularly violent episode broke out over the killing of a steer whose owner had not given consent, resulting in a fist fight between the owner and one of the authorities. Finally, on Wednesday, the first helicopter arrived. It brought nothing. It had come to find out what had happened to Yungay. However, by chance, the craft was piloted by the nephew of the doctor at Pashulpampa and did take out some of the wounded. One of its first passengers was Rosa Martínez, now at the edge of death after lying in the open for three days with a fractured skull, a crushed thorax, eight broken ribs, and a broken leg. The day after the avalanche she had been carried on a makeshift stretcher to Pashulpampa. She was flown immediately to Chimbote, where it was decided that her injuries were too serious to be treated in the makeshift hospital in that heavily damaged city. She was then flown to Lima, where she underwent a number of serious operations and began the long healing process.

Soon after the first helicopter arrived, more aircraft appeared in the sky, both helicopters and airplanes. The helicopters began ferrying out the wounded and the small children, and the planes began dropping food and blankets. The committees, which had been set up in both camps, took charge of distributing the first bundles of blankets, medicines, and food. Thus, when the first aid agency personnel arrived on the scene, the survivors had already taken the first steps toward recovery and the restructuring of their reality. They had walked, crawled, or been dragged away from a disaster that had entirely wiped out their physical and social milieu. Most possessed nothing more than the clothes on their backs, and some had even less than that. But, in those four days between the death of the city and the first arrival of aid, the survivors of Yungay had begun a process of recovery which will last for generations. They had replanted the seeds of their society. When aid finally arrived, the rehabilitative system of Yungay had already appeared in a nascent form.

The scope of the Yungay disaster was not known to the outside world for a full four days after the event. The earthquake had destroyed virtually all forms of communication between the Callejón de Huaylas and the coastal cities. Landslides had buried the roads in places and in other sectors, the roads had literally been shaken off their precarious mountain perches on the long winding route through the mountains. Work was begun immediately to clear and reconstruct the roads. For nine days and nights road crews worked feverishly up the roads into the mountains, clearing away rubble and encountering desolation and tragedy in every town on the route.

Telephone and telegraph lines were destroyed along with the roads. The only source of communication in the entire zone was a number of ham radio operators who were able to send a first report of the destruction on the evening of May 31 from Recuay and Huaráz at the southern end of the valley. Since each town within the valley was also cut off by the destruction, the ham operators in Huaráz had little idea of the horror that had stricken Yungay. The valley was totally isolated from the rest of the country, and each town within the valley was isolated from its neighbors. Understandably, the awesome tragedy preoccupied each settlement with their own crisis in the immediate postimpact period.

By June 2, a few Yungaíno survivors who had set out in search of help had made it as far south as Huaráz. They found the departmental capital in ruins with its own cataclysmic loss of 16,000 dead. The survivors of Yungay informed the ham radio operator at the Monastery of los Pinos of the fate of Yungay, and a message was sent to the government in Lima. These words were received in Lima with incredulity. The gruesome end of Yungay was simply unbelievable. In the two days following the earthquake, scores of aircraft had been sent into the air over the callejón. The first reports of Huaráz resemble descriptions of the saturation bombed cities of World War II, but all that could be reported for the Yungay-Ranrahirca area was that vision was totally obscured by thick clouds of dust which had billowed over 18,000 feet into the sky.

As time wore on in the days prior to any communication or aid from the outside world, the stress on the postimpact solidarity of the survivors began to tell. When aid did not arrive on the first two days of the week, attitudes of resentment and bitterness began to form toward the central government. An increasing number of flights overhead could be heard, but nothing was seen. The Yungaínos reasoned that, though it was impossible for airplanes to land in their vicinity, helicopters might be able to set down; at the orders of the subprefect, clear areas for helicopter landings were demarcated by long strips of red and white crepe paper found in the primary school in Cochahuaín. On the third day after the avalanche, there was still no contact between Yungay and the outside world. The sense of abandonment became profound. Concepts of personal private property, which had been submerged right after impact, now began to be asserted again.

Finally, on Wednesday, June 3, the dust had cleared sufficiently from the Yungay area for aircraft to get a view. The first photographs of the avalanche scar confirmed the destruction of the city to the outside world. A short time after the first clear flight over the city, the first helicopter landed near Pashulpampa.

The extent of the devastation of the earthquake, coupled with the gruesome news of the Yungay avalanche, staggered the entire nation of Peru. When the earthquake hit that Sunday afternoon, the population of Lima, all too well acquainted with the destructive power of earthquakes, had poured in terror into the streets, but little damage was suffered. Still, something hung in the air, and the city did not resume the normal activities of the day. People began to seek out their family members, aware that the awesome power that had spared them might have harmed loved ones in other parts of the city. But Lima had escaped. Then the reports came trickling in. And rumors accompanied them. Communications with the north were cut off. Chimbote was totally destroyed. Casma was said to exist no longer. There was no word from the Callejón de Huaylas. The entire nation became alert to the terrible potential of the earthquake.

Within three hours of the event, the president of Peru, General Juan Velasco Alvarado, called an emergency meeting of his council of ministers to organize emergency aid for the affected area, the extent of which was still unknown. The president and his ministers also made plans for an inspection trip north by naval vessel. As news of the destruction filtered into the capital, it became apparent that aid for the stricken area would be more extensive than first thought. By the time the death of Yungay was known, the government had already taken major steps toward emergency aid for the devastated coastal cities and Huaráz. On Friday, June 5, the National Emergency Committee was formed to undertake the immense task of organizing and distributing emergency aid to the thousands of victims. The National Emergency Committee set up command post headquarters in the national palace. Within hours of the earthquake offers of material and technical aid began arriving in Peru from nations of the entire world, and within days major international contributions of emergency food and housing, medical, and other forms of aid began arriving by air and sea. The postdisaster aid was to become a continuing factor in the devastated area, affecting most aspects of life for many years to come. The forms of aid and the structure and style of its delivery evolved on an ad hoc basis in the initial emergency period since Peru at this time had not developed any contingency plans or strategies for natural disasters, especially one of such enormous scale.

The immediate task of the National Emergency Committee was the rapid distribution of emergency relief to all sectors of the stricken area. In those early days, virtually all of Peru mobilized itself for this task. Collections for money as well as material were organized in the major cities of the country, and within days, sometimes hours, the assistance was on its way to the affected area. By June 5, seventy tons of emergency supplies had been parachuted into the callejón by the Peruvian Air Force, and over 400 injured people had been evacuated by helicopters. The Peruvian military was soon joined by air and sea units of the Argentine, American, French, Canadian, Brazilian, and Russian military, and a veritable air bridge between Lima and the Callejón de Huaylas was formed.

The airstrip on the outskirts of Huaráz at Anta was sufficiently repaired to receive flights of small transport aircraft by June 5. Four days later the engineers and their crews succeeded in clearing the roads through to the valley. Aid of every description was pouring into the major cities, but the thousands of tiny villages scattered over the Andean slopes, difficult under normal circumstances to reach, were still isolated. Helicopter flights from Peruvian coastal bases and the American aircraft carrier *Guam* were organized to survey the outlying areas for damage, ferry in medical teams, and aid and evacuate the wounded.

Food, water, shelter, clothing, medicine, and the burial of the dead were the priorities in the entire disaster area. Soon after the arrival of the helicopters, planes dropped bundles of aid to the Yungay survivors. Although some of the more fragile materials were dropped with parachutes, many bundles dropped without parachutes ended up in a useless conglomeration of condensed milk, rice, tea, chocolate, sweaters, matches, tuna fish, dehydrated carrots, and blankets. The clothes which had been collected in Lima were so old and dirty that, even in their miserable plight, the survivors were offended. According to one bitter Yungaíno survivor, the first substantive aid that Yungay received did not arrive until nine days after the disaster when the road was finally cleared and repaired. A group of young Yungaínos living in Lima had organized a collection and brought a truckload of clothes, medicine, and food. The problem of food was scarcely alleviated for the survivors of Yungay by the airdrops or the private donations of Lima Yungaínos. For a brief two-week period after the disaster, the Indian peasants continued to bring in their surpluses and give them to the urban survivors.

Although some of the survivors of Yungay from the suburban neighborhoods of Aura and Cochahuaín were able to salvage a few household articles from their ruined homes, the vast majority of people were left with absolutely nothing; everything they had ever owned lay destroyed and buried under the rapidly hardening crust of the avalanche. Consequently, virtually all of the material needs of the people encamped at Pashulpampa in the emergency stage had to be met from outside sources.

The first shipments of aid were distributed through the system of communal kitchens organized according to the origin of survivors. Within a short time, aid distribution was taken over by the subprefect. The National Emergency Committee divided the disaster zone into four food-distribution sectors. The representatives of the World Food Program of the National Assistance Board (JAN) and the Peruvian Red Cross were in charge of food distribution for the entire Callejón de Huaylas. These representatives in turn relied on the local leaders and ad hoc committees of survivors to assist them in the actual distribution of food.

The response of the world community to the Peruvian tragedy was overwhelming. Within hours of the event, commitments of material and economic aid began arriving in the capital. Shortly thereafter, disaster relief and medical teams from numerous countries arrived to assist in the rescue and reconstruction efforts. Reports were that cargo planes carrying aid from sixty-eight foreign countries and numerous private international voluntary agencies were arriving at the rate of one every two to three minutes in the week after the disaster (AID 1970:264). Since Peru had no contingency plans for a disaster of such magnitude, the influx of aid created serious organizational problems. Bottlenecks cropped up in the distribution process, which created severe shortages of crucial materials in several sectors of the affected zone. In many instances the capabilities of the Peruvian infrastructure were simply overwhelmed by the sheer quantity of aid, and materials began to pile up on docks and at airports, often waiting months and even years for distribution to the victims.

An appreciation of the magnitude of the organizational problems prompted the Peruvian government to form the Committee for the

Reconstruction and Rehabilitation of the Affected Zone (CRYRZA) on June 9. The CRYRZA was given absolute authority over all issues relating to the disaster and the disaster zone, including the distribution of all aid materials, the assignment of both national and foreign aid and medical teams, and control over such long-range questions as urban relocation and infrastructural development. The head of CRYRZA was also given ministerial rank, and the activities of all the ministries—health, housing, education, defense, and their subagencies—were placed under the direct authority of the CRYRZA in the disaster zone.

By the second week of June enormous shipments of food were arriving in the callejón. Much of this food was of a sort which, although appreciated by the victims, occasionally baffled them. Crate upon crate of canned goods were shipped into the valley and distributed to the refugees. Although most of the small stores around the callejón stocked various forms of canned goods, such as tuna fish, milk, fruits, and juices, such items were expensive and usually destined for the wealthy. Most of the valley's population were not familiar with canned goods, and if they were, they did not care for them. "We here do not know how to eat canned foods." (*No sabemos comer conservas aqui.*) Of course, when necessity dictated, the canned goods were consumed, but not with any great relish, and almost any substitute was rapidly chosen. The crates of Campbell's pork and beans which arrived in vast quantities often could not find recipients, and when they were accepted, the people immediately went to the nearest stream to wash the sweet tomato sauce away. Months after the emergency period had passed, stacks of the red and white cans of Campbell's pride could be seen gathering dust on the shelves of many small grocery stores.

Soon after the first shipments of food, large bundles of clothing and blankets, as well as crates of hard goods, such as pots and pans, cooking stoves, cots, and mattresses, arrived. This individually oriented aid caused many of the communally oriented adaptations of the emergency phase to dissolve, and people began to return to an improvised form of household living. Most of the dry and hard goods were gratefully received and put to immediate use. The Yungaínos felt a special sense of gratitude to and solidarity with all the distant international donors of aid. Cuban sweatshirts and plastic shoes were particularly appreciated. The sweatshirts were warm and had a variety of uses as nightshirts, undershirts, and pullovers. The plain, white sweatshirt became a prestige item, and some of the military personnel assigned to the disaster zone were seen wearing them. The sweatshirts were popular not only for their utility but also for the novelty of their donor and the sense of international brotherhood evoked. On the other hand, the used and dirty clothes and blankets which appeared in bales were held, often incorrectly, to be the cast-offs of the Peruvian upper class and were frequently disdained with righteous indignation. "I may be only a poor survivor, but I am not going to wear anyone's dirty rags," spat Violeta Mendez as she inspected some of the early arrivals of clothes. Such aid was considered an insult, an affront to one's dignity. Great bales of useless material arrived in the encampments throughout the valley, causing much bitterness and occasional hilarity. Yungay received a bale of several thousand used neckties, among which was the top of a woman's bikini bathing suit. Such things caused Yungaínos to question the attitude of the aid agencies in its assistance efforts. "What must they think of us to send us dirty rags and moth-eaten blankets? Do they think we are so low as to accept such garbage? Am I a beggar?" Such forms of aid, intended to help disaster victims, may compound the problems of psychological recovery by assaulting their self-esteem and engendering a resentful dependency.

Material aid in the emergency period in Yungay did a great deal to alleviate some of the most grievous hardships, but it was also unintentionally the source of continuing stress. Attitudes toward aid in Yungay were extremely varied almost from the first moments after the avalanche. Survivors soon began to prepare for the arrival of rescue and assistance in the initial four-day isolation. In fact, some resentment was expressed during that time by survivors when it seemed to them that no aid of any sort would arrive in Pashulpampa, and soon a sense of abandonment became another source of despair for the survivors as they listened to aircraft flying to other places above the mantle of dust clouds. Even the arrival of the first shipments of aid did not elicit any great displays of gratitude. From the very beginning of the aid period, the survivors of the Yungay tragedy had ambivalent feelings about aid, as do survivors of any severe disaster. A kaleidoscope of seemingly contradictory attitudes and emotions is evoked by the perception of oneself in desperate need. The necessity of accepting from others those things which normally one provides for oneself may undermine one's self-esteem. A disaster may demonstrate the inadequacy of culture to protect the individual from calamity, and the aid which follows disaster may demonstrate one's own individual inadequacy. On the other hand, aid that is organized on a mutual and informal basis does not compromise the victim's sense of self-sufficiency.

It seems almost inevitable that disaster aid at some time will become the focus of conflict. In severe disasters the conditions of trauma and loss are often so extreme that even massive aid can become merely a patchwork, stop-gap effort for a stricken population still insecure after the loss of personal community and the destruction of the physical, concrete aspects of their culture and society.

After the initial efforts to remove the wounded were completed, the Peruvian Ministry of Health began organizing field hospitals. Immediate steps were taken for the prevention of epidemics by spraying disinfectants in the areas around Huaráz and Yungay, where large concentrations of dead lay still unburied. The burial of the dead became more and more pressing in the Yungay area in the week after the disaster. Over four thousand Yungaínos, and as many as two thousand other people who had been in the city, lay half buried in the drying ooze of the avalanche. The area surrounding the battered cemetery was a ghastly charnel house of human remains, piled high and rotting in the warm sun. The actual burial of the Yungay dead was undertaken by a Yungaíno police officer who had been stationed in another region of Peru at the time of the disaster. He had rushed back to Yungay to find that his wife and most of his family had been killed. In desperate, driven fashion, he undertook the direction of the mass burial with the help of 300 Indian peasants, all the while methodically searching through the cadavers for the bodies of his family. Contingents of other policemen watched over the grisly process to shoot the wild dogs that came to scavenge the bodies. The desperate search for relatives brought people face-to-face with indescribable horrors, and many of the survivors bear the imprint of those first nightmarish weeks in their faces and eyes. They have seen things which are beyond description, and some will never recover. The police officer who directed the burial suffered an emotional breakdown at the end of the task. He was immediately sent to a hospital in Lima for treatment and recuperation from the ordeal. When he recovered sufficiently, his superiors gave him his choice of assignments anywhere in the country. He might have chosen the most peaceful, luxurious, and lucrative position in the urban comfort of Lima. He returned to Yungay.

The Calle Comercio in old Yungay. Photograph by Paul L. Doughty.

The church and palm trees of the "plaza de armas" of old Yungay. Photograph by Paul L. Doughty.

The four surviving palm trees of Yungay's plaza with the southern slope of Atma Hill in the background.

Huascarán and the path of the avalanche.

Family camping tents were the initial response to emergency housing needs.

Little outbuildings, gardens, and corrals for small animals soon gave the modular buildings of Yungay the look of an urban squatter settlement.

Estera (woven split cane) hut restaurants and bars along the road through Yungay camp.

The module buildings, built in 1970 to last two years, were eventually replaced in late 1974.

An Andean string band plays the waltz "Yungay" in the Restaurante Rosita.

Four survivors, three of them widowers, talking in the Restaurante Rosita.

Some Chupamaros and friends in the Restaurante Rosita.

Don Augusto Arévalo, his pain still etched deeply in his face, resides in Yungay, a hero, universally admired by his fellow citizens.

Many others, particularly the foreign volunteers who worked in the awful emergency period, were deeply appreciated and became the objects of heartfelt gratitude and affection. Approximately a month after the disaster, foreign medical teams from France, Italy, the United States, South Africa, and Russia were operating in the valley. In Yungay a Russian medical team administered to the population which by then had fallen prey to a high number of gastrointestinal ailments from contaminated water sources. Insufficient shelter in the frigid Andean nights also created conditions in which pulmonary afflictions became fairly widespread.

A warm sense of camaraderie as well as sincere gratitude developed between the Yungaínos and the Russian medical team staff during their three-month sojourn in the area. Although only one Russian, Tallin, could speak Spanish, all the team members are remembered affectionately, and tales of Russian drinking exploits grow more elaborate and legendary each year. The Yungaínos were very impressed with Russian drinking capacity. When they ran out of their own vodka, they astounded the Yungaínos, who are not modest about their own abilities to consume, by outdrinking the home team with the strongest forms of their own alcohol. Russians, in turn, gaped at Peruvian abilities to consume fiery hot food. Apparently, the Russians had brought much of their own food with them, including a spicy hot horseradish sauce which they used in modest amounts to flavor their food. They touted this sauce to the Yungaínos as much hotter than anything the local cookery could offer. One afternoon a group of survivors were drinking with the Russians, and Luis Alvarez, El Pillo, known for his sense of humor as well as his taste for hot food, asked to try the infamous horseradish sauce. With knowing winks for his compatriots, Tallin offered him the whole jar, gleefully anticipating the ensuing explosion. El Pillo casually examined the jar, and with a large serving spoon heaped great gobs of the sauce onto a piece of bread, which he calmly consumed, commenting as he munched away on its agreeable but mild flavor. The Yungaínos laughingly describe the Russian reaction as mute astonishment. They later compounded the joke by offering Tallin one of the most explosive varieties of pepper as "a local fruit." A decade later his reaction still makes for a good story.

While foreign medical and technical teams from Russia, the Netherlands, South Africa, the United States, and numerous other countries were being accepted and praised by the victim population, considerable resentment was felt toward many Peruvian volunteers and agencies. One Yungaíno reported to me soon after my arrival that some Peruvian doctors had worked in Yungay before the Russians, but they were actively disliked because of their refusal to touch their patients. Apparently, one doctor in particular constructed a fence of parallel ropes tied to two rows of stakes in the ground to ensure that no contact between himself and the patients was made. Safe from "contamination" behind this barrier, he heard complaints and prescribed remedies, all the while earning the undying hatred of the Yungay populace. Peruvian functionaries and administrators of aid programs were mistrusted and accused of employing the vast amounts of material aid for their own advantage. The newspapers were filled with accounts of the high-quality new materials which the international community had donated to aid the survivors. When bundles of old clothing and blankets arrived in Yungay and other cities and encampments, the people were not only insulted but also quick to accuse the national aid personnel of stealing the aid and selling it for their own profit. Survivors who had gone to stay in Lima with relatives returned from the capital with tales of stores in Miraflores, a wealthy district of Lima, burgeoning with new blankets and fine clothes that generous nations had sent to the victims of the disaster. In a sense, the aid was considered to be the personal property of the survivors. Administrators charged with allocating aid to where it would be most useful were considered to be unnecessary and dishonest middlemen. The military in particular was singled out as especially guilty of malfeasance in the distribution of aid. There were continual accusations that the army had taken the original shipments of aid, and the survivors had been given the army's used materials.

The cornstalk lean-tos of the first days of the disaster soon gave way to slightly more substantial pole-and-thatch huts in the area of Pashulpampa. The lean-tos, or ramadas, were only makeshift shelters to sleep in. After the general adjustment period of the camp, something more stable was required. People were acquiring clothes, cots, mattresses, food, utensils, blankets, and other articles, and these things had to be kept somewhere. Within days, people began constructing small huts with slender pole frames and thatch walls and roofs. *Quinchas,* more substantial structures with walls of laced reeds and plastered mud, were also constructed, providing more insulation against the cold. The rapidly forming community in Pashulpampa began to take on the very familiar appearance of an urban squatter settlement with its scores of cube-shaped little huts. Neither the ramadas nor *quinchas* came close to solving the major problem on everybody's mind: "What are we going to do when the rains come?" The rainy season in the callejón begins in late October and reaches its peak in January and February. The days of the rainy season are clear and bright until mid-afternoon, when heavy clouds shroud the mountain tops and the rain begins. The rains are torrential and do not cease until well into the night. The following day dawns clear, bright, and muddy. Neither ramada nor *quincha* would protect from the downpour completely. The rainy season is also the season of landslides when the earth on the steeper grades of foothills becomes loosened by the downpour and slips down the slopes, often wiping out roads. The rainy season landslides also take their share of human lives as well. The rain swells the rivers, which eat away at their rocky banks high above the valley and come roaring down the canyons carrying large boulders which crack and rumble ominously. Often these swollen rivers will knock out bridges. While the season brings much-needed rain for the crops of Yungay and the callejón, it also brings moments of discomfort, inconvenience, and occasional danger. In the aftermath of the earthquake, the rainy season would have a much greater impact.

The people's first concern was for shelter in the rainy season. The aid agencies responded with tents. The Peruvian army and other aid groups had established their own tent encampments close to the cities throughout the valley, and soon after that massive shipments of tents of all descriptions arrived for the victims, giving the callejón the rather deceptive image of a giant scout camp. As one moved north through the devastated area, encampments of tents of all shapes and colors appeared by the sides of the road. The Swedes and the Germans brought white and blue conical tents of a style vaguely reminiscent of the Middle Ages. The Peruvian army tents were the obligatory olive drab and were pitched in neat orderly rows. In Pashulpampa, the donation of hundreds of "Ted Williams approved" Sears and Roebuck family camping tents rapidly replaced the ramadas and many of the *quinchas*. Since the tents were distributed on an individual basis with little plan for spatial organization, the community soon became a disarmingly festive profusion of bright green and yellow tents, their canopies fluttering in the afternoon breezes. The random placement of the tents, their bright colors, the smoke of campfires, and the growing number of people arriving daily in search of assistance turned the encampment into a beehive of activity which belied the personal and collective tragedy of its populace.

The tents donated to Yungay measured approximately ten by six by five feet with a peaked roof supported by an external aluminum framework. The tents were said to be waterproof and probably would have been under conditions of normal use. In general, a family of four was allotted one tent. Single people were urged to group with others. Since many of the survivors of the urban area were the sole survivors of their families, the necessity to maximize the tents provided a basis for the early formation of postdisaster domestic units. Men who had been friends in old Yungay, whose entire families had been swept away, set up household together four to a tent. Women in similar conditions did the same, often with several orphaned children. Kinship, often of the remotest kind, provided a basis for the formation of a household under the protective roof of a tent.

The tents were a definite improvement over the ramadas, but they were far from an adequate solution to the problem of the approaching rainy season. August brought the first rains of what threatened to be a heavier than normal wet season, and many of the tents began to leak at the seams. After weeks of exposure to the sun and the onslaught of the season's first heavy rains in October, the tents began to lose their waterproof qualities and provided only minimal protection from the torrential downpours. They were too hot during the day and too cold at night. The zippered doors and windows also failed to withstand the constant use of permanent dwellers, breaking and snagging hopelessly and leaving the meager contents open to the increasing theft that began to plague the camp. It did not take long for people to realize that the tents were an inadequate solution to the problem of shelter. Many people began to make plans for the construction of their own housing of adobes or *quinchas*.

The arrival of the tents and the medical teams essentially marked the end of the emergency stage of the disaster in Yungay. Actually, by June 15, only two weeks after the tragedy, the Peruvian government had begun long-term reconstruction planning, and a week later, the shift from emergency relief activities to rehabilitation and reconstruction was underway. After emergency needs are taken care of, a disaster-stricken population is faced with the problem of establishing a system to care for the primary needs of the people while they attend to the tasks of reconstruction. This system, known as the rehabilitative system, is the stage where the institutions and life of the victim society are at least provisionally reorganized, and it may be long, expensive, and complex in terms of the problems encountered. Where disaster has been severe, few places are left to rehabilitate themselves. As Paul Doughty, an anthropologist who worked in the valley several months after the disaster, observed:

The number of public, international and private agencies at work in the area is truly extraordinary. There are more experts per square inch than fleas on a dog's tail and it would seem that every other vehicle has an official seal of some kind on the door. One notes also that, parenthetically, there appears to be a direct correlation between the velocity at which a car is driven and its official status, as opposed to non-public ownership. Thus, the people are confronted with infinite visits (if they are on traversible roads, of course) of dignitaries and engineers who hastily make notes, then disappear in the dust. The ones who arrive by car, of course, are less prestigious than those who drop in by helicopter. Those on foot are really in tough shape, but then again there seem to be few of these. The length of time passed in each place also correlated highly with the mode of travel; indeed, one would predict a perfect scale in this respect. It's likely that Galo Plaza established the record, alighting at most places for timed stays of 3.2 minutes (1970:10).

In cases like Peru where the devastation was truly great, the rehabilitative system may last indefinitely, and the experts and their work become a permanent fixture in the social landscape. The presence of such people and technology, which is often foreign or strange to local populations, may ultimately account for greater change than the disaster itself.

The rehabilitative system was especially problematical in Yungay because the authorities considered the camp provisional and warned that the entire population might be relocated to a safer place at any moment. This situation made any investment in permanent housing difficult. In addition, the surviving population of Yungay was already split into two groups in Pashulpampa and Aura. Since each location had a distinct political authority in residence, a sense of rivalry for aid as well as for the location of new Yungay rapidly developed. The subprefect sent orders to the survivors in Aura to come to Pashulpampa with all the aid they had received. He made it known that from that time on he would take responsibility for all aid and its distribution. The mayor of Yungay, living in a tent on the hill above the damaged houses of Aura, felt that he was under no obligation to comply with this order, and he and the others refused to move. Thus, an initial schism was created between the survivors of Aura and those in Pashulpampa over aid and authority.

With the increasing aid pouring into Pashulpampa, the influx of people attracted by that aid began to strain the resources of the area and agencies to support them. Consequently, a group of about two hundred was moved south to a tract of land called *Fundo Concepción* between Ranrahirca and Mancos. Shortly after that a group of survivors was established in Tingua, fifteen kilometers farther to the south. Thus, within three months of the earthquake, four separate populations were all claiming the name of Yungay in one way or another. A bitter rivalry over aid and structural importance within the province began to rage among them.

Among other things, the settlement at Pashulpampa had the largest population, and the subprefect of the province was in residence there. Since it was the largest, Pashulpampa had become the center for aid for the densely populated Yungay area. Pashulpampa also claimed to have the highest number of urban survivors, thus laying a claim on being the site for a new Yungay. The camp began to be called Yungay Norte by the reconstruction authorities.

Aura claimed to be the only part of Yungay that was still inhabitable. The disaster had rendered useless an effort to have Aura, previously considered to be a suburb of Yungay, incorporated within the city limits. Aura was almost as urban as Yungay had been. It was separated from the city by the Santa Rosa Creek, which was crossed by the Calicanto Bridge on the most important road into the city from the south. Although the mayor, Juan Beltrán, had by this time been transferred to a coastal city by his employer, the people of Aura felt themselves to be Yungaínos and deserving of full respect and benefits owed that status.

The people relocated to the *Fundo Concepción* soon erected a large sign saying Yungay Sur (Yungay South). Again, this camp claimed to have the most urban survivors, but they were not pressing for new Yungay to relocate there. Their main concern was that they had not been treated properly by the authorities and had not been given their fair share of aid as due survivors of the urban area and not peasants "like everybody in Pashulpampa."

The residents of Tingua also claimed the name Yungay chiefly because they had been settled there by the national reconstruction authority and told that Tingua might be the site of the new provincial capital of Yungay Province. Tingua also had one of the surviving Yungay physicians while Pashulpampa had none. Other Yungaíno families, on hearing rumors of relocation to Tingua, had moved there shortly after the disaster. Finally, Tingua had attracted people because it was the safest of all four locations. Pashulpampa was protected by a large hill, but the landslide had passed only 700 meters to the south. Just to the north of Pashulpampa was the Quebrada Ancash, the scene of the 1725 avalanche. Aura was located in between the two major lobes of the 1970 avalanche, between the buried cities of Yungay and Ranrahirca. Although somewhat elevated, Aura was directly in the path of any future cataclysm from Huascarán. Yungay Sur, located just south of Ranrahirca, looked into the jaws of Huascarán. No one was fooled into thinking that either of these two locations afforded any permanent safety from Huascarán. Tingua, though occasionally threatened by floods from the Santa River, was kilometers away from Huascarán and in little danger of landslides from any nearby peaks.

Thus, the four camps of Yungay each had reasons for being considered the most worthy of the name and the aid coming to Yungay survivors. Each also developed the particular identities of their populations and their leadership. Local wags were quick to seize upon these different qualities in describing each of "the four Yungays." Each camp was labeled with some variation of the word *pampa,* meaning a level area or plain in Quechua. Adding *pampa* as a prefix or suffix to an adjective or noun is a common way of forming place-names in Peru. Pashulpampa, or Yungay Norte, probably had the highest number of urban survivors, and their high consumption of alcohol quickly earned their camp the nick-name "Chichapampa." *Chicha* is highland corn beer. The urban survivors of Yungay Norte went through a six-month stage of extreme psycho-logical stress which was alleviated (or worsened), almost daily in many cases by consumption of colossal amounts of beer, pisco (a highly al-coholic brandy), and straight cane alcohol. Drunkenness was common in the other camps too, particularly Tingua.

In Aura, after the departure of the mayor for the coast, leadership

Existing cities and relocation sites in the Callejón de Huaylas was informally assumed by a committee of residents who had repaired their damaged homes and decided to remain. This committee was led by a strong-willed and intelligent woman who was determined to defend the interests of Aura against all who would attempt to deprive the area of status and aid. She clashed frequently with reconstruction authorities over the distribution of aid resources and gained considerable notoriety for her temper. It was not long before Aura had won the nickname "Brujapampa," or Witch-pampa.

Yungay Sur on the *Fundo Concepción* was, as were all the camps, originally a tent city. The Organization of American States donated a shipment of corrugated tin roofing sheets to the camp, and soon after the residents boasted of sturdy waterproof dwellings. Glistening in the sun like so many tin cans, Yungay Sur was soon dubbed just that— "Latapampa," tin-can pampa. The Yungay survivors who had moved to Tingua earned the undying enmity of the survivors in Yungay Norte when they began to pressure national authorities for the official designation of the provincial capital to be given to Tingua. While these efforts met with partial initial success, the general population did not immediately migrate to Tingua. The people of Yungay Norte chose the unflattering nickname of one of the most outspoken leaders of Tingua as the basis for "Monopampa," Monkey-pampa.

While all four camps, Chichapampa, Brujapampa, Latapampa, and Monopampa—were important in the reorganization of Yungay province, it soon became clear, despite government orders to the contrary, that Chichapampa, Pashulpampa, Yungay Norte, or simply after the passing of time, Yungay, was to become the province's most important urban settlement. It was in Yungay Norte that the only major efforts at providing a concrete rehabilitation system were attempted. However, the area presented problems which tended to offset the structural importance bestowed on Yungay Norte by the rehabilitation system. Geological reports indicated that while a limited area of Yungay Norte seemed reasonably safe from landslides, if a provincial capital was located there, the city would grow and spill over into dangerous areas. Thus, the CRYRZA was forced to supply structural and material support for a growing population in Yungay Norte, which may well expand into dangerous areas owing to immigration attracted by the very aid that was being supplied. Families from the hinterland who first sought help in Mancos, Tingua, or one of the other camps often obtained housing,

105

household articles, and food in Yungay Norte and consequently settled there. In essence, disaster aid reproduced the problems of intensified rural migration which cities all over the Third World are experiencing.

With the arrival of more and more refugees at the camps, aid and reconstruction efforts became more complex, and more bureaucratic steps were instituted to qualify for material aid. The institutionalization of aid is one of the markers in the transition from the emergency stage to the period of reconstruction. The process of registering as a disaster victim entitling one to residence in the camp, household necessities, and food allotments also became increasingly complex. Lost documents had to be applied for and signatures of local authorities had to be obtained on statements attesting to one's rightful status as a true victim. Documents, statements, and signatures, often on special stamped and expensive legal forms, had to be presented at the correct offices of the CRYRZA. The whole process of inscription became a demeaning and degrading experience for the traumatized survivors. Obtaining the necessary documents constituted an assault on one's integrity and honesty. It questioned one's right to receive aid and one's honesty in seeking it. A short time after the disaster, the word *damnificado* (victim or refugee) became almost synonymous with the words *vivo* (hustler) or *gorrero* (freeloader). The memory of those who did not suffer in the holocaust of May 31, 1970, proved to be exceedingly short. Adding injury to insult, the aid was often unfairly and inefficiently distributed. Once the pattern of aid distribution became established in the first year, social conflict, maldistribution, inefficiencies, and errors plagued the operations of the vast bureaucratic machine of the CRYRZA. One person commented wryly shortly after my arrival, "First the Earthquake, then the avalanche, and then . . . the disaster!"

Two serious problems plagued the community: adequate water supplies and shelter for the rainy season. A water system for both household and agricultural use was an urgent need of the growing population of the camp. Most of the irrigation canals supplying the whole lower sector of Yungay villages had been destroyed, shaken from their hillside niches by the tremors of the quake. The water available for household use from the small creeks and rivers was both highly contaminated and extremely muddied. In the six months following the disaster, medical personnel in Yungay reported that fully 65 percent of the ailments treated were gastrointestinal, caused by contaminated water. Faced with these acute water problems, the Yungaíno survivors began organizing themselves to deal with them. A young Yungaíno engineer, Juan Santoro, had been among the first Lima residents to arrive in the camp to help his stricken homeland. He undertook the design and construction of a reservoir and delivery system with the help of Indian labor. The system designed and built by local resources provided only two water spigots for the entire camp, and eventually fell far short of the needs for the rapidly growing camp.

Water and agriculture are simply two sides of the same coin in the callejón. Each community in the Yungay hinterland had to begin the task of rebuilding its irrigation system, and by November sufficient water was reaching a good many of the fields of the higher communities. However, many of the good bottomlands of the peasant communities surrounding Yungay were still without irrigation because the avalanche had destroyed the main artery of the water supply from the Ranrahirca River. The avalanche had moved right over the main system of irrigation canals. Again, Yungaínos, well aware that urban survival depended on rural agriculture, organized peasant labor forces for a rapid rebuilding effort. Irrigation water is the lifeblood of the whole section of Yungay district, located between the Ranrahirca and the Ancash rivers. This area surrounding the former location of the city, which now included the camp of Yungay Norte, depended upon the two main arteries of the irrigation system for water for crops. With water, this area represented a kind of breadbasket for the city. Without irrigation water, it would be reduced to depending upon winter rain, which would cut its agricultural cycle in half and permit only one major harvest a year.

When the national aid organization began to support labor for community reconstruction projects, the two main outlets of the irrigation system were major projects. The system devised to reconstruct the canals as well as many other community projects was a form of "Food for Work" program. Working with large donations of food from national and international sources, the nutritional support program, Apoyo Alimentario as it came to be known, operated on the principle that reconstruction in the towns and communities of the stricken zone would largely be a matter of local labor rebuilding those structures of community importance which were destroyed by the earthquake.

However, reconstruction efforts would have to be postponed for slack times in the agricultural cycle, and the rebuilding of important community structures would be drawn out over an extended period of time. Consequently, a system of food donations or payments was developed to maintain peasant laborers and their families while they rebuilt the most necessary aspects of their community infrastructure. Minimum daily requirements were worked out for flour, powdered milk, soy bean oil, rice, pasta, dried fish, sugar, and salt; and multiples of these were provided according to the number of people in the household of the laborer and the number of days worked on the project. Through this form of nutritional support enough peasant labor was concentrated to rebuilt the Yungay system of irrigation outlets and canals within a year.

Both the people and the government were well aware of the inadequacy of the tents for the coming rainy season. By the time an early and heavy rainy season arrived in October, the tents in Yungay were showing serious signs of wear. The rains swept in every afternoon and evening from the east, drenching everyone and turning the ground into a quagmire of reddish brown mud. Little groups of people, knit by kinship, friendship, or the bonds of common misery, would huddle together around a candle or a kerosene lamp in the leaking tents, talking quietly in the shadows as streams of water coursed down the sloping terrain of the camp, through tents, dousing fires, soaking everything. The rainy season and inadequate shelter brought respiratory ailments. The bright morning sun would begin to dry things out just in time for them to get drenched again when the rains began in the afternoon. The promised shelter program was eagerly anticipated.

At the end of June, the Peruvian government had announced the design of a housing program for the approximately 100,000 people left homeless by the disaster. The program had two parts: corrugated tin roofing materials were to be provided to rural people, who would erect their own house walls, and provisional prefabricated structures were to be built in the urban areas. When construction began for the prefabricated buildings in Yungay in late 1970, rural emigration increased even more. The population of the camp had grown to five times the original number. The buildings, funded by the Peruvian Red Cross and the Ministry of Housing, measured thirty meters long by six meters wide with a peaked roof at three meters, sloping to walls two and a half meters high. The houses were constructed of sheets of Mapresa—one-fourth-inch-thick asphalt-cement composition board—and red corrugated sheet roofing, all mounted on a metal framework. The organization of the "barracks" town, which Yungay was to become, involved creating a series of tiers or wide terraces on various levels of the hillside. The long buildings were to be located on these leveled terraces, which would be connected by a long, curving dirt road ascending the hill. The buildings were constructed in rows at a diagonal to the road and set into the terraces. There were three tiers or sections, each holding a different number of buildings: section A close to the road, the market, and the school; section B on the highest level of the hill before it became too steep for construction; and section C in between sections A and B on a middle level of the hill. Section D was set aside for the promised medical post donated by UNICEF. A fourth housing section, "E," was subsequently added to accommodate new migrants. In all a total of ninety provisional housing structures were erected with a total of 525 individual units. Ultimately, each tier or section acquired social significance affecting the overall integration of the community.

The construction of the provisional housing was traumatic for many people. Because the area close to the road out of old Yungay was judged to be in danger of further avalanches, the architects planned to clear the lean-tos and shacks from both sides of the road. Since most of these shelters were little stores and restaurants, their owners resisted this plan tenaciously. The engineer in charge attempted to explain that they would be given plots of land higher up where the market was to be located, but their resistance did not flag. "The avalanche has taken my home and family and now the engineer wants to take my place from me again," wailed one woman. After one confrontation, the engineer roared at the little gathering of protestors that if they would not let him work, he would drive the bulldozers and earthmovers over their straw shacks. He stormed off, muttering that he would see what the Lima authorities had to say about the problem. He had his way. The bulldozers crushed the few empty remaining shacks along the road as they leveled the terrain for the new market area. The little shacks had represented a beginning, a new start after the horror of the avalanche. The sight of similar destruction, this time at the hands of man, was still another blow. Although they were all eventually relocated in the prefabricated market structures, the handling of the situation by the authorities only contributed further to the stress felt by the survivors and worsened the rapidly deteriorating relationship between the people and the institutions charged with helping them.

The reconstruction of institutions and services in Yungay Norte began almost spontaneously after the disaster. The presence of the subprefect in Pashulpampa provided a locus around which the hundreds of refugees from rural areas as well as those few hundred urban survivors grouped. When the mayor of Yungay was relocated by his employer to the coast in mid-July, he transferred his authority to a provisional mayor, a survivor of Yungay living in Pashulpampa. The new mayor was a primary school-teacher and had been one of the principal merchants of the city. He soon became one of the foremost proponents of Pashulpampa as the site for the relocation of the provincial capital. With his succession to the mayor's office, both positions of maximum political authority of the province became located in Pashulpampa, operating their offices from two bright green and yellow tents.

A provincial council, named by the mayor, began operating in mid-August. The political authority of Yungay province was effectively re-established in Pashulpampa within two months of the disaster. In February of 1971 the national government formally named Rafael Moreno Alba, a large landowner, the official major of Yungay with his offices and provincial council in Yungay Norte.

Economic activity began to appear in the camp at Pashulpampa almost immediately after the disaster. Not two weeks after the tragedy, Indian peasants, who immediately after the disaster had given away their surplus food, began to sell their produce again in an open area in the camp. Many of those who had turned to selling their produce in the larger markets of nearby Mancos and Caraz began returning to sell to the growing population of the camp of Yungay Norte. The paved road emerging from the avalanche mud passed by the western border of the camp and within a month was soon lined with small cubical shelters of woven split cane sheets, which housed everything from dry-goods stores to tiny restaurants. As the camp grew from rural migration, the central market area became a daily hive of activity. People began to come to the camp not only for marketing but for social life as well. The little bars and restaurants in their straw shacks by the side of the road spilled their customers, plates in hand, onto the roadside where they sat and conversed in the sun. The interprovincial bus line, Expreso Serrano, established an office in the camp, a glistening corrugated tin building, which for a time was the largest structure in town. In quick succession two other major transportation companies followed and set up their own offices.

Two months later in August, the reconstituted provincial government of Yungay began to collect fees for the right to sell in the "plaza," an open area just east of the road. When the peasantry returned to the Yungay market in numbers, surviving urban merchants resumed the importation of manufactured articles from the coast. Rural store owners from the surrounding communities also began to establish their businesses in Pashulpampa. In December of 1970 the Ministry of Housing constructed and distributed the official Yungay Norte market buildings, consisting of ten prefabricated houses, each one divided into ten "modules" for stores, distributed to vendors on a first come–first served basis. The provincial government immediately took charge of these buildings, instituted rental charges for the stores and for ground space in the area enclosed by them, and appointed municipal employees to collect rents and maintain the hygiene of the location. Thus, six months after total destruction in Yungay, a marketplace of considerable proportions had sprung up. Not only had economic life been revived in the Yungay area, but the Pashulpampa market had grown to be the fourth largest market in the entire valley, an area of over 2,500 square kilometers and 150,000 people.

Despite the feelings of many people that God had turned his back on Yungay, a portion of land was set aside in the camp on which an open air church of logs and branches was built. The church had an altar of adobe bricks adorned with a rough wooden cross and a poster-paint depiction of Huascarán and the avalanche. Since Yungay's pastor had been killed in the disaster, a series of volunteer priests, espousing progressive roles for the church in personal and social development, ministered to the survivors with mixed results and responses. Many appreciated that the new priests did not charge for masses or confessions and that they chose to live with the people in makeshift shelters and tents. Others were disturbed by the egalitarian policies on aid distribution which the priests advocated. Ultimately, their potential for change was blunted by the arrival of a permanent priest of more traditional philosophy who chose to live in an abandoned house in Cochahuaín and charged for performing his religious duties.

Material aid pouring into the camp made Yungay a population center for the province. In response to this population growth the Yungay market rapidly became the economic center as well. The predisaster political institutions had been reestablished there by the presence of the province's maximum political authority. However, Yungay soon found itself in an intraprovincial struggle to retain the educational institutions of the province. This struggle proved to be an indication of things to come and became a key element in the formation of community spirit and identity in the arduous months ahead.

Within a month after the earthquake a provisional school committee made up of people from the entire province was formed, and at its first meeting, they decided that since school had been in session at the time of the disaster, it must be continued immediately at all costs. The only other urban center of the province, Mancos, had a relatively undamaged building with lights and water in which classes could be held. The committee ordered the province's national high school, the Gran Unidad Escolar Santa Inés de Yungay, to be reestablished in Mancos.

The Yungaínos protested this order vigorously on legal grounds, and the military governor of that sector of the disaster zone accepted their argument and ordered the high school returned to Yungay. A mass collective effort was organized in the camp to scavenge every available source for building materials, and a school of branches, scrap metal sheeting, plywood, and logs was constructed with the help of peasant labor ordered by the mayor. The people in Yungay viewed the transfer of the high school to Mancos as an attempt by Mancos to seize provincial power. They felt that relocating the high school in Mancos would be the first step toward relocating the provincial capital there. Actually, the conflict was a continuation of a long-standing intraprovincial rivalry and the desire of Mancos to be an independent province. The school conflict was the first shot fired in the latest battle Yungay was to fight for its political survival.

The struggle with Mancos for the provincial educational institutions was the preface for a further challenge which the rehabilitative system for the entire valley would present to the survivors of Yungay. Both rural and urban people alike faced a continuing threat in that the rehabilitative system authorities did not guarantee stability or permanence for the camp. Yungay Norte offered protection from further avalanches from Huascarán to the immediate south and from Huandoy to the immediate north in the form of 4,000-meter-high Atma Hill. However, the triangular area formed between the avalanche from Huascarán and the steep-sided canyon from Huandoy was quite reduced, and authorities speculated that if the provincial capital were relocated there, it would soon outgrow the safe area and spread into dangerous zones. Consequently, the aid authorities proposed that the new capital of Yungay be relocated in the camp called Tingua, some fifteen kilometers to the south.

The reaction to this project was immediate and definite rejection by the survivors of Yungay. Almost immediately after notification of the relocation scheme, the Yungaínos were soon busy at work painting and posting signs on the road and buildings at the southern edge of the camp. "Yungay Stays Here" and "Yungay Is Reborn Here" in broad white letters greeted citizen and visitor alike at the entrance to town. Aid personnel attempted to explain the need for such a step and outlined in careful detail that all the services and institutions of old Yungay would be fully reconstituted in a new city at Tingua, but to little avail. The survivors were adamant. Yungay Norte was the place where the majority of urban survivors had settled, it was the present location of the re-constituted institutions of the capital, and it was close to the original site of the buried city. They refused to budge. Many even threatened that if the Yungay Norte camp were dismantled for relocation, they would defy government orders and "invade" the avalanche scar above the old city in the manner of urban squatters.

This refusal to relocate and the resultant impassoned espousal of Yungay Norte as the only acceptable site for the capital became the *raison d'être* of the battered survivors of old Yungay and the community of New Yungay. The struggle in which they engaged the national government and other urban areas within its own borders was the most important factor in the formation of a new spirit and organization in the growing community. Not only had they been battered by the forces of nature, but now the forces of men were seen as conspiring to rob them of their birthplace, their way of life, and their identity. Few among the resident urban survivors were reluctant to enter the struggle, and soon the new rural immigrants and the highland peasants joined the effort to found and maintain a permanent capital city in Yungay, despite conflict and prejudice. Life acquired a broader focus. Individual survival was paramount in the aftermath of the disaster. Community survival became paramount in the aftermath of aid. Yungaínos fully understood

113

the necessity of bringing all their resources, however meager and tattered, to the struggle. The establishment of the social, economic, and political requisites of a capital city became the overriding concern of all citizens, and the efforts toward this end characterized life in the dusty tent and barracks camp for the next half decade.

Chapter 5
Yungay: A New Town
and New People

The settlement of Yungay Norte, which was to evoke such heartfelt allegiance from the survivors, was a visually un-prepossessing collection of long module buildings set into the red earth of the lower slopes of Atma Hill. The eastern border began where the hill's incline became too steep for the bulldozers to cut terraces, literally forming a back wall for the town. The southern boundary was another smaller hill which hid the avalanche scar from view. On the north was the Quebrada Ancash, site of the 1725 avalanche. The paved road which emerged strangely from the hardened edge of the avalanche passed by the lowest part of the town on its western border. This road had been quickly joined to a track, which had been bulldozed across the avalanche scar just up the slope from the surviving palm trees of Yungay's buried plaza. The now bustling market, most of the stores, the municipal offices, and the post office also housed in identical module buildings, either lined or were located close to the road. This road linked the new town to Caraz on the north and to the rest of the callejón and the outside world on the south. Beyond the first level of offices and stores, the tiers of residential modules set diagonally to the road ascended the hill. The once orderly rows and alleys so carefully designed by CRYRZA architects soon became clogged with little outbuildings of mud and laced cane, giving the town the cluttered look of an urban squatter settlement. The small outbuildings were constructed for cooking, workshops, keeping small animals, and a variety of other purposes not divined by official planners. The entire settlement was crosscut at several angles by blackened drainage ditches of raw sewage, and the roads and pathways among the buildings were littered with human and animal excrement. Higher on the hill on the southern border of town a pestilential garbage dump grew exponentially with the ever-increasing population.

In carving the tiers from the hill, the bulldozers had stripped almost the entire urban area of its vegetation. The later afternoon breezes lifted the unretained earth into great dust clouds, which tinged everything in the town with a reddish brown hue. The ascending rows of tan module houses with their light pink roofs rapidly blended into the surrounding red clay earth of the denuded hillside. When the rains came in October, the dull red color was not so much washed away as soaked into any porous or textured surface, such as house walls, shoes, clothing, or skin. Nevertheless the town's unappealing appearance did not deter rural migrants, and it was not long before all the module buildings were occupied and more had to be built on the town's northern edge.

Just as the appearance of new Yungay bore little resemblance to the old city, the people of the new settlement had also changed radically. The disaster had decimated the upper and middle classes of the district of Yungay. The little group of urban elites who survived formed the nucleus around which a new urban population, composed primarily of urbanizing rural people, began to form. Peasants, although escaping the horrors of the avalanche, saw their homes disintegrate in the quake. The all-important irrigation canals, often leading over several kilometers to distant fields, involving years of effort and no little engineering skills to construct, were destroyed in a matter of seconds. Large parts of community agricultural lands were covered by the avalanche, leaving survivors with nothing at all to fall back on in reconstruction. An urbanite may lose his home and his source of employment, but a peasant who loses his land may lose not only his opportunity to work, but also part of his identity. A peasant without land to work has been cut loose from the anchor of whatever meager subsistence and security it may have provided him but, as seen among landless laborers created by the development of modern large-scale agriculture, the peasant may lose the traditional community-based sources of social and personal identity.

The aid that reached the communities on the valley floor within two weeks did not reach some peasant communities for four months, and some not at all. Some peasant communities were totally destroyed but did not receive so much as a blanket in the aftermath. Thus, deprived of even minimal shelter, the peasants of many destroyed communities descended to the valley urban centers and refugee camps in search of aid soon after the disaster. Many peasants were told by urbanites that a tent, available for nothing to urban survivors, would cost 3,000 soles ($65.00) if they damaged it. For the peasants, it was far preferable to live in a makeshift dwelling than to run the risk of indebtedness on this scale for an article which was sure to be damaged in continuous use.

In general, in order to receive aid, an individual, regardless of community origin, had to be certified as a true *damnificado* (victim), a process which involved documentation of one's status by the subprefect, notarized secondary documentation, and formal presentation to authorities of the petition. Indian peasants recounted how after numerous trips from their village to distribution centers, only to be refused aid time and again for bureaucratic technicalities, they finally stopped going. The trips seeking aid were wasted time and money.

However, rural people felt that if one were already residing in the Yungay camp, aid would be much more accessible. Once residence in the camp was established, the earthquake victim certificate could be more easily obtained, and they could then obtain housing without strings attached and other forms of aid from the National Assistance Board. In the first month before the tents arrived, it was possible to move into the camp by building a lean-to on the edge of the settlement or near relatives or friends. When tents, food, clothing, medical aid, and later prefabricated housing began arriving, peasant earthquake victims who had been living in the ruins of their hamlets began moving into Yungay in a steady, daily flow. As in normal processes of migratory movements, most of these people came from nearby foothill villages rather than from the *alturas* (heights). The people of the higher, more distant communities tend to be more indigenous in language and culture and, hence, less eager and well equipped to deal successfully with the urban environment than people from the lower communities. It never occurred to Arturo Cantaro, living in his partially reconstructed home in Timbrac, to move into the camp. He was well aware that his Indian identity would make housing and other aid difficult to obtain. The less indigenous people of the lower communities are most ready and able to take advantage of any opportunity to migrate and cope successfully with the non-Indian urban culture. The cholos, like Augusto and Meche Angeles and the Tamaríz brothers, took advantage of the disaster and housing aid to migrate to an urban area, fulfilling a much-desired goal for the non-Indian members of highland rural society.

Once the rural migrants became established in the camp, they were loath to admit their rural origins for fear of losing what aid they had already received or being deprived of future benefits of urban residence because they had not been residents of old Yungay. Although urban survivors said repeatedly that there could not have been more than 300 people who escaped the holocaust of May 31, and some of these had departed for the coast shortly afterwards, the population of Yungay less than a year after the disaster was approximately 1,800, roughly 60 percent of whom claimed urban origin.

Within a year the camp had grown to approximately 40 percent of the population of the old city. Almost two-thirds of those people were under the age of nineteen. The old city, according to the 1961 census, had approximately 50 percent of its population under the age of nineteen, as well as a slightly greater percentage of women (54.5 percent) over men (45.5 percent). The balance of the sexes was altered in the aftermath to 52 percent male and 48 percent female. Interestingly, the number of births in the province did not decrease proportionately after the disaster. Even though approximately 25 percent of its population was lost, the total number of births in 1971 in new Yungay was 89.4 percent of an average taken from birth certificates from 1960 to 1965. The birth rate per thousand people does not drop after the disaster, but remains relatively constant. The birth rate in 1961 was 37.23 and in 1971, exactly one year after the disaster in new Yungay, was 35.22. One reason why these statistics do not decline significantly with the mortality of the disaster lies in the fact that the rural population survived more or less intact. In 1961, for example, only 18.6 percent of the registered births were urban in origin and in other years for which statistics are available urban births never exceeded 31 percent of the total. Thus, the disaster did not seriously reduce the population responsible for approximately 80 percent of the births in the district, which was the same group now rapidly repopulating Yungay.

From a socioeconomic standpoint, the new population was not only predominantly rural in origin, but also largely lower class. The old city as a bastion of the regional elite and its servants was being replaced by a town composed of people of a much humbler origin. The upper levels of Yungay society had been decimated, with the exception of a few notable cases. The uppermost stratum, the traditional landowning aristocracy, was rarely in residence in Yungay before the disaster. Their presence on any kind of permanent basis was totally out of the question after the disaster. Some members of the old families now living in Lima came up to Yungay after the disaster either for curiosity's sake or to pay homage to dead relatives. Most scanned the desolate panorama of the avalanche and the grimy reality of the camp and declared their intention never to return. Yungay for them will always be that picturesque little city of whitewashed houses and red-tiled roofs with the lovely palm-shaded plaza and the view of majestic Huascarán. One woman, who came to place a memorial on the avalanche scar, visited the dusty barracks settlement and declared in a voice curiously tinged with both scorn and despair, "This is not Yungay and it never will be."

There is a sizeable group of traditional upper-class Yungaínos living in Lima who became fervently committed to the foundation and flourishing of a new town in the location of the camp. Maximo Carrillo Guevara, the surgeon who was a frequent visitor to his homeland before the disaster, was now an ardent proponent of new Yungay, organizing shipments of aid and fund-raising events in Lima and visiting the new community for both pleasure and information on which to base further efforts on its behalf. Aurea Terry de Fernandez, an upper-class woman married to a Lima physician, organized fund-raising efforts and tirelessly sought homes in Lima for the many Yungaíno orphans. Her visits were also frequent, but the melancholy of her feelings about old Yungay displayed none of the scorn for the new city which characterized so many others of her class. She and Carrillo Guevara, whose sister lives in the new town, were voices of encouragement and support for the new city.

The provincial elite was now more in evidence in Yungay Norte than the traditional aristocracy. As a class they suffered much higher mortality than the aristocracy because they lived in Yungay. The surviving elites have shown mixed reactions to new Yungay. Some of them have also left the area to live in Lima and other coastal cities. The area's largest landowner, Rafael Moreno Alba, was designated the new mayor of Yungay Norte by the government, but complained often that his duties kept him from his economic pursuits, and eventually delegated the majority of his responsibilities to his lieutenant mayor, a young primary school-teacher. Several members of the provincial elite were instrumental in organizing the new market, and others served as temporary mayors or president of the Civic Committee, the liaison group to CRYRZA. They

119

continued to take active roles in politics and were considered to be the new town's leading citizens.

Juan Antonio Mendez, considered Yungay's best doctor, perished in the avalanche. Two other physicians also died. The surviving two soon abandoned the Pashulpampa camp and left, one for Lima, the other to Tingua, much to the disgust of the remaining elites in Yungay. Roberto Falcón became an intermittent visitor to Yungay, alternating between Lima and Yungay. His one surviving child, a small son who was visiting his maternal grandmother in Lima during the disaster, stayed there while Roberto traveled back and forth between the two cities. He felt unable to leave Yungay altogether, but was unable to undertake any new direction in life either there or in Lima.

Emilio Robles, whose family survived in the district capital of Matacoto, became a vocal community leader in the aftermath of the disaster. He had been in Huaráz on the day of the disaster and had narrowly escaped being crushed by a falling building. He became the leader of a liaison committee between survivors and the national aid coordinating agency. He set up a law office in a tent and then moved it into a module building. Much of his work had to do with helping people establish claims to property and securing the proper documentation for refugee status. Before long, Emilio had disinterred his car from the rubble under which it had been crushed in Huaráz. The roof of the late model Dodge had been totally flattened and the interior ruined, and it had lost most of its blue paint. But the car's motor was not seriously damaged, and it was not long before Emilio had it on the road again. This strange apparition of an automobile, its flattened roof pounded out in strange shapes, without windows or windshield and moving at a crab-like diagonal bias because of distortions of its frame, became a familiar sight in the valley as Emilio pursued his mission of leading the reconstruction of Yungay.

The number of people who controlled the political and economic power of Yungay city, district, and province was drastically reduced. Although the elites constituted only a relatively small number in the encampment, the degree of social, economic, and political power they manipulated decreased only slightly. They occupied the most important formal political roles, and, informally, their opinions and judgments were of great importance and were sought out before any decision was made. Economically, they tended to wield a rather understated, but totally understood power in local business as well as agricultural affairs. Socially they were paid the utmost deference, addressed as "don" and "doña," or "señor" or "señora" by all but their social equals and were referred to as "nobles," as they were before the disaster. As individuals their power and prestige diminished little in the year following the disaster. As members of the upper classes they may have lost most or all of their material possessions, but they did not lose their social position and the benefits which may accrue through that position. Every surviving member of the upper classes was able to call upon a network of resources, not always available to the rest of the population. Credit from official sources, monetary gifts, and other support from family or properties in other parts of Peru and other demonstrations of class solidarity minimized the loss of prestige and power. However, their small numbers meant that in the decade since the disaster the ranks of the elite have filled out with individuals who, before the tragedy, would not have been considered their social equals. Many of these upwardly mobile people have come from the middle sectors, and a few have leapfrogged into elite economic status from the lower classes.

The middle sectors also suffered extremely heavy losses in the landslide since most members of this group—the lower-echelon white-collar employees of the government and banks, policemen, and many primary schoolteachers as well as skilled blue-collar workers—were urban residents. However, there were more survivors from the middle sectors since a small segment of this group were rural dwellers, maintaining homes in the more immediate suburban villages.

While Antonio Flores had not lived in the rural suburbs, he had been one of the lucky few who successfully outran the avalanche. After the emergency period Antonio and his half-brother Javier had gone to Lima to stay with relatives and seek work. His parents died in the avalanche, and he felt that life in Yungay was no longer possible for him. Although the life of Lima with its bustling modernity appealed to his active spirit, the conditions of life in the crowded, dirty city began to oppress him, and he and Javier eventually returned to Yungay to take up the posts of treasurer and secretary of the municipal and provincial councils. While fully qualified for the jobs, they had been among the only surviving candidates acceptable, and the provisional mayor of those early months had asked them to return to contribute to the reconstruction of their homeland.

In Yungay some of the blue-collar skilled laborers such as mechanics, truck and bus drivers, machine operators, and other higher paid manual laborers survived because their jobs often took them outside the city. At the time of the tragedy, Rodolfo Armendariz was driving the Lima-Pomabamba route for the interprovincial bus line Expreso Serrano. It had been a good route for him to drive since it took him through the callejón and Yungay on his way to the remote northern districts of Pomabamba and Piscobamba, which had just recently been linked to the rest of the province by road. The day of the disaster Rodolfo was resting in Lima after returning from the north. His normal schedule usually meant one or two days of rest in Lima or in Yungay every three to five days. He was due to take a bus north on the first of June. Since the earthquake had destroyed all roads to the callejón, Rodolfo and other Yungaínos in Lima rode in trucks up to the coastal town of Barranca, and set out on foot into the mountains from there. They walked for three days and nights over the rugged peaks of the Cordillera Negra, many without any provisions at all, to reach their homes. They discovered the death of Yungay at about the same time as the rest of the world on June 3. Rodolfo lost his parents, his brothers and sisters, his wife, and all but one of his four children. His thirteen-year-old son, Miguel, had survived in the circus. Rodolfo and Miguel returned to Lima within a short time. When the roads were opened up and the bus and truck lines began to run between Lima and the callejón, Rodolfo began to drive for the bus company again. Since accommodations in the cheap hotel where Rodolfo usually stayed in Lima were poor and depressing for both him and Miguel on a permanent basis, they returned to Yungay where they were joyfully welcomed by their fellow urban survivors. His rough-and-ready style and his boisterous sense of humor, although somewhat subdued by the tragedy, were highly valued by his friends struggling not only with their grief but also with the increasingly miserable conditions of the camp. He was seen by many as embodying much of the positive in the *serrano* spirit—rough, unsophisticated, but durable and sincere. His unflagging spirit and profane defiance in the midst of the camp's misery were often the only things that kept the individuals who formed a little community of grieving widowers around him from psychological disintegration.

In Yungay, middle-sector people became increasingly visible in positions of responsibility in community affairs. In the year following the disaster they did not move into positions of actual political or economic power, but rather became functionaries in formal political and economic structures. While this kind of responsibility was not out of the ordinary for the white-collar middle sector, it was rare for the blue-collar people. The town council of Yungay Norte camp in the year following the tragedy had eight white-collar middle-sector members, four of whom were primary schoolteachers, and four blue-collar members of the total fourteen positions. Blue-collar people began to interact with the political and social elites of Yungay in a professional or occupational sense, and particularly among the males, in a social sense. The marathon drinking bouts in the year following the disaster saw grief, alcohol, and common Yungaíno identity temporarily erasing predisaster differences in social status. However, the political positions middle-sector people occupied were purely functional and carried very little decision-making power. Nonetheless, their increasing public activities were a measure of the degree of mobility achieved by middle-sector people and the dependence of Yungay Norte in general upon their ranks for the general functioning of society.

One of the most numerous groups in Yungay Norte after the disaster were the lower-class mestizos. These individuals characterized by their "non-Indianness" included small farmers, artisans, small store owners, and a few primary schoolteachers. Since most of these people lived in the rural "suburban" communities, they survived in considerable numbers. In fact, in the year following the disaster many foothill communities lost a considerable percentage of their skilled labor and artisans to the refugee encampment. Almost one-quarter of the family heads surveyed (91 percent of the total) in Yungay changed their occupations in the first year after the disaster. Within months of its existence Yungay Norte had a full complement of hatters, shoemakers, carpenters, barbers, tinsmiths, and bakers. Other lower-class mestizos lost their farmland under the avalanche, migrated to Yungay, and became part of the large proletariat class which suffers from severe underemployment. Any work gang organized of community men for town maintenance included a considerable number of lower-class mestizo laborers as well as cholos and Indians.

The entire family of the hatter, Miguel Mejía, was miraculously spared by their visit to the village where his eighth child had been born, but he had lost virtually everything else. His home, his shop, his tools, everything with which he supported his large family was buried by the avalanche. For a while after the disaster, he and his family subsisted on aid donations. They received a couple of tents, some camp beds and blankets, pots and pans, and a stove which he complained did not burn hot enough to cook anything. After several months of this dependent existence, Miguel journeyed to Lima to secure a loan to buy new equipment for his hat-cleaning business. His quest was unsuccessful. Just when things began to appear really desperate, the CRYRZA began construction of the prefabricated housing. Miguel obtained work as a laborer for fifty soles a day, just barely enough to feed his family. His diligence on the job, however, impressed the engineer in charge, and he was made a foreman with a raise of salary to eighty soles a day. With the extra money, Miguel was soon able to make a down payment for part of a new set of tools and forms for his hat-cleaning and blocking business. Since his family was so large, Miguel was given two L-shaped rooms in a module building. He converted one L into an I for a workshop, and the other L and the fragment became the living quarters for his family of ten people. With the rapid growth in population, Miguel soon acquired customers for his trade. A petromax lantern in his module rooms could again be seen burning into the late hours as he cleaned and blocked hats for the next morning, while his large family slept peacefully in the next room.

When Rosa Martínez had been airlifted out by the first helicopter to arrive in the Yungay area, few people believed that she had any real chance to survive. She had lain grievously wounded and only intermittently conscious for three days after the avalanche. The helicopter had taken her immediately to Chimbote, which the earthquake had also devastated. She was then flown to Lima and was admitted to the National Police Hospital. In the following months she had two operations to set the multiple fractures she suffered. After the second operation she was sent to a convalescent home. By October she had recuperated sufficiently to leave the home and had sought out a sister-in-law who lived in one of the squatter settlements on the outskirts of Lima. From here she began a desperate search for her sons among all the hospitals and groups of survivors from the callejón in Lima. By December she had exhausted all the possibilities of locating her sons and had abandoned all hope. Her intense grief at the loss of her sons and the hardships of life in the urban squatter settlement soon began to tell on her, and she made plans to return to Yungay. With the smallest of loans from her sister-in-law in Lima, she returned one grey December day to Yungay. No one was expecting her when she descended from the Expreso Serrano bus on which she had been given free passage, but word of her arrival quickly spread throughout the camp. "Rosita Martínez has returned." She had become known in Yungay as "the first survivor," and many people walked down from their modules to the road to greet her. She was dressed in black and her demeanor was solemn. As people welcomed her, her eyes filled with tears as she spoke of returning to Yungay to be with her dead sons. Her plans were to begin again, to start a small restaurant in town to maintain herself so she could live out her life in Yungay close to the grave of her sons. Soon after her return, Rosa and some friends had constructed a small restaurant, which soon became an important gathering place for survivors to drink beer and talk in the late afternoons and evenings.

While the Restaurante Rosita became a meeting place for many urban survivors, the migrant cholos, the most numerous social group in Yungay, tended to congregate in the general vicinity of the market where some of them had established little general stores. The cholos and those few Indians who had come down to live in Yungay constitute the lower class of the community. Since the cholos were already in a transitional process, they were among the most flexible and adaptive to the emergency conditions after the disaster and have been among those most able to emerge successfully from the harrowing experiences of the disaster. Their enthusiastic embracing of Western entrepreneurship equipped them well to succeed in the unsettled conditions of the refugee camp. The opportunity to urbanize which the establishment of the camp offered was immediately seized by a large number of rural cholo farmers, artisans, small shopkeepers, and laborers. Their aspirations and their mobility had equipped them prior to the disaster to urbanize. The disaster and subsequent reconstruction provided the opportunity to urbanize which rural cholos had awaited.

Augusto and Meche Angeles were among the first rural people to arrive in the makeshift camp at Pashulpampa. Augusto and his two surviving children had made their way from their shelter in Cruzpunta over to Pashulpampa a few days after the disaster, and Meche had arrived on the fourth day after her trek over the Cordillera Negra. The landslide had covered half of their lands and the other half was now without a source of water since the quake had caved in all the irrigation canals. Returning to the land was all but impossible for them. Once they established themselves in the camp, they began to work. Within a month Augusto had sold all five of his surviving animals for 16,000 soles ($480.00) and had set up a *ramadita* (lean-to). With an additional 2,000 soles in savings, which he had dug out of the ruins of his home, he set off for Huaráz, the departmental capital, to buy stocks for his "store." He began with three cases of beer, four cases of soft drinks, noodles, sugar, and salt. At first, business was poor, but little by little as the camp grew, things began to pick up. Within six months he was able to expand into the market module and "make enough to live on as well as some to save." As he happily said, "I'm going to continue with this business. I'm not going back to the other one. I am now a merchant . . . one who has his own store. . . ."

Augusto and others like him were soon to constitute an increasingly powerful group of cholo entrepreneurs in the Yungay market. The reality of their economic progress was based on a very shrewd assessment of the needs of the community and their own capabilities. In the general store business Augusto and the other cholo entrepreneurs had a clear field to operate in. The refugee camp was growing rapidly and aid was covering certain basic needs, but other secondary necessities such as soap, salt, and sugar, as well as some slightly less necessary but none-theless highly desired items like beer presented very promising markets. The overall reduction in the number of merchants to sell these things after the disaster was certainly greater than the reduction in the volume of trade, since many highland peasant consumers had survived. That the great majority of the clientele for this type of business survived, however miniscule each individual purchase may have been, provided Augusto and others with the opportunity to increase their scale of operations rapidly. The high mortality of the disaster reduced the number of sellers in relation to buyers. Some economic theorists consider this a necessary condition for accumulation of capital and development in peasant economies (Belshaw 1965:82).

Augusto's success has been rather remarkable. He expanded his business to include some wholesale activity and beverage distribution. However, the heart of his rapid economic success was still his own store. Augusto and Meche had one module measuring six by three meters, just like every other module in the market buildings. Their store contained an incredible variety of products stacked on shelves along one six-meter wall. Cans of milk, tuna, peaches, sardines, salmon, and the unappreciated Campbell's pork and beans in tottering dusty stacks, rows of bottles of pisco, vermouth, alcohol, guinda, algarrobina, and other local drinks, packages of soap, cigarettes, matches, household remedies, detergents, batteries, prophylactics, all climbed the wall in colorful profusion and seemingly little order. A narrow passageway for customers to walk separated one wall with merchandise from the other. The other wall was reserved for commodities packaged in bulk and sold by the liter or kilo. Beverage bottle cases reached the ceiling. Large oil drums of kerosene and alcohol, seventy-kilo sacks of salt, rice, and sugar, heavy paper bags of various kinds of pasta noodles, rose also to the ceiling. Bags and drums that could not be stacked provided what little seating there was in the store. The store was open at both ends, one entrance from the paved road and the other from the market interior. At the street entrance stood a glass-faced, battered wooden counter. Behind the counter, on a stack of beer cases sat the one luxury item—a portable radio. In the evening Augusto, Meche, and friends, all sitting atop the sacks and barrels of the store's merchandise, would talk and listen to highland music by the light of a Coleman lantern.

Augusto attributed his good business to personal relationships in part and in part to good business practices. He stated that other businessmen may not have done as well as he has because they do not have clients. "I have clients. I sell to people from everywhere, from the people of the heights to the people of the town, because I give them *peso completo* [full weight for their money]. I don't cheat." There is no question that Augusto's own rural and cholo status has served him well in this cholo community. While almost every merchant in old Yungay knew enough Quechua to interact with the Indian peasants in the economic framework, Augusto and Meche often lapse into Quechua themselves when they feel like it. Their ability and occasional preference to speak Quechua, their own recent peasant identity, which it has not yet occurred to them to repudiate, and their generally friendly and helpful personalities attract people to them. Such gestures as Meche knitting a baby sweater for the infant of a friend right after the birth of her own child do not go unnoticed in this small community. While they enjoyed economic success, their life-style changed very little, and their standard of living was not visibly higher than many camp inhabitants. He did not build a home away from the grimy camp with their new wealth. Augusto and Meche lived, as everyone else did, in the cramped and drafty modules of Yungay, suffering equally the mud and the dreariness of life in the barracks town.

However, Augusto's standards of economic behavior, at once a stimulus and product of his increased resources, have left his peasant origins far behind him. His entrepreneurial spirit, perhaps first evident when he worked his way up from delivery boy to baker in three years, has been able to find full expression in the disrupted and relatively open economic conditions after the disaster.

About all Elena Olivera was able to salvage from her collapsed home in Huantucán were an old frying pan, some clothes, and a blanket or two. Since the Pashulpampa camp was established within a few minutes walk from her house, she and her son, Rolando, took a tent there while they rebuilt their small adobe house in Huantucán. In a short time the house was rebuilt, and she and Rolando moved back to their village, which by that time had the burgeoning settlement of Yungay encroaching on its doorsteps. With a growing population to feed, it was not long before Elena began to work again. Since the earthquake, Elena has had to diversify her merchandise somewhat to include other vegetables, fruits, eggs, and soft drinks in her permanent stall in the prefabricated market buildings. This need to diversify is a direct result of the postdisaster conditions. Before the disaster, Yungay had a high percentage of non-producing professionals, commercial people, artisans, and laborers. The disaster annihilated all but a few of this specialist population, and the new refugee camp is now possessed of a high percentage of producers. Agriculturalists now make up about 15 percent of the urban population, and many other people supplement other professions and trades with small-scale farming in their free time. Consequently, the crop-importing middlewomen have found the market for agricultural products greatly reduced not only in scale but in demand. Elena complains often that since the disaster many of the people who live in Yungay have their own *chacras* and rarely have to buy anything in the market. "Here business is bad now. Before in Yungay five or six seventy-two-kilo sacks in a day were not enough because there were so many rich people. Now, not one sack in three days do I sell. The town is pure Indian now, and they eat from their own fields."

Thus, Elena had to diversify. Her room in the prefabricated building in the market regularly displayed varied fruits and vegetables as well as eggs, herbs, and soft drinks. However, her capital outlay for other products never approximated that of potatoes because the risk of loss from spoilage is greater. Also again, as before the disaster, Elena is caught between the coastal wholesaler and local price controls. She may buy a twenty-five-kilo crate of coastal tomatoes for 170 soles and sell them for seven soles a kilo, receiving only five soles a crate for profit because the market inspector will not permit any higher prices. The market still does not allow her to achieve as satisfactory a standard of living as before the disaster. Now, as she put it, she "survives," but, because of the limited amount of business, that is all she can do. Her level of subsistence is still above that of the *revendadoras* like Juana Machco, who continues in unaltered fashion her meager commerce.

The disaster and the trials of reconstruction had a great impact on the economic attitudes of the working classes of Yungay. While the poorest levels of Yungay society have always struggled grimly to survive from day to day, those slightly better off suffered a heavy blow to their ambitions and confidence. Elena laments:

Life? this is not life! There is nothing to work for now. I just work to eat, not to save. Before, I worked to save, to have a little something. Ahhh, now I just work to live, to eat. I have no desire to work for anything more now. Anyway, the market is poor now and gives one only enough to survive.

The Tamaríz brothers, who had watched from their fields in Yanama Chico the huge mass of the glacier break off the north peak of Huascarán, lost almost half their land in the avalanche. While their parents are able to subsist on the remaining portion, the three brothers were forced to seek a means of support in the Yungay encampment. Although all three had worked in agriculture, the loss of their land pushed them toward another form of livelihood. The skills and experiences accumulated during their sojourns on the coast enabled them to begin a new form of livelihood in the Yungay market. They began to sell clothes in the marketplace on a patch of ground close by the permanent stalls of larger clothes shops. The apparel they sell is of the cheapest variety, consisting of rough cotton shirts, handkerchiefs, socks, crudely cut and stitched blue denim pants, aprons, blouses, and skirts. Most of their customers are highland peasants, as they themselves once were. They started in the clothing business by getting to know the wholesalers who supply the larger dealers. Obtaining stock through credit from the wholesalers, the three brothers work to sell enough to live on and pay the wholesalers a little each time they visit from the coast. They estimate that they sell about $110.00 worth of clothing to Indian peasant clients each month. Of that gross income, approximately $22.00 a month is left to split three ways after meeting expenses, thus affording them little opportunity to reinvest or get out of debt. Their business provides them with their *pan del dia* (daily bread) and little else. In one sense, the Tamaríz brothers have transposed a subsistence economy from the highlands to the urban market. Forced out of agriculture by catastrophe, their meager resources and the structural difficulties of the peasant market limit their enterprise to a scale of bare maintenance and perpetual debt.

The Tamaríz brothers are typical of a large group of migrants to the new city of Yungay, and indeed of the entire disaster zone. The disaster provided a combination of "push-pull" factors for migration. In the case of the Tamaríz brothers, the avalanche pushed them from their rural home, but each of them as very young teenagers had experienced the world beyond the borders of Yanama Chico. While the Tamaríz brothers, and many others like them, were rural and agricultural in origin, they were not monolingual Quechua-speaking Indian peasants. They had shifted their gaze from the little community to the wider society. They had already altered their values and goals and acquired new skills to cope with the demands of the national society. They were cholos, bilingual, non-Indian in dress, sometimes literate, and economically ambitious. Waiting in the wings, they saw and used the disaster and the aid that followed as an instrument of social mobility. Many have used relationships acquired while working in cities or on the coast to obtain credit to finance an attempt to leave the marginal existence of peasant agriculture for a life in the city. The commercial vacuum created by the high mortality of the disaster constituted a magnetic pull factor for migration to the Yungay encampment. Although the disaster exiled the Tamaríz brothers from their homeland, they had, in a very real sense, been readying themselves for the journey for some time.

Thus, for the migrant cholos, the vast majority of the new city's population, the move to Yungay, dusty barracks camp that it was, constituted the anxiously awaited first step on the ascending journey from rural poverty. The sad reality of the camp was that successes as Augusto Angeles had were for a lucky few. Life for most migrants in the camp became a hard, dreary struggle to maintain oneself and family without losing the treasured foothold in an urban context. For some, like the Tamaríz brothers, there was no turning back. Their past was buried with their land under the avalanche in Yanama Chico.

Relatively few Indians migrated to Yungay after the disaster, even though much Indian land was buried or lost because the avalanche and earthquake destroyed irrigation outlets and canals. Without irrigation water, the number of harvests was effectively halved. Half of normal production for these farmers, whether mestizo, cholo, or Indian, was not going to provide subsistence.

The few Indians who took the leap to urban life found themselves relegated, as expected, to the lowest jobs in Yungay society. Epifanio Cántaro's first job was hauling water for the restaurants that established themselves by the roadside. He was paid eighty cents a day and meals. Later in January of 1971 he received the same wage for helping to build Rosa Martínez's restaurant. When the barracks buildings were built, Epifanio was able to get work as well as one of the module rooms for himself and his wife and two small children. Although more than a hundred million dollars were devoted to reconstruction and development of the disaster zone in the first two years alone, little of it filtered down to the poverty-stricken populations. Construction work that began with the module buildings in the latter part of 1970 bogged down in a prolonged planning and oranization process. Particularly in Yungay, where the camp was considered provisional pending studies of geologic safety, there was only intermittent employment for the working classes for almost two years. Epifanio and his family survived on the edge of starvation thanks to food sent by his in-laws in distant Timbrac, food donations in Yungay, and the little his wife could make as a reseller in the market. The first years in Yungay for the Indian and other migrants were years of hardship and misery. Without work and with little to eat, Epifanio, his wife, and children suffered in their damp, dirt-floored module room. Their only possessions were an old table and chair, a one-burner kerosene stove, and some worn and soiled blankets. They had arrived in Yungay too late for the aid distribution of household goods. Epifanio's plight was shared by many others. While most of the adults survived these miserable conditions, many migrant children, particularly infants, succumbed that first year to the pulmonary and gastrointestinal diseases which afflicted the entire population.

While relatively few Indians migrated to Yungay in those first two years, as the most numerous group in highland society, they cannot be discounted as a significant factor in the new city's growth. The peasant population, predominantly Indian, was the life-force behind the cities of traditional highland Peru. It was the peasantry that would ultimately provide the labor to rebuild Yungay. It was the peasantry that grew the food to sustain the urban population. While Indian farming was largely oriented toward subsistence for the family, the small surplus marketed by the woman of the family provided a little cash for manufactured necessities. In the aftermath of the tragedy, Indian women returned to the Yungay market by the hundreds selling their small amounts of foodstuffs. While each woman sells only small quantities, the sheer number of participants in the daily and Sunday markets ensures a relatively steady supply of food to Yungay.

The Indian also represents one of the major consumer groups for the market. Like their participation as vendors in the market, their participation as consumers is also extremely limited by their relative scarcity of funds. The sheer numerical preponderance of Indian peasant consumers, however, makes them an important buying force for manufactured articles. The cholo and mestizo owners of general stores stocked large amounts those products, usually basic necessities such as matches, kerosene, small tools, dyes, sewing articles, and rubber tire sandals, which are most sought after by the Indians. In addition, the large Indian population constitutes an important consumer population for the services and institutions of the new city. The church could not survive without continued Indian participation both in ritual and in the material contributions of cash and labor. The market revenue, which constituted over 80 percent of the province's internally generated income, is derived largely from the rents charged to Indian vendors. The many administrative functions of the municipal offices, such as keeping records of births, deaths, marriages, and other legal matters, were in part supported by Indian clients. The province's educational institutions, including more than forty little two-year schools in highland communities, were taught and administered with national funds from Yungay, providing considerable employment for urban people.

In sum, it is clear that the old city of Yungay could not have existed without the large peasant population which surrounded and nourished it. It is even more clear that the new city of Yungay could not have survived its first week, much less its first year or decade, without the active participation of the predominantly Indian peasantry living in the surrounding hillsides.

Chapter 6
Pride and Prejudice
in Reconstruction

The forms and nature of social relations among the new people of new Yungay began to take shape rapidly. In the days immediately following the avalanche, rural people flocked to Pashulpampa, drawn to the authority and organization represented by the subprefect and the doctor. They came by the hundreds, some grieving, some in shock, some empty-handed, some carrying a blanket or other salvaged possessions from their destroyed homes. Soon the green fields of Pashulpampa were filled with the remnants of old Yungay and many others who would become the population of new Yungay. The urban survivors soon became aware of the increasing numbers of rural victims and attempted to ascertain the origin of everyone in the encampment. Roberto Falcón and Asunción Montoya, among others, drew a rough map of the city and, when people claimed to have been residents of Yungay, they were asked to locate the approximate position of their homes on the street plan. The urban people were determined to find out how many real survivors of the tragedy there were in the camp. The Yungaínos, *netos y natos* (authentic and by birth) as they came to call themselves, were convinced that very few urban residents had survived the avalanche. After the official establishment of the encampment, the efforts to fix the number of survivors were continued, and further lists of authentic Yungaíno survivors were compiled, none of which contains more than three hundred people. It is likely that at least several hundred more survivors were either out of the city and never returned after the disaster or returned long after the attempt to list survivors had terminated. In any case, it is reasonably sure that no more than 15 percent of Yungay's approximately 4,500 people survived the disaster.

Everyone in the camp acquired disaster identities, which became crucial in the formation of the new society taking shape on the hills of Pashulpampa. One was either a survivor, a *sobreviviente,* an authentic Yungaíno who had survived the certain death of the avalanche, or a *damnificado,* a victim or "injured" person who had suffered only the effects of the earthquake. Survivorship placed one at the center of this mammoth tragedy which had riveted the attention of the world. In a sense, *sobrevivientes* saw themselves as symbols of the strength and tenacity of humankind to survive the harshest blows that nature or circumstances can deliver. They were survivors, not merely victims. Most survivors clearly were urban people, although peasants whose communities had been crushed by the avalanche on its way down the mountainside were included among this elite of sufferers. The *damnificados* were almost entirely rural, since suffering only the effects of the earthquake meant that one's home was not located in the city or in the path of the avalanche. This group was to become socially and materially important in new Yungay. In the immediate aftermath, when the new community was in the process of formation, the survivors of Yungay wanted to know the community origin of everybody in the camp to be able to differentiate according to their perceptions of need and loss when aid was to be distributed.

When aid did start coming in significant quantities after about two weeks, it provided an additional element to these two groups. *Sobrevivientes* saw themselves as far more deserving of aid than the peasants who had suffered only the effects of the earthquake, and who had, at least in theory, been able to salvage some of their possessions. Thus, in addition to one's disaster identity of *sobreviviente* or *damnificado,* differences in the quantity and quality of aid that each should receive began to color each concept with shades of honesty or dishonesty.

In the eyes of the "nobles" of Yungay, there were very few survivors of the urban area in the camp. Most who claimed urban origin were considered to be imposters, exploiters of the tragedy seeking to get something for nothing. In addition, the middle- and upper-class survivors who remained in the camp considered themselves to be surrounded by "Indians," a term which was used most often to express one's scorn for somebody of the lower class. The fact is that most people who claimed Yungaíno origin were from the rural areas, but were most definitely not Indians, but rather the more transitional cholos. Most of the urban survivors chose to ignore the difference, if they saw it at all, and labeled the rural migrants as Indians. Their hostility toward Indians and other rural people who had *sobreviviente* status was tempered somewhat by the traditional paternalism which had characterized predisaster rural-urban interactions.

Many rural people did hasten to adopt Yungaíno urban identity since they felt, with some reason, that they might be short-changed or left out entirely when aid was distributed. In assuming *sobreviviente* status, the rural *damnificados* acquired another aspect to their identity in the eyes of the *gente decente*. Not only were they less deserving of aid, but in receiving aid "properly" due the townspeople, they were also dishonest. The rancor of many townsmen over having to stand with rural people in the long lines, sometimes over two hundred people long, for blankets, pots and pans, and food was often bitterly expressed. The sudden leveling of status compounded the shock and grief they suffered in the tragedy. One old man, his face contorted with rage and eyes brimming with tears, choked out, "Why must I stand in line? Who am I? An Indian?" The lines for aid were felt to be a further indignity heaped upon the shoulders of a people already traumatized by their profound loss. Some refused to stand in line at all, simply moving to the head of the line as befitting their perception of the social order. Others never reappeared after the first distribution of aid, preferring to go without or purchase whatever they needed rather than suffer the indignities of the lines. Those wealthy Yungaínos who had resided in the suburb of Cochahuaín, which was not damaged by the landslide, accused the rural people of looting their houses after the avalanche. Even while the Indians were engaged in the grisly job of burying the thousands of Yungaíno dead on the landslide, bitter accusations that they were stealing wedding rings and other jewelry from the bodies were being leveled at them.

The urban survivors unleashed all their bitterness and sorrow on the rural people who migrated to Yungay and even on the Indians who stayed in their own communities, but received aid. One survivor complained:

The disaster has put some people up and some people down. The Indians are way up now. When did they ever have beds, sofas, tables, stuffed chairs? They did not even know what *calamina* [corrugated metal roofing sheets] was before the disaster and now they have them all, and they are fat. We, who had everything, have nothing and they now have everything.

The attitude that "the Indians never had anything to begin with, so why should they get help now?" was very common among middle- and upper-class survivors during the period of initial aid. Rodrigo Montoya, a Peruvian anthropologist, who filed a report on social and physical conditions a month after the disaster quotes a survivor:

The Indians are those that are benefiting most from the aid. We, the decent people of Yungay, are only about one hundred persons. The rest are all Indians. They ought to give more to us, the Yungaínos who have lost everything. The Indians have everything they need, and besides, they are accustomed to live as they do (1970:8).

At the same time, according to Montoya and other witnesses, it was quite clear that the middle- and upper-class survivors of Yungay were receiving more aid than the Indians of the rural sectors. Again, Montoya quotes a *damnificado* from the neighboring village of Punyan: "We from Punyan went to the subprefect to ask him for some aid and he told us to eat dirt, to eat shit, because there was no food for us, because they say there is not enough for the peasants" (1970:8).

The hostility between some groups of urban survivors and rural people became even more severe as the year progressed. While most major planning and construction for Yungay was delayed, pending studies of the location's geologic safety, some work on housing, irrigation canal reconstruction, and road clearing was funded. These projects paid wages two to three times higher than average Indian wages and created a labor seller's market. The point here is that the Indian peasant suddenly had the ability to choose how to allocate his labor. They were no longer dictated to by townsmen on the issue of wages. No longer could an Indian be told that he would work for sixty cents a day and meals. Indians who were not satisfied with employers' offers could refuse with impunity. Their labor was no longer a quantity to be delivered on demand to the townspeople. The aid agencies' wages or the nutritional-support program severely curtailed the exploitation of Indian labor by urban centers all over the valley. Indians now expected to be paid in cash or kind for their labors in the city of Yungay. Townspeople experienced a sense of outrage, of righteous indignation when an Indian refused to perform labor at the menial wages traditionally paid. One woman, complaining of the Indians who had come to the camp, said, "They haven't lost anything and now they are so fat on the aid that they received, that they won't work, even if you pay them 100 soles [$2.00] a day. They won't even carry anything for you if you ask them; even if you pay them, they won't do it." This alteration in traditional social patterns between urban people and peasants was a major factor in the considerable hostility toward rural people in the aftermath.

Survivors were not entirely consistent in their hostility toward the rural migrants. On the one hand, an hacendado who had lost most of his family and lands in the avalanche, could bitterly reflect on being "reduced to this misery after what we had." Sweeping his arm over the vista of the camp, he exclaimed, "And these people! Shit! All from the hills. What can you do with these people. They are shit! Yungay will never be anything because there are no more 'decent people' left. We are the last." However, a fellow hacendado, speaking in his most rhetorical tones, responded, "It is our great mission in life to educate them, to 'culturize' them. And by doing this Yungay will rise again."

To many urban survivors, to be consistently critical of rural migrants was tantamount to abandoning any hope for Yungay's future. They saw themselves as the base of leadership upon which the new city and its rustic population would be reborn. They tempered their resentment toward the rural migrants with a paternalism couched in professions of faith in Yungay's future.

The hostile attitudes and occasional actions that characterized intergroup relations in the early life of the camp were by no means a one-way proposition. Lower-class people sharply criticized, albeit only to and among themselves, the behavior of the more traumatized urban survivors. Some urban survivors had economic resources outside the province and did not have to work for a living. Others, among them several teachers, were able to return to their jobs within three months of the disaster. The economic resources and the fact that aid planning and delivery fell far short of involving everybody meant that many urban residents had time on their hands to contemplate the tragedy of their loss and the misery of their surroundings. Alcohol was a major means of coping with grief. Heavy drinking among the urban survivors as well as among some rural people soon became a serious problem. The consumption of beer alone jumped from 24,649 cases in 1970 to 31,100 cases in 1971, even after the province had lost 25 percent of its population. Since beer is a relatively expensive drink consumed largely by urban men rather than by rural people, the per capita intake for the urban area was colossal. Drinking was almost always done in groups, and the marathon drinking bouts often resulted in fights, crying fits, verbal abuse, and other problems. As El Pillo put it, "The disaster was the real drunk. Everything else is just to cure one's head" (*curar la cabeza*). Many lower-class people singled out the teachers as particularly guilty of excessive drinking. One market woman complained to me, "All they do is drink all day, and half the time they don't even show up for work at their schools. They are terrible examples for our children."

Even some of the middle-class urban survivors who had opened stores in the market often closed up in the afternoon or left others in charge to join their companions in the cantinas. A number of upper-class individuals had accepted positions of responsibility on aid or municipal committees and because of their heavy drinking had failed completely in their duties. The criticism and accusations of drunkenness, irresponsibility, and abuse of authority at the urban survivor group by the lower-class migrants, however, was rarely overt and never reached the ears of the people being judged.

While peasants and urban poor could hardly make direct allegations of malfeasance against the notables in charge of distribution, they were very often able to make their discontentment known through other middle- and upper-class people with whom they had patron-client relationships. Their patrons, usually politically or socially opposed to those distributing, could then voice the discontentment, inequities, and ultimately the accusations of malfeasance against those in charge of the distributions. At times, the climate of hostility and accusations grew so acute that many community leaders refused to have anything to do with the distribution of aid and simply signed their responsibilities over to the town council or subprefect's office, which in turn received their due share of accusations of favoritism and malfeasance.

While virtually all aid that reached Yungay was controversial in a social sense, no program provoked as much conflict and hostility as the provisional shelter program of the Ministry of Housing. The promise by the reconstruction authorities that provisional housing would be provided for all *damnificados* in Yungay was perhaps the most compelling attraction for rural peoples in Yungay. The tents were tearing and leaking, and their zippered entrances began snagging and breaking quickly. People anxiously awaited a shelter program. However, once the module construction began, people all over the valley showed an initial reluctance to occupy the houses. Before construction was begun in Yungay, many people requested that they be given or loaned the money to buy materials to build their own houses. CRYRZA ignored these requests, and it was not long before Yungay leaders were proclaiming that the module dwellings were an insult to human beings. "We are not animals to be put in stables. These houses violate the privacy of the home and the sanctity of the family."

Although the houses had dirt floors, no running water or electricity, little protection against the cold and damp, were not entirely waterproof, offered little security against theft, and became cracked and drafty soon after construction, even the dissatisfied Yungaínos had to admit that the provisional houses were an improvement over the lean-tos and tents. However, the distribution of the housing in all likelihood exacerbated the dissatisfaction with the material conditions of the dwellings. The distribution of the housing units was the responsibility of a group of Housing Ministry social workers. These young women were recent graduates of Peru's major university schools of social work. They had worked tirelessly in a variety of aid programs since a few weeks after the disaster. They were young, idealistic, and eager to assist. They were also imbued with the egalitarian ethic of those whose work and goals are social change. Their egalitarian ideals brought them into immediate and abrupt conflict with the urban survivors, who were operating under and attempting to reinstate the traditional system of social stratification and privilege in the camp.

During the construction of the module buildings the social workers had visited Yungay on a number of occasions. Gradually as people learned of their mission in the community, they began to make acquaintances among the population. As their visits became more frequent during the construction process, they were often invited by urban survivors for refreshments in the lean-to and shack restaurants along the road. One hot afternoon, while I was taking a break in one of these establishments, all four social workers assigned to Yungay arrived. The owner of the restaurant rushed to greet them at the door and with great cordiality ushered them to their seats at a table not far from mine. They ordered soft drinks and began to relax in the shade of the palm-thatched roof. When the drinks were brought, they reached for their wallets to pay, but the owner quickly protested that such distinguished guests would never have to pay in Yungay. After all, since they were providing such a generous service to the people of Yungay, it was the smallest favor he could extend to them in return. They protested that they must pay, but he would hear none of it, and ultimately they had to accept his hospitality. It was clear that such a gesture made them uncomfortable. They were concerned about accusations of favoritism once the actual housing distribution began. While their apprehension was well founded, they did misinterpret the gesture. People in general in the Andes often attempt to mitigate the impersonality of official interactions with personal relationships. Where bureaucracy is infamous for its slowness and inefficiency, often the only way to get anything done is by knowing someone within the bureaucratic structure. The owner of the restaurant was not trying to bribe the social workers. He was merely trying to establish a personal relationship with them, which would hopefully facilitate what he expected to be a long and arduous bureaucratic process to get a provisional dwelling.

Finally in mid-November of 1970, the social workers set up shop in one of the dwellings already constructed for the high school, and people began to arrive to register for a dwelling. The social workers initially stated to all who arrived that the apartments were to be allotted on a first-come, first-served basis and in fact, proceeded to register and allot houses in this fashion. Word of this policy passed rapidly around the camp. In shocked tones, urban survivors asked how such a policy could be possible. Within days of the initial distribution, the social workers began to receive complaints from urban survivors, saying that they did not want to live next to Indians or peasants. One afternoon, a local official of some importance stormed into their offices brushing aside the people who were in line to register. He proclaimed that he did not want any peasants to be inscribed for housing in the community and that he himself wanted to choose the location of his module apartment. One of the social workers, somewhat taken aback by his stormy entrance, coolly told him he would receive a house where there was a vacancy and that all those people with documents certifying their refugee status would receive a house in similar fashion, whether they were peasant or not. "We are all equal in the eyes of God," she told him.

"We are not equal," he roared at her.

Soon more and more "decent people," survivors of the city, began complaining of their treatment at the hands of the social workers. Many were outraged at even having to come and register for the housing, fully expecting the social workers to come to their tents to allow them to choose their homes. The rural people did not seem particularly perturbed about the location of their new homes, but it became a very thorny issue for the urban survivors. "I am an authentic Yungaíno," one man stated adamantly, "and I want to be in the city, near the road and not up on the hill with the peasants."

Since the housing registration offices were fast becoming the locus of the most volatile social issue of the camp, I began to drop in to watch the progress of the distribution and talk with the social workers in the afternoons. One afternoon, just before closing, a couple came into the offices with their elderly widowed mother. By their dress, they were obviously urban but no longer wore mourning clothes. The old lady, however, was dressed completely in black, a solemn, somewhat stout figure with white hair. With her hands folded in front of her, she had an air of ultimate resignation and sorrow about her as her vigorous daughter and son-in-law began making their demands known. They wished to get a module room for their mother, but, they stated primly, "with nice neighbors, please."

For Maria, one of the two social workers on duty that afternoon, it had been a truly arduous day, assigning houses and receiving complaints in a community which was rapidly growing more hostile to them each day. Her patience was just about exhausted as she flipped through the housing files. When the couple reiterated their desire to get their mother a home close to "nice" people, Maria looked up sharply from the files, glared at them, and pointed at me. "Is he good enough for you?" she exasperatedly asked. The obvious implication was, "Is he white and 'decent' enough for you?" The couple and the old lady were mortified, and there were embarrassed murmurs of assent as Maria assigned them the house next to mine.

The old lady never moved into her house, and, although I often saw her in town, I probably saved us both embarrassment by never asking her why. She was either too embarrassed by the encounter with Maria in the housing office, or she did not like the neighborhood, since my home was located in the last row of buildings in the highest part of the camp on the hill, definitely a peasant neighborhood. There is also the possibility that as a foreigner, of exaggerated stature and strange appearance, I had an ambiguous status and was therefore not "decent" enough by local standards. Whatever the reason, my neighbor ended up being a young man from the peasant community of Arhuey who had migrated to Yungay. On occasion he was joined by his wife, who stayed in Arhuey to tend their fields while he began an ice-cream business. Every morning by 5:30 Antogenes would buy a large block of ice brought down by Indians from the glaciers of Huascarán or Huandoy. By 6:30 he would be happily grinding his barrel-size ice-cream mixer to the tune of his favorite record, "Five Flowers," played at full volume on a battery-driven phonograph. By 8:00 he would be pushing his tricycle with the ice-cream cooler mounted over the front wheels over the rough grounds of the Yungay market, selling ice cream to children and marketers until early afternoon.

If there is one overriding memory I have of my life in my module room, it is the high-pitched whine of the singer of "Five Flowers." The first verse, "Five flowers do I need to pronounce your name" was the first thing I heard every day for eight months, followed shortly by the gravelly chorus of the ice-cream mixer, easily penetrating the one-fourth-inch-thick walls of our module building. Those thin plywood walls, which separated each room from the next, allowed no secrets from one's neighbors, and gave the Spanish saying "pueblo chico, infierno grande" (small town, big hell) more truth than ever.

The distribution of the housing became an ever more acute situation as time wore on. Whenever the social workers indicated the essential equality of all humankind in response to complaints of housing next to peasants, the retort was invariable from urban survivors, *"No somos iguales!"* (We are not equal!) repeated again and again adamantly.

Despite the uproar and conflict over housing, possession of a module home came to signify the concrete substance of one's identity as a Yungaíno. For rural migrants the apartment became the symbol of their newly acquired identity as urban Yungaínos. *"Tengo mi módulo"* (I have my module) became a characteristic statement of identification with the city. However, often, upper- and middle-class individuals chose to erect their own adobe structures on the edges of the barracks city instead of occupying the module which they had been assigned. Some even went to live in other cities, leaving their rooms locked and vacant. However, possession of a module, even unoccupied and locked, was also symbolic of upper-class urban identification, and when the social workers ordered the lock sawed off the apartment of a particularly prestigious urban survivor who was living in Caraz and assigned the accommodations to a mere peasant, it created a scandal. "How could it be possible?" exclaimed those who had originally befriended the social workers. "They were such nice girls at the beginning. How could we know that they would act in such a barbarous fashion?"

The murmurs and grumbling soon became shouts, and the confrontations began to verge on violence. Ultimately the conflict became so bitter that representatives of the urban survivors denounced the social workers to the Ministry of Housing. The social workers also went to Lima and formally requested the removal of one of the principal leaders of the province. Hostility between the social workers and the urban survivors became so sharp that eventually the social workers refused to come to Yungay to assist with the distribution of doors and windows for the houses as well as with other organizational aspects of the project. They feared for their safety in the refugee camp. Even people who had been initially friendly with the young women were baffled by their obstinate performance of their duties. Many urban survivors shook their heads in wonder that the social workers should attempt to distribute the houses on a totally egalitarian basis.

In the first few months after construction, the camp became divided into "high rent" district and "slums" or their equivalents in a refugee encampment. Sector A soon became known as the neighborhood of the upper class, though as things later proved this was hardly the case. Sector A was closest to the market, the high school, the prefabricated medical post, the provisional town hall, the bank, the post office, the water outlets, the public telephone, and the road. Sector C became the neighborhood of people from the lower foothill communities. Sector B, highest on the hill, farthest from the center of town, but also, ironically, the safest and least muddy when the rains came, was supposedly the Indian neighborhood.

Despite early characterization of sectors as belonging to one or another social group or class, neighborhoods eventually became more integrated. The urban survivors were initially so few and the rural survivors so numerous that social integration in housing was inevitable. Initially pockets of urban survivors existed among the mass of rural people only in Sector A. However, with the passage of time urban survivors who had temporarily gone to live on the coast with relatives returned and were assigned housing where vacancies existed in the now stabilized system. Ultimately, the result was that upper- and middle-class survivors tended to be grouped throughout Sectors A and C with very few located in B. Not many new relationships were formed as a result of this de facto housing integration, and relationships among neighbors of different social, economic, and ethnic status exhibited most of the formal characteristics typifying such relationships in the pre-earthquake situation.

Neighborhoods or barrios began to form, often according to the regional origin of migrants. Where urban survivors clustered in Sector A, street names from old Yungay were posted at corners of the passageways between module buldings. Migrants from the foothill communities of Pampac and Utcush clustered in Zone C and formed a committee to protect their interests in aid distribution and urban services. A module room was acquired for use as a chapel for patron saints whose images had been salvaged from the wreckage of the communities' chapels.

While prejudice and hostility toward the Indian masses certainly played an important role in the conflicts in the aftermath, it is important to remember that the urban survivors had suffered a unique tragedy. The disaster had snuffed out in seconds their entire social reality and had left them naked and alone on a rustic hillside. The people were overwhelmed by loss and the suddenness with which their lives have been irrevocably changed. Their lifeways, their values, those elements of their existence that lent meaning and significance to their lives were thrown into chaos by the destructive force of nature. When the collective body and individual versions of these elements, the "mazeways," are invalidated by disaster, the mental health of individuals and the social health of a community are endangered. The status-leveling effects of the disaster endangered, among other elements, certain traditional social values of urban survivors. Their hostility toward rural migrants was a response to the "disordered" reality the disaster had imposed upon them. In the traditional highlands the differences between townsman and Indian were clear enough to rural and urban people alike. When those differences, which constituted important means of identification, became not only blurred but apparently meaningless, the reaction was dismay and hostility toward those who were attempting to impose a system which was in violation of all that they understood as true and proper. We may not agree or sympathize with such hierarchical sentiments, but we must recognize the discordant and disruptive effects on the psychological state of urban survivors. In essence, the disaster not only destroyed the material reality of their community, it also threatened to upset their social reality and in consequence, much of the remaining emotional stability of the urban survivors. The perception of what appeared to be a radical alteration of the social landscape in the aftermath of the massive physical destruction was terribly unsettling to urban survivors. I can remember tears of rage and bewilderment on the contorted faces of urban survivors as they spoke of the changes in the social conditions in the province. My own reaction fluctuated between sympathy and dismay. The loss and pain experienced by these people, dressed in the black of mourning for their lost families, evoked my profoundest sympathies. The stream of hatred which many of them unleashed on the Indian and rural migrants dismayed me and eroded my sympathies. It was some time before I was able to perceive these hostile reactions without considerable though unexpressed hostility of my own. Ultimately, it became evident that while the order of the social hierarchy was backed by profound sentiment, the extreme hostility directed toward rural people was more the product of the pain and chaos which urban survivors were experiencing during the first year. Scapegoating is a common phenomenon in the aftermath of disaster. While the avalanche could not be blamed on the Indians, part of the rage and misery of urban survivors at their unhappy conditions in the aftermath was directed at them because they were seen as beneficiaries. Whether or not rural people benefited from the disaster is a doubtful issue.

Much of this postdisaster social conflict conforms to behavior in other disasters. Immediately following a disaster, there tends to be a heightened degree of social cooperation and unity in initial emergency activities. Groups that would otherwise maintain strict social distance close ranks and cooperate for the good of the totality. In Yungay a unity and cohesion did develop among the group of survivors in the first two weeks following the disaster. Authority was respected. Property was shared. Work was undertaken in common regardless of social barriers. However, once the major crisis has passed, it is common for conflicts within the system to reappear, often in exaggerated form, which may ultimately be a symptom of changes being ushered in by the disaster (Barton 1970:309). The disaster threw the status system out of balance, as is illustrated by the *sobreviviente* woman who complained: "The people of the heights, the Indians, never had anything, so why should they get help? On the other

147

hand, we, the real Yungaínos, have lost everything so we should get more."

The distribution of some individual aid on a more or less egalitarian basis contradicted the established value system of the urbanites, who demanded and expected preferential treatment. When this treatment was not forthcoming to the degree anticipated, conflict with those seen to be in competition, hostility toward those in charge, dismay, and further social and emotional disintegration were the result. Thus, the initial and many of the continuing efforts for rehabilitation and recovery were in partial violation of the traditional status arrangements and produced and exaggerated tensions and frictions that had already existed in the community (Oliver-Smith 1977b).

The aid personnel and programs in the housing project faced a dilemma. In essence, the housing program could have conformed to traditional patterns of stratification and minimized the effect on the already badly traumatized urban population, or it could have implemented the project according to the egalitarian principles it was trying to establish, violating the norms of the dominant sector of society and further traumatizing the survivors of Yungay. As it stands, the implementation of the program along egalitarian lines, although it resulted in bitter conflict and stress for all involved, probably did less harm to urban survivors than perceived at the moment. As the year progressed and the newly emerging city faced further challenges, the degree of intergroup hostility declined considerably.

While overt hostility between rural migrants and urban survivors diminished with the passing of time in the first year, middle- and upper-class people still continued to express scorn and disdain toward the urbanized peasants in conversations among themselves. The countrified accent and ungrammatical Spanish of many rural migrants were often ridiculed among groups of urban survivors, sometimes in a good-natured fashion, but sometimes with considerable venom.

There was also tension within classes. The *sobrevivientes* of Yungay, with the exception of a very few upper-class individuals, eventually came to consider themselves as a cohesive group. "We the survivors of the city of Yungay" prefaced many a town resolution as well as many a drinking bout. This group, drawn together through common origin and disaster identity, suffered from some internal dissension as well. The trauma of the disaster and the insecurity resulting from life in an unstable social as well as geographical situation over a prolonged period stimulated considerable tension, bickering, backbiting, and feuding among the urban survivors.

Varying business success in the aftermath created wide rifts in the survivor community. Through luck or perspicacity a few individuals began to enjoy substantial increases in income after the disaster. A number of general-store owners and two beer distributors, one of them a much-bereaved widow, were subjected to venomous gossip and hostility because of their economic successes, particularly from those who had once been well off, but who, through bad luck, mismanagement, or psychological trauma, had failed in their efforts to rebuild their economic base. Successful entrepreneurs were covertly accused of having robbed the bodies of the dead or of having excavated the houses of the rich in Yungay, taken their wealth, and buried them again. Very often psychological reasons were used to explain success or failure after the tragedy. People down in their luck stated that they felt unable to enter into business or trade with the same degree of enthusiasm or skill. They lacked the will, the strength. "It is not like it was before when one had the desire to work, to build. There seems to be no reason now to work for anything more than enough to live on." They accused those who enjoyed economic success in the aftermath of not having suffered, of being cynical and lacking respect or sentiments for the dead. The feeling was that if one had been truly affected by the tragedy, one would not be able to bounce back as quickly as those people. They had no deep feelings. They were superficial and crass. Since the disaster, however, most people reported that they had experienced a loss of memory, the loss of ordinary abilities such as counting or making change in a store, and a general nervousness and inability to sleep and often were awakened in the night by dreams. One recurrent theme throughout the internal group conflicts was one's relative loss and deprivation from the disaster, as well as others' dishonesty in receiving aid. Sudden differences in income levels brought about through varying degrees of loss evoked a great deal of hostility among the survivors. A number of people had escaped the avalanche because they lived in Cochahuaín, the wealthy suburban area just north of the town. The subprefect and a few of the larger landlords and cattlemen lived in Cochahuaín. Although most of the houses were made uninhabitable by the earthquake, the landslide's momentum carried it only to the back garden walls of the southernmost homes. The owners of these houses lost the use of their houses, but not all their possessions. Those residents of Cochahuaín who remained in Yungay were often the object of considerable hostility from those who had lost all their worldly possessions. Most of their families were intact, and many had salvaged most of their goods from their homes, although they accused the Indians of looting while they had taken refuge on the hill in Pashulpampa. Their losses, like those of the rural masses, were seen to be considerably lighter than the losses of those who had lived in the city, and when these people received aid, a great deal of anger was provoked among the rest of the urban survivors. In many cases, the new conflicts were based on old predisaster hostilities as well.

Many kinds of aid in postdisaster situations, particularly aid for individuals, become a source of serious friction in systems with marked social differences. Aid donation and reception are viewed from unique subjective positions and are given to heavy emotional overtones. Equivalencies and inequalities are always tempered by local social values and perceptions of loss and deservedness. Where there are social tensions within a system, aid is very often seen to favor rival groups. Where the society is highly stratified, as in highland Peru, the distribution of aid according to principles which violate standing priorities of values can lead to considerable social conflict (Barton 1970:308–15).

Often the mission or purpose of aid is perceived differently by donors and receivers. Donors and administrators of aid most often see the purpose of their efforts to restore everybody in the stricken community according to need to a minimal level of self-sufficiency. The people of the stricken community, particularly those who were well off, may see the purpose of aid as a replacement of losses. The question also becomes one of relative deprivation. If rich and poor receive equal aid, the relative positions of rich and poor are in all probability closer than prior to the disaster. In a stratified society, individual aid perceived to be distributed along egalitarian lines runs against the goal of the middle and upper classes, which ultimately is the maintenance of relative class position (Barton 1970:308–15). Consequently, any individual aid that rural people received was not only undeserved but dishonestly accepted in the eyes of the "nobles," and any aid that urban people received was the result of graft and influence in the eyes of the humbler people in new Yungay.

That aid was extended to rural people at all was, from the urban point of view, an indication of changed statuses, which may, in the last analysis, be a correct assessment of things. The urban survivors felt threatened by this potential change in the order of social life, and this threat provoked them into some fairly overt expressions of anger and hostility toward the peasantry in general. By outwardly proclaiming their superiority over the peasants, urban survivors were reaffirming their place in a social order which had been profoundly upset by the disaster. Belittling the peasant, while proclaiming one's privileged status as a surviving Yungaíno became a way of reconstructing the order of one's social universe. In the aftermath of the disaster, with so many strangers around and everybody reduced to the same material conditions more or less, if one didn't proclaim it to the world, one's treasured identity might go unnoticed.

CRYRZA organized local committees of notables to oversee the distribution of aid in each community. When the urban Yungaínos themselves took over the distribution of aid, the internal dissension did not abate markedly. One section of the camp, occupied primarily by migrants from a destroyed hamlet near Yungay, formed a committee to protest the favoritism with which the aid was distributed. "We have asked help from CRYRZA and also from the Yungay Women's Committee, and there was no just distribution from them. When the food and other goods arrived, we wanted to get them distributed in exchange for work in the camp. The Women's Committee said the aid was only for widows and orphans, but they gave out the stuff only to their servants."

Aid, then, stimulated friction and competition rather than cooperation. It continued to be an irritant in social interaction and community organization. While alleviating emergency needs in camp, aid also served as a catalyst for a return to an exaggerated form of predisaster social stratification. Urban survivors saw themselves for the first time in competition with rural people for the basic necessities of life. This perception of competition stimulated an even stronger affirmation of urban superiority than had existed before the disaster.

Aid was also seen in a highly political perspective. Those in charge of distribution were seen to favor their friends and political allies to the exclusion of other urban survivors with whom they had quarreled. The question of "need versus loss" arose even on an individual basis. Many people who ostensibly had little need for the articles being distributed collected them each time they were distributed and later sold them. Accusations of theft and complicity in theft by leaders ran rampant through the camp when aid goods were being stockpiled in the camp for distribution. Even the modules became subject to graft.

In one instance, Felicia Ocaña, a chola woman who sold fruit in the market, was assigned a module next to that of a large landowner. Before she had a chance to move in, he took possession of it, seemingly by virtue of his eminent position in society. He used the module as a warehouse for potatoes from his haciendas. In desperation, Felicia sought out an unoccupied module in a section not too distant from her original one. Within a week of moving her meager belongings into the module, its assigned owner, another landowner, complained to the social workers to throw her out. He had no intention of living there. It was also to be a storeroom. While the social workers deliberated on the case, Felicia, who had been an informant of mine off and on during my stay in Yungay, asked for my advice one day when I stopped to buy an orange from her at her roadside stand. She also asked me to intercede for her with the social workers. In the Andes when one faces powerful opposition, the tactic most often adopted is to acquire relationships which are of equal or greater power for assistance. Felicia had obviously assessed her chances of prevailing against two landlords as nil and, because we had been friendly, decided to enlist my assistance. As a foreigner and a *decente,* she considered me to be an equally powerful and influential person. Although I doubted that I could prevail against two landlords either, I said I would speak to the social workers. A mutual interest in each others' activities had brought us together for coffee on a number of occasions, and I felt comfortable enough with the beleaguered social workers to broach still another housing problem with them. Whether it was my intervention or, more probably, their own sympathies for the poor and disadvantaged I do not know, but a few days later Felicia effusively thanked me when I stopped at her stand for another orange. The social workers had told her she would not be evicted for a sack of potatoes. If Felicia Ocaña believed that my influence had carried the day for her so did the two landowners. One never spoke to me again, and the other was only barely civil from that time on. When I told Rosa Martínez the story of Felicia and the landowners, she said, "What do you expect from an hacendado?"

Although each small conflict had its villains and victims, depending upon the person telling the tale, the villain in the eyes of all survivors was CRYRZA, the national government's ministry-level aid agency. It is safe to say that even when the CRYRZA implemented a successful project, admission of that fact by victims throughout the disaster zone was often grudging. As soon as the emergency phase of aid handled largely by the armed forces and the National Emergency Committee was over, the government established the CRYRZA for long-term reconstruction with its president and offices in Lima. In other words, "business as usual" for both coast and sierra: bureaucratic centralization and stagnation everywhere. During the first year following the quake, CRYRZA commissioned a variety of studies by experts who would make short-term site visits, shudder at the conditions in which people were living, and return to Lima as quickly as possible. Tales abounded in Huaráz of "very important people" who would arrive with lucrative contracts for the design and reconstruction of cities, drive around the city for a day, and disappear, never to return. Months, and sometimes years, later a report would be submitted and filed, never to be implemented. While experts rushed up to the callejón and back as quickly as they could, the resident representatives of CRYRZA attempted to implement whatever projects they could despite the bureaucratic hamstringing from Lima. As 1970 ended with little more than the pressboard modules actually in place, grief was replaced by outrage at the stagnation and inability to act of the CRYRZA. This anger and the conflict it generated became crucial factors in effectively working through the grieving process for many victims. The grief and frustration of the survivors were vented in tirades at aid officials, and new adaptations and adjustments were articulated in the conflicts with CRYRZA.

The grand promises made by CRYRZA officials so gratefully believed in the early months soon began to evoke a hostile cynicism from victims. One afternoon after passing an elaborate CRYRZA project sign coming home in the back of a truck from Caraz, one urban survivor commented to me, "What an elegant sign!" "Yeah," piped up his companion, "that's what the CRYRZA is best at—elegant signs. And receiving fat salaries. All those *señoritos ingenieros* [elegant little engineers] who don't do anything and get 35,000 soles [roughly $500] a month."

"Brother, if all the aid that came from foreign countries had really arrived, this place would be back on its feet and more by now. What happens is that instead of letting the aid come directly to us and letting us distribute it fairly, Lima decides who is going to get the aid, so . . .

153

like the Cuban hospitals, a little piece to Yungay, a little piece to Caraz, and the bulk of it stays in Lima."

A few days later, Antonio Flores and I were trudging up the muddy slope to our modules in the late afternoon. "Ahh, tocayo [the term of address for a person with the same first name], we are really getting screwed in this aid business. Look at us here in this miserable mud and filth, and they tell me that the aid is piled up in mountains down in Lima and even in Huaráz, and none of it gets here." As we reached the second tier of modules and started down one of the alleys between two buildings, Antonio looked around furtively to see if anyone was close. With dark rapidly approaching and a light rain falling, very few people were still outside. Stepping under the scant protection of a module roof overhand, Antonio handed me a folded piece of white paper. "Go ahead. Read it," he urged me, grinning maliciously. "I got this from a friend in Huaráz yesterday."

I opened the sheet of paper to see that a poem or song had been typed on it. The title was *Yaravi Ancashino*. A *yaravi* is a Peruvian form of song, usually associated with sadness or lamentation. It read in Spanish as follows, with my own crude translation parallel.

La promoción "terremoto"	The "earthquake" regime*
trajo sismo y destrucción	brought tremors and destruction
y aprovecho el alboroto	and took advantage of the tumult
para su ROBOLUCIÓN . . .	for its Rob-olution . . .
Al pobre damnificado	To the poor refugee
muy poco es lo que le dan	very little is given
porque el molido han guardado	because the very best
los de la JAN** para Juan . . .	is saved by the JAN for Juan** . . .
los dolares por millones	The dollars by the millions
llegaron del mundo entero,	arrived from all the world,
pero los muy picarones	but the rascals here
dicen que ya no hay dinero . . .	say already they are gone . . .

*Literally, the earthquake "class."
**JAN (Junta de Asistencia Nacional)—National Assistance Board for Juan (Juan Velasco Alvarado, President of Peru [1969–75]).

Zapatos, remedios, ropa	Shoes, medicines, clothing
no han llegado a su destino	haven't reached their destination
porque mucho fue a la tropa	because much went to the troops
y al vendedor clandestino . . .	and to the black market vendor . . .
Chile, Colombia, Ecuador	Chile, Colombia, Ecuador
ayudaron como hermanos	assisted us like brothers
pero el cuantioso favor	but the bounteous favor
solo llegó a pocas manos . . .	only reached a few hands . . .
Nixon nos mandó frazadas	Nixon sent us blankets
de las que usan en Vietnam	like those used in Vietnam
pero aquí fueron cambiadas	but here they were replaced
por las viejas que nos dan . . .	by old ones that they gave us . . .
Los tiranos comunistas	The communist tyrants
tambien nos aprovecharon	also took advantage
mandando propagandistas	to send us propagandists
que a unos ensartaron . . .	who hooked a few . . .
y así la cruel realided	And thus the cruel reality
de tanta miseria y muerte	of so much misery and death
es que Ancash se quedará	is that Ancash remains
abandonada a su suerte . . .	abandoned to its fate . . .
Ya que los damnificados	So that the refugees
con desengaño y tristeza	with disillusion and sadness
ven a los privilegiados	watch the privileged
comiéndose su pobreza	eating from their poverty
Pueblo Infeliz sin derechos	Unhappy people, without rights
sin carne, aceite ni pan	without meat, oil or bread
estos son los reales hechos	these are the true facts
que no desmiente la JAN!	Let the JAN deny them!

The content and tone of many of the verses revealed the fact that the disaster had clearly become a political issue to the survivors as well as to the government. Both the right and the left sought to use the diaster and the aid programs to criticize the basic political stance of the national government. The government itself was attempting to use the devastation of the disaster to carry out some profound structural reforms and to institute a pilot development program which would not only rehabilitate the area, but significantly develop it as well. For this reason, government spokesmen argued, it was necessary to carry out so many time-consuming studies in the first year, even while so many people lived in such abject misery. The conservative right-wing elements of provincial highland society accused the left-wing government of taking advantage of the disaster to heap even more suffering on the property-owning classes, who had already suffered so heavily in the cataclysm. The far left, who had seen social revolution come to the Callejón de Huaylas in an act of nature, unleashed a torrent of criticism at the government when their organizing activities were curtailed and their leaders ordered back to Lima. When the social revolution failed to materialize to their expectations, the radical left wing labeled the so-called revolution as reformist in content and the military government as fascist in intent. A number of Yungaínos began to feel that the lack of real aid for Yungay was based on the city's traditional association with the APRA party and its antimilitary stance. While always careful to state their general support for the government, the Yungaíno survivors also tended to reflect the conservative claims of victimization and found the blame for the lack of progress in their scorn for the military and the Lima bureaucracy. However, in Yungay, political questions were clearly secondary to the material consequences of government policy.

As one of the verses of *Yaravi Ancashino* states, the Yungaínos saw their "cruel reality of so much misery and death" as an abandonment to the fates. Yungaínos, punished so severely by nature and now seemingly in constant conflict with the government and its agents, felt abandoned in their struggle to survive. When the threat of relocation became a real possibility, the conversations of survivors began to resemble those of a besieged and surrounded army. The whole valley swarmed with aid personnel, engineers, architects, social workers, administrators, sociol-ogists, social "promotors," and others with even vaguer titles and func-tions, living and working all over the callejón, but after the emergency period not one ever came to Yungay to live. During the first year and a half, engineers, architects, and social workers came on day visits to design, build, and distribute the module buildings and the meager public facilities of the camp. In Yungaíno eyes no one ever spent any more time there than they absolutely had to. The survivors felt like lepers, and the sense of increased victimization, this time by human beings, grew deep. As Emilio Robles put it, "We, who have suffered most of all, we should get at least some psychological help. CRYRZA should at least send us a psychologist to help us get over the emotional trauma that we have suffered." At least one and a half years passed before anyone with a function even remotely resembling mental health rehabilitation appeared in camp on a consistent basis.

In that year and a half following the avalanche when the Yungaínos were experiencing their most intense grief and suffering, I was unaware that my residence in the camp had meant anything beyond being a rather curious but friendly presence in a place and time with more than its share of strange things and people. I was led to a different conclusion by the reaction of people when someone attempted to rob my module. In early February I had decided to take a week's vacation in Lima. While I was gone, a boy about nineteen years old attempted to rob my home late one night. He broke the padlock on my door and was discovered trying to break the lock of my trunk by a neighbor who chased him down and turned him in to the police.

Within minutes of my return, before I had even been informed of the robbery, people began to approach me with apologies. The gist of what was expressed was that Yungay had been shamed. Rosa Martínez, full of indignation, said people were very bitter about the robbery, and it had been the main topic of conversation in town while I was away. "People were asking, 'How could anyone do that to our friend, Antonio?'"

El Pillo told me, "We were very worried about your study . . . if you had lost any of your papers! But," he counseled, "since you didn't lose anything, don't press charges. It was his birthday and he probably didn't have any money to celebrate." Others were not so charitable. "He has shamed Yungay. Lock the little son of a whore up. He's been stealing for years." I decided not to press charges in the end. I also began to understand the significance my study had acquired for the Yungaínos, who felt abandoned by all the official agencies. At least somebody felt they were still important.

In their continuing battles with the aid agencies, one phrase which constantly cropped up in conversations or in public diatribes and condemnations was *"No nos han dado nada!"* (They have given us nothing!). My first reaction to this claim was to be somewhat dubious. To stand anywhere in Yungay was to be surrounded by donated material aid. The clothes that people wore, the food they ate, the dishes they ate from, the houses they lived in, all in large measure had been given them by the JAN, CRYRZA, the Peruvian Red Cross, AID, the OAS, or a number of other institutions hell-bent on giving things to the disaster victims. It seemed incredible to me that any of the survivors could claim that they had been given nothing, and yet I listened to that lament over and over again throughout my stay. In my early months there I had almost begun to believe that the Lima cynics were correct, that disaster victim status was becoming just a way to stay on the public dole, and the *damnificado*'s complaint was simply a tool to extract more goods from the aid agencies. Although disaster aid hardly put anyone on easy street, it was still difficult to understand how they could claim that they had received no aid.

It was not until Rosa Martínez locked horns with the wife of the president of the republic that I began to understand what the victims meant. In early February of 1971, *La Prensa,* one of the major Lima newspapers, sent a reporter to the callejón for interviews with victims. In Yungay he interviewed, among others, Rosa Martínez. She had been back in Yungay slightly more than a month. I was there. She told him of her experiences on the day of the avalanche and of the ordeal of her healing process. "My paisanos and my relatives have helped me with what they have been able to open my restaurant," she said, spreading her arms wide to indicate the laced cane hut which housed her enterprise. "Not one pot, not clothing, nothing have I received, except for the medicines," she told the reporter (*La Prensa,* February 16, 1971:5).

Rosa's statements and those of a number of other Yungaínos were printed in a variety of articles spread over several pages of *La Prensa* several days later. Shortly thereafter, *La Prensa* printed another article which quoted Sra. Consuelo Gonzalez de Velasco, the president's wife, refuting the claims which Rosa had made concerning the aid which she had not received. Rosa's name, according to Sra. de Velasco, appeared on several lists of people who had received specific articles of aid. When Sra. de Velasco's contentions were read to Rosa, her attitude was both righteous and amused by her sudden celebrity and her debate with Peru's first lady. She said that she was not going to refute the fact that she had received two beds, but she said that the help she really needed— help to get her business going—was not given to her. Rosa added that she would have even taken the aid in the form of a loan. She said that she did refuse the second-hand clothes, adding that she may be poor and not have much, but she was not going to wear someone else's rags.

"They have given us nothing" was a phrase which reflects the disaster victims' perception of aid. It essentially meant, "They have given us nothing of use, nothing which will allow us to return to a state of self-sufficiency." Survivors of Yungay, particularly the cholos and poorer mestizos, almost unanimously complained that what they needed was help to get back to work. *"Hay que trabajar para vivir"* (One must work to live). Beds and blankets, stoves and pots are all very well, but they do little to earn one a living, and earning a living became the crucial issue quite quickly after the emergency period had ended. What they got were repeated donations of material goods, often of inferior or inappropriate quality, distributed by the CRYRZA, the JAN, and the leaders of Yungay's upper classes. The distribution lines were humiliating; they were often treated shabbily by the people in charge, being pushed and shoved along through the distribution stations by the people in attendance, and their obvious dependency on this impersonal system was degrading to them. Instead of material aid, many people repeatedly asked for loans, or grants of capital, to allow them to build their own homes, to replace their lost tools, to reopen old businesses or begin new ones. It is noteworthy that those people who did have a little capital or were able to secure loans from relatives or friends outside of Yungay almost always used the money for these purposes.

What the Yungaínos were telling the aid agencies with their lament was not "give us another teflon frying pan," but rather "help us go back to work." Postdisaster assistance, while focusing on material concerns, must also attend to the crucial social and psychological consequences of disaster. Disaster victims must be given the opportunity to demonstrate renewed effectiveness as individuals and communities. If people are shown that they are powerless to defend themselves from nature, the first measures of assistance after emergency needs should be designed to reestablish a sense of personal and community integrity and self-sufficiency as soon as possible. Recurring waves of material donations create patterns of dependency, lowered self-esteem and morale, and conflict within and among social groups and sectors. Paternalistic forms of disaster aid which do not involve the recipients in decision making, management, and implementation, risk compounding the psychological and social impact of disaster.

Thus, while aid to Yungay helped to restore the basic material conditions of life in terms of shelter, food, clothing, and other necessities, the form and structure of delivery contributed to a deterioration of social relations in the community and between the community and the aid agencies of the government. Hostility and conflict are common between disaster victims and aid agencies and personnel, who are perceived as outsiders with little understanding or compassion for the stricken population. CRYRZA and its representatives became the focus of concentrated hatred and anger throughout the disaster zone. On the one hand, the dependency on CRYRZA not only engendered intense hostility, but also hindered psychological rehabilitation of individuals who saw themselves frustrated at every turn in their attempts to return to self-sufficiency. Although it gave material goods, CRYRZA also impeded the victims in their attempt to regain self-esteem and integrity through the control the agency exercised over the victims' lives. On the other hand, at the community level, the hostility and conflict with CRYRZA, particularly after the relocation issue arose, stimulated a remarkable sense of solidarity and cooperation on projects relating to reconstruction of the provincial capital in Yungay. Indeed, the difficulty of negotiating one's way through rapid change is often articulated and ultimately resolved through conflict (Marris 1975).

It can be argued that given its task, CRYRZA and the agencies that succeeded it accomplished quite a lot, particularly if one visits the callejón today, more than fifteen years later. However, in that crucial first year, little beyond a bare survival minimum was provided, and much was done to undermine the disaster-shaken morale and self-esteem of the victims even further. Finally, in November of 1971, a full eighteen months after the disaster, President Velasco Alvarado decreed that CRYRZA would move its center of operations to Huaráz, to the disaster zone itself, "so that CRYRZA personnel would feel the cold, hear the cries of the needy, and experience the needs themselves and, therefore, work more rapidly." Velasco himself admitted that up to that point what had been accomplished in the disaster zone was "very little, almost nothing" (*La Prensa*, November 25, 1971:2). The Yungaínos, immersed in their tragedy and the misery of life in their module camp, were in complete agreement.

Despite the horrors and loss of the disaster and the hardships of camp existence, life in Yungay went on in a peculiar blend of tension and tranquility. A strange, crisis-alert kind of normality began to impose itself. The situation of Yungay was unsure, unstable. No one knew from one day to the next whether or not the camp would be relocated against its will by the government. Indeed, no one was completely sure that the glacier would not come crashing down the mountainside again. Rumors of cracks in the glacier circulated rapidly, and stories of hidden volcanoes about to erupt in the hills made people pause. The heavy thunderstorms that year rumbled in the mountains and the swollen rivers growled and crashed ominously high in the canyons. People were ready for the potentiality of another disaster. The sound of jet planes passing 30,000 feet over the valley on their way north is suspiciously like the sound of an avalanche, and people searched the sky for confirmation that it was, in fact, only an airplane this time.

Since traffic was open throughout the callejón, there was a constant stream of new people through the camp. People traveling to other parts of the area often stopped for meals and rest in the community. With the disaster relief efforts large numbers of coastal Peruvians and foreigners added another source of variety to the people passing through Yungay. And yet, despite the tension which accompanied existence in a disaster area and the bustle of traffic through the community, life in Yungay possessed an underlying tranquility. There were the mundane little chores of life to do as well as many of the common little pains and pleasures of existence. "People must work," they said. "If we don't work, then we will die."

And what work there was, was done. There were crops to be sown and harvested, things to be bought and sold in the market, trucks to be driven, people to be fed. In the afternoon men gathered in a favorite store or bar to chat and drink a beer, and women talked in the market or while washing clothes at the drainage ditches or water outlets.

Bars and restaurants became one of Yungay's principle industries owing to the number of single people and fragmented households. Stores, bars, and restaurants served as meeting places for the many solitary people in the camp. The lonely hours of the evening could always be filled with conversation with friends, and a bowl of hot sheepshead soup at Rosa Martínez's restaurant would take the chill out. Augusto Angeles's module store brought people together at night, to talk quietly together, muffled against the cold in blankets and odd coats and jackets which had come in clothes donations. Since the module rooms had no electricity, the brilliant light of the Coleman and Petromax lanterns in the stores and restaurants were beacons of warmth and comfort in the cold, black Andean nights.

Conversation rarely strayed far from old Yungay, the disaster, or the aftermath. Memories of happy events and lost friends or family were recounted tirelessly as people worked through their grief. The little social gatherings in stores, bars, or homes offered a context for personal rituals of catharsis in which grief, anger, and frustration could be vented in safe circumstances. The behavior of others in the aftermath was also a favorite topic of conversation. People were subjected to criticism for marrying too soon after the disaster, for allegedly receiving unneeded aid, or for drinking heavily and neglecting responsibilities. While criticism and gossip could be harsh, people tended to be understanding as well. The phrase that an individual had been *malogrado por la tragedia* (wasted or damaged by the tragedy) often accompanied criticisms. Almost all Yungaínos felt that their mental health and behavior had been adversely affected by the disaster, and this tended to temper their criticism with concern for the person, particularly in cases of heavy drinking.

Drinking was a serious problem in the first year after the disaster. On the whole, those most affected by the disaster, the upper- and middle-class survivors of Yungay who lost all or most of their families in the disaster were the heaviest abusers of alcohol in the camp. On the other hand, those men in particular who did not lose their families, especially their wives, in general participated less in the drinking bouts. Essentially, the more intact the family structure, the less likely the individual was to have a drinking problem. Groups of male friends would start drinking in the afternoons with a few bottles of beer and end anywhere from four to eight hours and several cases later in drunken tears or fights. Although the drinking bouts often ended badly, in their initial stage there was good-natured conversation. Humor was by no means absent either, whether in the form of barbs at others present or simply funny stories about camp life or even the disaster itself. One of the favorite stories dealt with the schoolteacher who was in the shower when the disaster struck and escaped by running naked through town. When he reached safety at the cemetery, he had to borrow one of the many skirts worn by Indian women to cover himself. They laughed uproariously about Clementina, who put up a great show of mourning for her lost husband and ten months later gave birth to a baby girl, alternately explaining the child as "a remembrance from her Alberto" (her deceased husband) or accusing the Russian doctors of impregnating her with injections.

On one occasion, many times since recounted, a group of friends who had been drinking went up on the avalanche scar on a cold grey afternoon. They walked in silence around the palm trees and shattered church tower for a new minutes. One of them, suddenly seized by oratorical fervor, looked fiercely up at the beclouded peaks, shook his fist and, pounding his chest, shouted, "Accursed Huascarán, vile traitor, assassin, come and devour another Yungaíno breast!" At that very instant, the sound of a small glacial avalanche came faintly rumbling down the canyon. The orator's friends will never let him forget that he ran right out of his shoes. He ruefully admits to his rapid flight but adds that the donated shoes were far too big for him anyway.

While humor did not pervade the Yungaíno attitude, it often tempered both anger and grief. *Raspadilla,* a paper cone of shaved ice from the glacier covered with sweet syrup, is a favorite snack in Yungay. One afternoon walking by the market I passed one of the older survivors of the city, a dignified old gentleman in a wide-brimmed straw hat, enjoying a cone of *raspadilla.* Seeing me, he waved his cone and called out with a twinkle in his eye, "I am taking revenge on Huascarán, eating him a little bit at a time."

El Pillo, the rascal, was one of those who lost all his family in the disaster. In the year afterward, he was on an emotional roller coaster, drinking heavily and alternating between periods of black depression and high humor. In his circle of friends, it was his biting humor that often kept the level of hilarity up in drinking bouts, and when the alcohol took effect, it was just as often his plummeting spirits that turned them into crying jags or bitter arguments. On one occasion not long before I left Yungay, I was drinking with El Pillo and his friends. He had just told a joke and then turned it on one of his friends, causing even more hilarity. Smiling at me, he commented quietly, "You know, Antuco, in the midst of all our misery this year, we've had some laughs."

There were a number of pastimes which permitted the Yungaínos a bit of distraction from their unhappy circumstances. Transistor radios, relatively cheap and easy to obtain, were prized possessions. News and music from Huaráz and Lima stations helped alleviate the sense of isolation that pervaded the town. The major national and international soccer matches drew groups of men and some women together in the homes of radio owners. The town council purchased an elaborate and expensive public address system with four powerful speakers located throughout the camp. When not used for public announcements, Antonio Flores, the council's secretary, would often play popular and folk music on the system. "In all this sadness, we have to give the people a little music so they won't get depressed," explained Antonio.

Even in the first months after the disaster, soccer provided a distraction from the conditions of camp life. A miniature soccer field was laid out not far from the lean-to church, and pick-up games were common. As time went on, Yungay reorganized its sports clubs. Starting some six months after the disaster, the five original clubs reformed the soccer league. Almost none of the clubs had enough surviving members to field a team, and subsequent recruitment drives were very competitive, drawing upon formerly rural people for the new membership. Although a number of clubs had difficulty obtaining minimal membership numbers, ultimately enthusiasm for the league grew to a point where they not only rejuvenated the original five clubs, but created three others from Mancos and the two satellite communities of Musho and Tumpa.

The soccer field is perhaps the most visible context of social equality that exists in Yungay. The degree of social integration was higher than in any other community organization or social institution. Clubs were composed of people from cholo and lower-class mestizo backgrounds as well as from the middle and upper classes. Soccer games invariably brought out large numbers of spectators, and truck owners donated their vehicles to transport teams and spectators to matches outside the district. The healthy existence of the soccer league was interpreted by many as a symbol of the determination and strength of spirit of the community to survive and prosper.

As other community organizations reformed in the aftermath, they also provided social events for the enjoyment of the general public. The parent's association of the school system organized very successful fund-raising events such as bingos and dances, which brought people together in community action as well as social activity. The market syndicate organized a number of kermesses, a kind of outdoor meal and party to which tickets are sold for food and drink and the opportunity to dance and enjoy oneself in the company of one's friends and community. These and other organizations provided contexts in which one could break the atmosphere of tragedy and the miserable conditions of camp life with a little fun, and it was always for some good cause. Yungay was becoming a settled community with a regularized social and organizational life, despite its unsure future and the dangerous potential of its environment.

People still spoke of the earthquake and the avalanche as though they had happened the day before. They exclaimed to each other about the noise, the violent shaking, the dust, and lack of water afterward, and they also talked of the possibility of it happening again. As though to reaffirm for themselves the benefits of their environment, they extolled its beauty, the clean air, the good climate, the rich soil, but they recognized the dangers as well. For them few places in the entire valley are safe. "When death comes for you, it doesn't matter where you are," one survivor fatalistically told me.

They are frightened of the possibility of further avalanches, but they do not consider any place as safe. As another Yungaíno put it, "There are some places in the callejón that are safer than others, but there is no place in the callejón that is truly safe. Well, for that matter, there is no place in the world that is safe. The only place that is safe is to be in the air."

The vulnerability of the area to further avalanches was amply demonstrated to us all one rainy evening in February. When I left my module early in the evening for dinner down at Rosa Martínez's restaurant, a huge rainstorm suddenly broke loose. It poured great sweeping sheets of rain down upon the camp. Lightning flashed and thunder rumbled up and down the canyons. The streets quickly turned to mud and then to swamps, the water and filth of the streets gushing over into houses. When I arrived at Rosa's, now thoroughly soaked, a group of friends were already there, Chico Romero, Maria Alva and her husband, Emilio Robles, Rodolfo Armendariz, and Rosa, as well as a table of people I didn't know who were very drunk. Everyone was wet and shivering.

Rosa served me a bowl of hot chicken soup as she had the others, and we sat and ate, hunched around a table which had been strategically placed to avoid the drops of water trickling through the leaky roof onto the dirt floor. The conversation was subdued except for a little nervous laughter about the downpour and the thunder off in the canyons. The thunder's rumble would mask the sound of anything more dangerous coming down the canyons. Chico Romero, who had finished eating, sat quietly among us, shivering, his face dark. Cursing the rain, he stood up and said he was going to head home. The only fit place for a night like this was bed, even though it too was damp. Saying goodnight to everyone he left the restaurant and climbed the slight grade to the street. Suddenly, he reappeared in the doorway of the restaurant. Eyes wide, he gestured to me and said, "Antonio, come here! Quickly!"

I went to the door and up into the street with him. He asked me if I heard the noise. There was a heavy, deeper rumbling sound coming from the direction of Ranrahirca Canyon, the path of the 1970 avalanche. I called Rodolfo to the street, and the rest of our little group followed. The entire street became crowded with people. The rumble grew in intensity and volume, now sounding like an enormous locomotive coming down the valley. We stood there on the road for a moment. Was it an avalanche or wasn't it? Nobody seemed to know. I thought to myself, "My God, are we going to wait until we see it to start running?"

The roar now seemed to be coming from a point directly ahead of us on the road, which disappeared in the darkness into the avalanche scar, but it seemed to be moving laterally rather than toward us. And then it seemed to be coming from the river, below us and to our right and past us. When we realized that whatever it was had passed us, someone pointed to the hill above the camp. It was alive with tiny lights, steadily moving upwards, and we could hear moans and cries of fear from women and children.

By this time the rain had let up, and the many groups of people who had remained on the road began to talk together. Some said it was an avalanche. Some said it was just rocks in the Ranrahirca River and scoffed at the fear of others. Several trucks arrived shortly, and the drivers were questioned, but they had only been in Aura and knew only that the road over the avalanche scar was intact. Someone mentioned the possibility of an avalanche in Mancos or even Carhuaz much farther to the south. Nobody knew. Some people showed a blistering scorn for those who were afraid. Others had comforting words for some of the women who were crying.

Some people were bitter and fatalistic. "Hell, let it take us. So we die. So what?" Rosa Martínez quietly told me that she thought that we would all finally go together. She said she did not care if she died. Miguel Giraldo said he thought we had had it, and Maria Alva was crying. The drunks in Rosa's never left the restaurant. One of them screamed at the top of his lungs that he wanted the avalanche to take him because he wanted to see all his friends from Yungay again.

166

As things calmed down, the subprefect cranked up the Swedish generator for the camp's few street lights for a few hours. People began walking up and down the road together, quietly talking, trying to calm themselves. The lights on the hill started slowly moving down. I began walking home. At the row of module buildings below my own, I met a group of people who were discussing the night's events. Chico Romero said that he had returned to his module and found his seventy-five-year-old mother quietly weeping. One woman said that the people had run screaming up the hill, wrapped in blankets, barefoot and carrying lanterns, leaving their homes wide open. "It's the children, the poor little ones [pobrecitos] I feel sorry for," she said.

By the time I reached my module, Antonio Flores was on the public address system, announcing that there was no danger and that people should return as quickly as possible to their houses because of the risk of robbery. As people descended the hill, a neighbor commented that the people who had climbed the hill were alarmists. He and many others felt that the present location of the camp was safe, and half of Huascarán would have to come down to reach us here. I remember taking some reassurance in this opinion, which was fairly general among the middle- and upper-class survivors. The next day we found out that a huayco, an avalanche of rock and mud along the river's path, had swept away the bridge over the Ranrachirca River and everything on both banks for thirty meters.

The people took heart that Yungay was never really in danger. Yungaínos were always alert to the dangers presented by the peaks of the Cordillera Blanca, but the concerns of everyday survival in a location that seemed to offer as much security and future to them as any seemed to take precedence. Few if any people left the camp as a result of the huayco of February 1971.

Thus, amidst the misery of camp life, the instability of their situation, social conflicts, their grief, and the potential dangers of their environment, the people of Yungay adjusted as best they could and worked out a semblance of normality under conditions of physical and psychological stress. The attitude of most people was that life must go on. The environment doubtless held risks, but for them, all environments do and theirs had distinct advantages as well. The community was made up of dirty and drab module buildings, but nonetheless it was a physical foothold in the world where only months before there had been nothing.

Social events and activities again became necessary and desired aspects of life. And there were people, with whom one had relationships of both conflict and cooperation, hostility and affection. Few people in Yungay became social recluses after the disaster. Although more people lived alone afterward, they sought out the company of others frequently. The need for contact was perhaps felt more deeply. Although gossip and criticism could be severe, it was often tempered with compassion by the oft-repeated phrase *malogrado por la tragedia*. Everyone felt emotionally damaged by the disaster, and this sense of common affliction created a community of sufferers. They had bitter conflicts, but they recognized common bonds with each other. The people of Yungay recognized and articulated their need for each other and for the cooperation of everyone for the survival of the community.

Chapter 7
Beginning Again:
Grief and Renewal

When a disaster strikes, one of the first concerns of people everywhere is for the safety and welfare of their families. As the earthquake shattered Yungay, many people said that they felt the day of judgment had arrived. Friends and families knelt, embracing each other, amidst the fury of the destruction, and resigned themselves to death. Others, who were not with their families, immediately began to search for them. Most died in the futile attempt to extract their loved ones from the rubble before the avalanche engulfed the city. Some survived, but only a few with their families intact. Still others simply fled, with no thoughts but escape.

In the initial period after the avalanche, much effort, most of it tragically in vain, was dedicated to ascertaining who in the widening circles of family, kinship, and community had survived the holocaust. Often this search was complicated by the fact that one member of a family might have been working on the coast or in another town when the disaster struck. Many people walked for four days and nights from the coast over the Cordillera Negra only to find that they were the sole surviving members of entire families. Evacuation procedures, particularly of the very young or the wounded, led to several individuals being "lost" for three or four months in Lima while surviving relatives in Yungay believed them to be dead and buried in the avalanche. Even up to a year later, the instability and uncertainty of the postdisaster situation and the traditional geographic mobility of the Andean population fragmented many families in Yungay.

When Yungay received its shipment of tents, many households had begun reforming in the lean-tos. Nevertheless, the tents also contributed to the creation of new households and family groups. Under normal conditions in small Andean cities such as Yungay, the household was made up of a nuclear family of approximately four people, although occasionally recently married children would live for a while with parents (Doughty 1968:30). Many households from the middle class upwards also had resident servants, often brought down from landholdings in the city's hinterland. The typical Indian household of the region also consisted of the nuclear family, but occasionally two nuclear families of related individuals would make up a household (Stein 1961:127). In Yungay the high mortality suffered in the disaster and the unsettled conditions of the aftermath contributed to a variety of new makeshift forms of household. Fully 60 percent of those families claiming urban origin did not conform to the traditional pattern, and 40 percent of the rural families in the camp were atypical. When I took my initial census of the population in December of 1970, almost 35 percent of the households were headed by widows or widowers, and almost 70 percent of them were from the urban area. Frequently, a number of orphaned siblings, led by the eldest, formed a household. This was fairly common since many parents remained at home on the afternoon of the avalanche while their children went off to the circus in the soccer stadium, which suffered only partial damage. Orphaned cousins or widowed uncles and aunts were taken into families as well. Many families consisted of a husband and wife who lost children and several nieces and nephews orphaned by the disaster. There were also families that consisted of grandparents, who survived because they lived in the hinterlands, and orphaned grandchildren of urban parents. Sometimes, surviving couples took widowed brothers and sisters into their modules, and occasionally godparents and godchildren formed new families. Some families combined many different kin relationships to form a household such as one consisting of a widower, his two children, his sister-in-law, five nieces and nephews, and a business partner. After the construction of the modules, household size averaged between four and five people, but several households had as many as eleven or twelve members. There were also many households of single individuals, most of them widows or widowers.

While these households were in the process of forming, and in some of the less traditional ones for a considerable time after, the ordinarily clear lines in the division of labor became blurred. Tasks that were clearly within the realm of female labor were carried out unselfconsciously by men in households without women. However, in most of the cases in which the household regrouped with a relatively normal distribution of the sexes, the traditional division of labor by sex was not long in reappearing.

Friendship also played an important role in the formation of post-disaster households. Rodolfo Armendariz, El Pillo, Miguel Giraldo, Ricardo Urteaga, and Shamu Mendez had all been friends and drinking buddies before the tragedy. El Pillo and Ricardo were also cousins, although fairly distant ones. Virtually everyone of them had lost all or most of their families in the avalanche. Rodolfo's eleven-year-old son had survived in the soccer stadium, and Miguel Giraldo had a daughter in Lima as well as an illegitimate son whom he now chose to recognize. El Pillo had lost everyone in his immediate family—his parents, his wife, and his children. He had relatives in Ica who helped him from time to time. Ricardo and Shamu had lost all their immediate families but had relatives in other parts of Peru.

After the disaster, each of these survivors made their way back to Pashulpampa within a few days. When the tents arrived, they clustered theirs together around a common cooking fire on the hill above the ramada church. Living together, mourning together, drinking together, these widowers soon became known in the camp as an informal group and then a household. The implicit leader of the group was Ricardo Urteaga since he had probably had the highest social position of any of them in old Yungay. However, the conditions of the aftermath reduced the degree of social distance among them, and their household was more egalitarian with little deference paid to predisaster social positions. In fact, some of the favorite and frequent targets of El Pillo's wit were Ricardo's social standing, dignified demeanor, and intellectural inclinations. The drinking exploits of these five and the friends they gathered around them became legendary in a very short time.

In the afternoons, the five would gather in one of the cantina shacks for a friendly glass of beer. The conversation would be genial, behavior would be correct, language would be formal, and the humor would be good-natured and at no one's expense. As the afternoon shadows grew darker, and the number of empty Pilsen bottles increased, the tone and atmosphere would change. Issues were argued more passionately, language became more florid, and the humor both more biting and obscene. By the end of the afternoon, everybody would be drunk, Ricardo would be declaiming to the world in poetic and impassioned terms, standing, pointing a finger to the sky, eyes blazing, condemning the ignorance and brutality of all who surrounded him. El Pillo would be ridiculing him, his rapier wit somewhat blunted by alcohol, but losing little of its effect for the group. Rodolfo would try to outshout Ricardo and would occasionally subdue him by sheer volume. Shamu Mendez, the bookseller, would try to reason with Ricardo, to argue with him as rationally as their drunkenness would permit. Miguel Giraldo would witness all this, slouched back in his chair, eyes narrowed, disdain for everything around him etched in his sharp features. Without warning he would explode, impugn the manhood of all those around him, and then subside again into his black depression. As night fell, the drinking would slow down as some of them fell asleep where they sat or wandered off into the night toward their tents. Occasionally all five, sometimes roaring with anger or sometimes even hilarity—it was often hard to tell which— sometimes wracked with the sobs of overwhelming grief released by the alcohol, would return together to their tents, disturbing all those around them, waking the children, and drawing the curses of their neighbors down upon them. El Pillo said once that the only reason to drink now (after the disaster) was to get drunk. "What the hell, why not? I've lost everything in life, why don't I just keep on getting drunk? We get drunk, and we remember our loved ones and cry and the liquor comes out the eyes."

Although Yungay and present conditions dominated conversation, other topics like politics were commonly dealt with in the lengthy afternoons of conversation of the five friends. Around this time in late 1970, the Uruguayan guerilla group, the Tupamaros, were making headlines for their daring revolutionary activity in Montevideo. The name *Tupamaros* was taken from an eighteenth-century Peruvian rebel called Tupac Amaru. Since Tupac Amaru was also the symbol of the Peruvian military government's "revolution," the name was in common usage in Peru as well. One afternoon as the friends were initiating another drinking session, the topic of the Tupamaros came up. All admitted that since they were "communists," they were bad, but they really had style and daring. They were macho. As the conversation ranged around the recent exploits of the Tupamaros, a number of men were invited to sit down and *"chupar"* a little beer with them. The verb *chupar* in its slang usage means to drink alcohol, usually heavily. The coincidence of the two words *chupar* and *Tupamaros* in the context of this heavy drinking

172

and tightly knit group of friends who now saw themselves as independent of society's opinions soon gave birth to the nickname "los Chupamaros." While it is untranslatable to English, the term came to acquire a great deal of significance, largely positive to those who bore it and negative to those who grew tired of their drunken bombasts and disruptive behavior.

Ricardo, Rodolfo, Miguel, El Pillo, and Shamu were the Chupamaros, loved or scorned, and occasionally both, eventually by most people in the camp. When the module buildings were being distributed, they acquired one entire building of eight rooms for themselves up on the second tier above the road. Since they had a building on the end of the tier they had a little space in which to make a garden. When the ramada church in the field was knocked down to make way for the modules, Ricardo took the cross and planted it in front of their garden. Much of the work of installing doors and windows on their modules was carried out by carpenters whom the Chupamaros hired, but the work of the garden was begun by El Pillo with help from the others. They planted a few trees and bushes around their front doors, but the plants eventually succumbed to lack of care. While Shamu began a new store and Rodolfo soon got a temporary job as a labor gang boss for the CRYRZA, the other three individuals neither had nor really needed work. They had other resources on which they could depend. For these three it was extremely difficult to focus their attention on any tasks. A number of projects were undertaken, like the garden, and then dropped as their enthusiasm for them waned. The group, the Chupamaros, the friends who lived and drank and cried together, was the only thing that provided support for those blasted lives that year. The focus of that support was their dedication to the survival of Yungay.

The bond of friendship was the tie that kept many people from complete emotional collapse in the aftermath of the tragedy. Friends comforted each other in their grief. They held each other when grief threatened to overwhelm them, when they lost control and succumbed to their loss in frenzied agonies of hysterical sobbing. Friends who felt the same pain cared for each other when the pain was greatest; they provided sympathy, understanding and, most important, presence. Presence meant sharing, and sharing in the context of Yungay meant understanding.

A short time after the tragedy Roberto Falcón's brother came up to

173

the valley and took him back to the coast. According to Roberto, the two of them traveled around the north coast of Peru together as his brother attempted

to get me through the rough time. After a month I came back here, and I spent six months living with my great friend Guillermo Mendoza who was also a teacher. Then Guillermo was murdered, we suspect, by a man who thought Guillermo was sleeping with his wife. His death really shattered me. It was the last straw because he had lost as much as I had, and we kept each other from going to pieces. I couldn't sleep, I lost weight . . . three months of this. How could I work? Impossible! Since his death I eat and sleep where hunger and the night catch me. I also drank a lot, but now [January 1971] not so much. I had to leave the drinking because you can't live that way. My life is very undecided now. In Lima I was offered considerable credit for work towards another degree and a job besides, but my spirits wouldn't permit it. It is probably better for me to come back here where my students would be as traumatized as I am, and we can dedicate ourselves to getting better mentally.

Friendship and common suffering created ties which kept people from breaking down and knit them into the fabric of new households. In the broadest sense, these elements also reintegrated people who had lost everyone into the life of the new community. When Rosa Martínez returned to Yungay after her long convalescence, she had only very meager resources with which to start her restaurant. Since she had arrived so late, the social workers apologetically explained that all the restaurant places in the module marketplace had already been distributed. However, Rosa was not abandoned in her difficulties. The Chupamaros and others, among them Don Epicho Bellido of the Expreso Serrano, immediately pitched in. Don Epicho told her, "We are not going to leave you without help."

He cleared a spot for her on the road just north of the Expreso Serrano office, and one of the CRYRZA labor bosses gave her twenty sheets of corrugated plastic roofing material. Other friends, Rodolfo Armendariz and El Pillo among them, began a collection of money and materials for her and within a short time, they had built a rough shed of logs and branches with a plastic roof close to the tin shack which housed the bus company offices. Within a day they had scrounged a number of pots and pans for her, and I gave her a primus stove and some utensils that I was not using. I had completely outfitted myself for householding in Yungay but had found that eating in the many restaurants which grew up in Yungay was not only less time-consuming, but also more appetizing, even in the worst of times. Restaurants were also good places to meet people and talk. Within a few days, Rosa with the help of her friends began serving meals. Quite a large number of people, the Chupamaros, other widows and widowers, and I among them, made *pension* contracts for all our meals with her. In addition, Don Epicho told all his bus drivers to inform their passengers that the best place to eat when the bus stopped in Yungay was the Restaurante Rosita. Wherever Rosa went in the first few months after her return, she was treated warmly and affectionately by all in Yungay, regardless of social class. As she said, "With work I hope to get over my sadness. I live with the avalanche and the faces of my sons who died in the avalanche." Rosa may be bonded to Yungay by the faces of her dead children, but her survival and continued life in the camp was assured by the response of the community to her. Her life, in many ways, became symbolic of the life of Yungay in the year following the tragedy. She was "the first survivor" of the avalanche, and people in the community were not about to let her succumb to the aftermath. The kinship of common experience and the friendship awakened in people by her indomitable spirit throughout the community were vital elements of support in Rosa's efforts to rebuild her shattered life.

In old Yungay people related to each other through rituals of compadrazgo, and such fictively bonded individuals were always important elements in each others lives emotionally, ritually, socially, and economically. The death of compadres (coparents) and *padrinos* (godparents) in the disaster engendered feelings of great loss, sadness, and vulnerability among the survivors. In old Yungay as in much of Latin America, compadrazgo was a system by which usually unrelated individuals were bound together through the sponsorship of another person or couple passing through an important ritual even in the life cycle. The compadrazgo relationship institutionalized a set of mutual obligations between compadres and between *padrinos* and *ahijados* (godchildren). It was a sign of respect to be chosen a godparent. In return for the respect and gifts received, a person was expected to become the "spiritual parent" of the child and support him or her with gifts and assistance. Theoretically, the godparents were responsible for a baptized child should something happen to the parents. There were a variety of events in

175

which compadrazgo relationships were considered necessary such as baptism, holy communion, marriage, confirmation and particularly among the Indians, first hair-cutting, and first nail-cutting. Compadrazgo involved a linking of members of the same class in horizontal relationships or of members of different classes in vertical relationships.

The loss of compadrazgo relationships among townspeople was profoundly felt, particularly among the poorer classes. Most lower-class mestizo and cholo survivors lost the compadrazgo relationships they had established with great care with the powerful classes in Yungay. As Miguel Mejía said to me one afternoon in his hat shop, "In the old town there were families who made sure you were all right—rich families who protected you. Marcial Benítez protected me. You remember him? He had the Bazar Benítez on the Calle Comercio? Well . . . now there is nobody to protect us. The rich people in the market now are all new and from the countryside, and one does not have sufficient confidence to ask for help or loans." Miguel feels alone and defenseless in the world without his compadres. Looking at his healthy brood of eight offspring, from Felipe at fifteen to Beatriz not yet a year old, he moaned, "Look at them, poor little ones, alone, without godparents."

The loss of compadres and other ritual kin is also felt deeply by those on the superior level of the compadrazgo relationships. Rosa Martínez, whose family losses in themselves were very devastating, told me that she felt lonely without her ritual kin, "I have no more compadres, no more ahijados, all dead, all buried in the avalanche. I am lonely. Who will care for me? Who will keep me company when I am old? I am alone in the world now."

The compadrazgo relationships therefore had different meanings for the different participants. For the poor, compadrazgo was a hedge against unforeseen difficulties, someone to rely on in case of need, and a link with social power and prestige. For the godparents the relationship might mean the continued clientele of a family in one's store, or the receipt of small gifts and services, but in some measure at least, compadrazgo relationships with many people constituted an affirmation of one's status in the community. The visits of compadres and *ahijados,* and their deference, respect, and affection, were important manifestations that one was esteemed and meaningful. While upper-class people often complained that their responsibilities to their ritual kin were more bother than their worth, they were rarely dismissed altogether.

About six months after the disaster, new compadrazgo relationships began to be established in the camp with great pleasure on everybody's part. Her new compadres and *ahijados* would come to visit Rosa in her restaurant. While none of the respect due a compadre was missing, the enjoyment and gratification in the relationships for all were clear. To be a *padrino* is to be respected and esteemed. To have a compadre or a *padrino* is to have a buffer against the world when needed. After the disaster people in general felt a deep personal loss at the death of their ritual kin, but equally profound was the sense of despair at the loss of the protective social barrier which ritual kin relationships constituted in Yungay life.

The celebration of life-cycle events and rituals, particularly those involving compadrazgo relationships, also offered the beleaguered and traumatized survivors an opportunity to renew old social usages and customs reaffirming the continuity of their lives with the past. The living must continue with life, and birthdays and baptisms and their ritual celebrations are part of life. In the first three months following the tragedy very few celebrations of these events took place. Conditions were too raw; life was too uncertain; wounds had barely begun to heal. However, in October and November of 1970, birthdays and baptisms began to be celebrated in traditional fashion, and not long after weddings began to take place. When the module houses were built and a relatively steady state, regardless of its essential misery, began, the celebration of these important events in the life cycle became socially important again.

Baptism often takes place quite late in the child's life. In December of 1970 one of the high-school teachers had his three-year-old daughter baptized and celebrated the event in traditional fashion. The baptism was in the ramada church at eleven o'clock on a bright Saturday morning. After the ceremony, the assembled guests walked from the church to a rural home not far from the camp. The house, which belonged to the teacher's country cousin, was a typical rural Peruvian dwelling with one large room and storage areas in back and on the second floor. A part stone, part adobe brick wall (*pirca*) encircled the house. A courtyard or corral area was partially shielded from the bright sunshine by a lattice-work of palm fronds. At the edge of the corral was a small grove of graceful eucalyptus trees. Although the formal invitation, a small card with little silver angels and the names of the child, the parents, and the godparents printed in silver letters, had indicated 12:00 noon, I arrived

177

much earlier than most at 12:30. Straight-backed chairs had been set out under the shade of the palm latticework, and benches of wide, split logs were arranged around the courtyard. To the back of the courtyard near the house two men in rustic homespun pants, white cotton shirts, and sandals were laboring over a fire on which a great number of earthenware and metal pots were steaming. A battery-powered phonograph blared rock and roll and Peruvian popular tunes from a table near the center of the corral.

My host invited me to a glass of beer, and I drank several before the other guests finally arrived about an hour later. Then many cases of beer were brought out, and the guests began to drink in traditional highland fashion. One person opens a bottle, pours himself a glass, toasts the person next to him with the bottle, and passes it on to him. After drinking his beer down, usually in one draft, he swirls the remaining foam around "to clean" the glass and shakes it out on the ground before passing the glass to the person he toasted. Under these customs, drinking becomes a highly formalized and public activity. Since you are being toasted, it is extremely difficult to refuse to drink without offending, and if you do not pour yourself a sufficient amount of beer, your reluctance is duly noted and criticized. Under these conditions in about an hour everybody is well on their way to being drunk. The state of drunkenness is no cause for shame and no reason to cease drinking. After an hour of beer, we were all served several small glasses of *capitán,* a volatile mixture of *pisco* and sweet vermouth. The *capitán* was followed by a three-course meal of *papas a la Huancaina* (cold boiled potatoes in a cheese sauce) followed by *escabeche de pollo* (cold chicken and potatoes in a sweet onion sauce) and finally, the *pièce de résistance* of all highland feasts, *picante de cuy* (spicy barbecued guinea pig with potatoes). The meal, of course, was accompanied by more beer, and by four o'clock in the afternoon everybody was very well fed and in high spirits. After the meal the little girl was brought out. Her dark brown hair was tied in many small locks by red ribbon bows. One woman carried the child and another held a metal tray on which lay a pair of scissors. The child was passed from guest to guest, each cutting a lock of hair off and placing some amount of money on the metal tray. The gifts varied from a few soles to several hundred. The child went round all the guests twice and was almost totally shorn and very upset about the whole business by the end of the second round. Then, in the fading hours of the afternoon, the dancing began. Some people were reluctant to dance because of mourning restrictions, but most eventually succumbed to the chance to enjoy themselves a little. The music at the beginning was rock and roll and popular *criolle* music, as it is called. As the party progressed, the music became "tropical" rhythms, *cumbias, merengues,* and other Latin styles. By nightfall, one lone Coleman lantern revealed everybody boisterously shuffling and stamping around in the corral dust to the strains of highland *huaynos,* and happy conversation continued on to past midnight.

While these events were excellent opportunities for the Yungaínos to forget their sorrows for a few moments, often the vast amounts of alcohol had different effects on different people, and difficulties, arguments, fights or hysterical grief could mar the festivities. Another baptism about a month later took place in Yungay's largest restaurant. The restaurant itself was a small building of one dingy low-ceilinged room of whitewashed lace cane and mud with a kitchen area in the back. It was really nothing more than a large rectangular *quincha,* constructed by the side of the road to attract travelers. All the tables had been pushed together to form one long table for the approximately fifty guests. This fiesta was a considerably more formal event since it was the baptism of the granddaughter of one of the town's wealthier citizens, a man whose entire family had survived the avalanche because they had lived in suburban Cochahuaín. Despite the formal atmosphere, the proceedings followed essentially the same pattern as the earlier fiesta.

At the banquet table I was placed between two men in their early thirties, both in black, both survivors of Yungay. As the festivities proceeded, I noticed that the man on my left was becoming progressively more introspective and quiet amidst the general chatter of the party. Since we had met earlier, I began to talk to my solemn companion about the baptism fiesta. Glancing around at the dingy walls of the restaurant, the ingrained dust thrown into high relief by the brilliance of the Coleman lantern, and the shabby dress of the participants, he muttered sadly that in old Yungay such a fiesta would have been an elegant affair, involving many more people. Baptisms were happy events to celebrate. He was quite moved by these thoughts, and suddenly reached across in front of me and grabbed his friend on my right by the sleeve. "Doesn't it seem like a dream, Juanito? Doesn't it seem like we will walk out that door and walk the same streets and see the same people as before?" His eyes filled with tears, and he struggled to control his emotions. Juanito touched his arm and urged him in a low and sympathetic voice to calm himself. Juanito continued his conversation with others while the man on my left lapsed into the total silence of his memories. For the survivors of Yungay, the resumption of normal social life was a bittersweet process. As people tried to reconstruct traditional patterns, the obvious differences in their lives made for painful transition. If anything softened the agony of their grief and the misery of their present conditions, however, it was the resumption of social activities and relationships. Life had to go on, and births and baptisms and the rituals and the relationships created and formed around such events, one's compadres, one's god-kin, were part of life and important elements in rebuilding one's personal community and life.

Certainly one of the chief means of rebuilding was marriage and its varieties of forms and expressions. A home, marriage, and a family are expected norms in Andean society, and to people who lost all these things in one violent moment, remarriage and new families were very much desired. In the early months after the tragedy, both men and women would openly long for the joys of hearth and family, and people spoke of their departed spouses with great respect and love. Although mourning traditions in the Andes normally require a year's wait before remarriage, many people simply established households together in the camp on an informal basis. This cohabitation, or *convivencia,* is fairly common in Peru among the lower socioeconomic groups. In one of the neighboring districts of Yungay, at least 19 percent of the men and 15 percent of the women live in consensual unions without benefit of either civil or religious ceremonies (Doughty 1968:32). In the year after the disaster in Yungay people of all classes were establishing consensual unions.

Julia Cáceres, a widowed primary schoolteacher, and César Obregón, a widower also, established a household within a few months of the disaster. Julia had taken her two children to the circus the afternoon of the avalanche. She had wanted her husband Esteban to accompany them, but he preferred to stay home and listen to the soccer game on the radio. César drove for an interprovincial transport company and was on his way to Lima from the southern city of Tacna when the earthquake hit. He lost his wife and all his children. César had been a good friend of Esteban's, and when the module dwellings were distributed, Julia and César applied at the same time and were given contiguous rooms. As the months passed, César was often seen walking with Julia in the camp, shopping in the market with her occasionally, or playing with her young children in the dusty alley next to their module building.

I remember on more than one occasion when César was having a beer with a few of us at Rosita's, Pedro or Julita, Julia's children, were sent to remind him of some responsibility or errand for the household they now maintained in common. Inevitably, the child's mission would evoke much laughter and many sarcastic remarks about César being a *warmi-mandarán,* the Quechua word for *henpecked.* A little embarrassed, but smiling, César would rise from the table with a sigh, far more of satisfaction than reluctance, and departing to the good-natured and more than envious joking of his widowed and solitary friends, would accompany the child home.

The question of remarriage and surviving children was one that weighed upon the minds of the widowed in Yungay. Benjamín Figueroa and Roberto Falcón who both wanted to remarry after a year, discussed their anxieties about this issue with me. Benjamín, who was now both father and mother to his one remaining little daughter Margarita, was concerned that it was "going to be tough on our remaining little ones with stepmothers. And we will have more kids and that will also be tough on them because their brothers and sisters won't have the same mother."

Roberto explained, "Siblings [*hermanos*] who are of the same mother are closer than siblings of the same father, but different mothers. The mother unites them. But, in our case," he said, pointing to Benjamín and himself, "our children will have different mothers, and the little ones who have lost their mothers may not feel close to the children of new wives. It will be hard for them." César Obregón's newly acquired stepchildren respond to him as they would to their real father, and he has made every effort to get close to them. Since Pedrito remembers his father a little, and he knows that his father and César were good friends, César has tried to tell him as much as he can about his father. There seems little attempt to bury the past in terms of lost parents or spouses. They are remembered with love and respect, regardless of present circumstances.

People who had not yet formed new unions or households often idly wondered about whom their prospective mates would be. Passing a quiet afternoon with Rosita Martínez, who had been a good friend of his wife, Rodolfo Armendariz said he was very curious about whom his new wife would be. "Will she say, 'He is not as good as the first one!'? " Rosita responded glumly that nothing would ever be as good. Everything after would always be worse than before.

Not everyone was as distraught as Rosa in those early months. The disaster for some had brought suffering in a compounded form. Luis Cordero Paredez, for example, was widowed twice, once by the avalanche of 1962 when his wife Josefina and their two children were buried in Ranrahirca while he was working in his Yungay bookstore, and once again, when his second wife Mélida was awaiting the birth of their child in the Yungay hospital·on May 31, 1970. On that day Cordero was in Huaráz where he narrowly escaped being crushed by a collapsing wall in the earthquake. Cordero then moved to Caraz, where he wanted to reopen his bookstore and printshop. A reporter for the newspaper *La Prensa* interviewed him when he went to Lima to negotiate a loan for the purchase of new printing machines from the Industrial Bank. When asked if he contemplated marriage for the third time, he laughed and responded, "Why not? I still feel young and I can form a household . . . now it's a simple matter of finding someone who is interested. . . ."

Most people wanted to remarry, or at least establish new households formed around consensual unions. Leo Ruiz said he was going to wait one more year and then marry the daughter of the straw boss of a small hacienda he had in the hills. He said the last time he had married a Limeña, but this time he was going to get married in the *chacra,* in the fields. He was nervous about how his relatives in Lima were going to receive such a union since he was forty-two years old and eminently *decente,* and she was a comely chola of eighteen. It never happened.

Some of the consensual unions formed during the year were formalized in both church and civil ceremonies after the required year or more of official mourning. Often these marriages and consensual unions had an economic base as well as an emotional one. Many business undertakings, particularly commercial ones, require two people. In one case, a woman vegetable exporter and a man who had lost his store in Yungay but survived with his panel truck established a profitable business relationship as well as a household. In the case of Rosa Martínez, her friendship with the dead wife of Rodolfo Armendariz served initially as the basis for companionship between Rosa and Rodolfo. As their relationship deepened, they began to live together in the back rooms that Rosa eventually added to her restaurant. Before he got temporary work with CRYRZA, Rodolfo handled Rosa's finances and occasionally waited on tables while she took care of the cooking. When Rodolfo went back to work as a driver for the Expreso Serrano, he continued the policy of recommending the Restaurante Rosita to his passengers when they made a rest stop in Yungay. Rosa's restaurant made money because of her unstinting efforts, but it was dawn-to-dusk hard labor. When Rodolfo returned to work for the bus company, he was not there much of the time to help either. Rosa complained that the restaurant business in Yungay was a life of pure drudgery, a life of journeys between market and stove. They both still had to live in the restaurant back rooms for security reasons.

Despite the tremendous disruption of the disaster, marriage patterns for the province as a whole were not disturbed in a major way. In fact, compared with statistics from predisaster Yungay, marriages increased after the disaster. Probably many if not most of these marriages formally registered with the civil authorities were between rural partners. One explanation of this increase is that a great many consensual unions of the rural area were being formalized religiously and civilly. Almost 70 percent of the rural or poorer people I spoke to felt that the disaster was "a punishment from God," and the increase in marriages may have been a form of propitiation by formalizing what the church regards as a sinful relationship. I am acquainted with a number of cases where rural consensual unions among non-Indians were formalized after the disaster in response to pressure from priest, parents, or a *padrino*. One such couple had been living together for over ten years and had five children.

As mentioned earlier, the number of births in Yungay did not decline for much the same reason that marriage rates increased. However, another important consideration in the birth increase is that children are much desired in the Andes. Children are felt to be the natural result of marriage, as central to the institution as the husband-wife relationship itself. While more people are concerned with controlling the number of children they have, not having children at all is never considered, and childless couples feel the lack acutely and are pitied by others. Since so many people lost their families, including their children, once a relationship had been established, the next step in rebuilding family life was having children.

While life went on in Yungay—babies were born, people got married, work was done—much of the life in that first year was devoted to emotional as much as physical survival. The formation of new households and homes and the birth of new babies were important aspects of both physical and emotional survival, but most of the survivors were far from through the difficult process of coping with the awesome changes in their lives. During that first year, grief and mourning were crucial aspects of both behavior and identity for the survivors of Yungay as well as focal elements of the emerging culture of the new community.

The disaster had brought loss of some kind to everyone in Yungay. In some cases, for example the migrating peasants, the losses were less severe. Most peasant families had survived intact, but their material losses had created greater physical hardships and forced migration to the refugee camp for some. Even for those who had leaped at the chance to urbanize, even a voluntary change occasioned some feelings of loss for old and comfortable ways of doing things. The major losses, of loved and valued people as well as of all material possessions, were clearly suffered by the urban survivors. They had lost their community. And they had lost aspects of self, aspects of social and personal identity. All of these losses caused various forms of grief. The year after the disaster was a time of bereavement during which people worked through their grief, sadness, and suffering which follow any loss. Yungaínos mourned the loss of their loved ones, their homes, their community, and those aspects of self in acts of private, personal anguish as well as in public rituals in the community.

At the death of an important person, or the loss of a valued object or aspect of self, the grief that ensues appears to be a general pattern of human behavior regardless of culture. Death, like other forms of permanent loss, presents an ambivalent problem to survivors which is manifested in the conflicting tendencies seen in the grieving process. Survivors, to use Marris's phrase, want "to incorporate the dead and banish them" (1975:91). Survivors want to hold on to what is significant in the past because it is fundamental to understanding and making the present meaningful. When a person, object, or aspect of self passes permanently from the present, it takes with it the part of the survivor that was made meaningful by its presence.

Thus, there is a conflict about how to cope with loss, particularly in death. The meaning and importance must be retained without retaining the dead. Marris cannot be improved upon here:

. . . the continuity of life cannot be re-established until the nature of the disruption has been made clear. The loss must be insisted upon, otherwise the value of the lost relationship may seem disparaged, threatening all such relationships which still survive; but it also must be made good, and the bereaved must be led to re-establish themselves within society . . . for while the dead must be dismissed, the values they represented in all their relationships must be preserved (1975:34–35).

Grief then involves a process of negotiation between these two conflicting impulses of allegiance to the past and commitment to the present. The working out of grief swings the bereaved between these two tendencies until the conflict is resolved by incorporating what was valuable in the past with new commitments to the present in a meaningful existence. The alternative for the bereaved involves a life wholly or partly frozen in the past (Gorer calls this "mummification"), chronic grief, apathy, withdrawal, and a variety of other pathological behaviors (as quoted in Marris 1975:31).

The resolution of this conflict beween past and present appears to be facilitated by rituals of mourning, which seem to be the universal human response to loss and grief. How grief is expressed and how the mourning process for working through grief is structured are widely variable. All societies provide their members with guides to appropriate behavior. Ritual observances and practices such as funerals, wakes, periods of mourning, modes of dress, and forms of condolence are culturally defined channels of grief and mourning for the bereaved (Peretz 1970:16).

In the face of their awesome losses the Yungaínos suffered agonies of grief. Grief was expressed in many ways as individual personality characteristics and coping techniques varied. People expressed their grief alone in solitary tears or together with friends in reminiscences evoking cathartic expressions of emotion. Crying publicly in Yungay for men or women, drunk or sober, was no shame. In that sense, the general Latin American cultural pattern permitting men a greater measure of emotional expression was probably conducive to a generally healthy process for men of working through grief. People spoke openly of the tragedy and cried when it affected them. One rainy afternoon in February I sat with

Chapter 7

Rosita Martínez, Rodolfo Armendariz, Miguel Giraldo, and a Yungaíno woman visiting from Lima in Rosita's shanty restaurant. We were drinking coffee and talking of the summer I had spent in Yungay four years before. They all wanted to know how much of old Yungay I remembered. Did I remember the open air restaurant *Los Claveles* (The Carnations) where they served terrific *picante de cuy?* Of course, I replied, smiling. "One does not forget memorable food like that quickly."

A shadow passed over Rodolfo's face. "There doesn't pass a day when one does not think of these things. Of these things, of the good things of Yungay, then of the earthquake, of the landslide."

"And my wife and kids . . . so close to safety," added Miguel hoarsely, a rising inflection of anguish in his voice.

"And my daughter," said the visitor from Lima. "I always thought if one of my daughters died, I would die also, but one learns to accept, to resign oneself. But walking by the landslide is sometimes hard, but, you know, going to visit the landslide can be a help also. One goes to the landslide and cries hard and comes back tranquil."

Tears were often evoked in the course of ordinary conversation if the subject happened to turn to the tragedy in the old city. Because Rosa Martínez's survival was so miraculous she was often asked for the details by people from the valley who had known her before the disaster. I recall one particular occasion on which a woman from Caraz sat with Rosa for almost an hour, peppering her with brutally direct personal questions about her rescue, her survival, and her loss. As Rosa related the part of her story which dealt with the death of her sons, her voice choked and the tears began to flow down her cheeks. She did not interrupt her tale, however, and attempted to staunch the tears with the sleeve of her black sweater. The Carasina persisted in what I was beginning to feel was an intolerably insensitive line of questioning, and I began to think of ways I could delicately interrupt for Rosa's sake. In a short time, the lady from Caraz took her leave, embracing Rosa and telling her in a light-hearted voice to "be strong and accept" and to come visit her in Caraz. As I watched her leave the restaurant, I saw Rosa retreat, still crying to the back of the kitchen area.

Several hours later, I was talking with some friends, among them Rosa's companion, Rodolfo, about what happened. I was having misgivings about my own questions which had occasionally elicited tears from Yungaínos. When I told them about the Carasina and my misgivings about talking about painful issues, Rodolfo smiled and said, "Don't worry. It's okay. Crying for us is a *desfogue*" (a release; Oliver-Smith 1979).

This began a general discussion of crying among the group. The question was raised as to who dealt with their crying best. El Pillo said that he couldn't talk when he cried, and Rodolfo said that when he cried, his face got redder and his throat choked up, but when Miguel cried, "he keeps right on talking and his neck doesn't swell or anything." Everyone was amazed by this and Miguel smiled. They all agreed that when you come back from crying on the landslide, you feel a great deal better. Pablo added that his days for crying on the landslide were Tuesdays and Fridays.

Since grief is part of the total experience of every survivor, the various expressions of grief were topics of frank and open discussion. One's grief and the grief of a fellow survivor were part of the common experience which bonded people in the aftermath. They were all suffering together, and if one could be there when grief and pain began to push hard on a fellow survivor, one shared it, one let him speak or cry or roar drunkenly in his anguish. Sooner or later one's time for grief and pain would come, and there would be someone to listen.

One of the bitterest losses for many urban survivors was the loss of an aspect of social identity, an integral part of one's individual mazeway. The socially elite classes of Yungay considered themselves to be the custodians of culture and breeding in the old city. With the disaster, they suffered a sudden and radical experience of social leveling. They lived in modules like cholos just in from the countryside. They suffered dust and heat, the cold and rain and the mud and the filth in ragged and dirty clothes, just like everyone else in the camp. Whereas before they had enjoyed a social and economic dominance, in the aftermath most of the markers of their elite status had disappeared. Leo Ruiz, whose grief drove him to three- and four-day drinking marathons, once had a run-in with one of the nonlocal police, who locked him in the module jail for the evening. When he told us about it the next day, he wept, partly from grief and partly from rage. With the tears rolling down his cheeks, he cried, "I am a real Yungaíno, from the plaza de armas! They know who I am. Ahhh, God! We who were the representatives of Yungay, what are we now? Shit! Just shit!"

Yungaínos also grieved for their community and their lost way of life. As Wallace explains, we learn to love our way of life, our surroundings,

187

and the contexts in which we obtain the necessities and satisfactions of life. We identify with and love our culture because it is associated with all the benefits of life. When our culture is shown to be ineffective or is destroyed, we suffer loss and grieve as though we had lost a loved one (Wallace 1957:24). Yungaínos grieved not only for people but for places and objects that no longer existed and for customs that were no longer viable in the camp's environment. The constant reminiscences about this chapel, that street, the little corner store, or a stroll in the plaza were ritual expressions of the value and significance of the lost past. Such expressions and the translation of the values they represent are crucial to resolution of the grieving process. Much in the same way that we recount the virtues of loved ones at their deaths, Yungaínos continually lauded their lost community as they grieved for their lost way of life, thereby establishing the importance of the values it represented for the future.

Many people of all ages complained of other typical grief symptoms such as apathy, withdrawal, restlessness, nervousness, loss of memory, and the inability to concentrate. Others had physical symptoms: headaches, shortness of breath, dizziness, and loss of appetite. Insomnia plagued some people and nightmares others. Occasionally, when I would work late, huddled in my sleeping bag for warmth, writing notes or reading by candlelight, the silence of the sleeping community would be split by the tortured wail of someone in the throes of a nightmare. The walls of the module buildings were thin enough for the sound of the quiet weeping of the awakened dreamer and the muffled words of solace of their companions to be heard by neighbors. Many said that they dreamed often of the disaster, of trying to escape the avalanche as it descended upon them. I had that dream myself once, just before I was to leave the community. People would awake with shrieks of horror from these dreams, which would sometimes awaken others, and the stillness of the night would be shredded by a brief cacophony of screaming babies and howling dogs until they, the dreamer, and the rest of the community subsided into sleep once more. The night was the most difficult time for people living alone. Before she started living with Rodolfo, Rosa often spoke about what it felt like to be alone. During the day, there was so much to do in the restaurant that she did not think much about her solitude, but when night came and people abandoned the streets, she would realize how alone she was. Before the disaster, she and her eldest son would talk over the events of the day and make plans for the following day before going to bed. Now she had no one to talk to at all at night, and she was plagued by thoughts of her past happiness and her present miseries.

For most people in Yungay the symptoms of trauma persisted in varying degrees through the first six months, in some up to a year after the disaster, and in a few still continue many years later. However, only a few people seemed to succumb to chronic depression. For some people, particularly men, grief took the form of anger and aggression directed at self and others. During the first six months of the camp, the main street of bars and restaurants would be the scene of fistfights and arguments between drunken men. Sometimes the arguments and fights would be between camp residents, but occasionally there would be a conflict between a Yungaíno and someone who had chosen to live in Tingua or Yungay Sur. These people were considered traitors, and when they came to Yungay for market or to visit relatives, they occasionally became the targets of verbal or physical abuse.

Survivors seemed to direct a great deal of anger at themselves. The violent behavior of many of the heavier drinking survivors occasionally resulted in minor injury to themselves. Men who would appear to be drunk to the point of immobility would suddenly explode in a frenzy of violent activity, running amok, causing injury to themselves and others, before collapsing or being subdued. Grief and anger drove Aquelino Huamán into such frenzies. I witnessed one of them. It was a dark, cool, clear night in November, a rare thing, for we were well into the rainy season by then. I was having a late cup of coffee with friends in Arcadio Chavez's restaurant on the edge of the highway. We sat talking quietly at one of the bright blue tables in the dim light thrown by a kerosene lantern. The lantern's flame cast an orange tint on the tan estera walls contrasting with the darkness of the shadows in the corners of the room. Several other groups of people sat quietly, drinking beer or having a late dinner. Most of them were dressed in black.

"Angelita!" Something between a shriek and a sob came out of the darkness beyond the open door. A figure in black rushed in, stumbling, crashing into the first table, sending dishes and people tumbling to the floor. It was Aquelino, in a grief-stricken, drunken hysteria. He crossed the room, eyes clenched tightly shut, and pitched headlong into another table, again scattering its contents to the hard-packed dirt floor. His eyes now wild and rolling, his mouth contorted and trailing a stream of saliva, he shrieked the name of his dead wife again and again as he launched himself toward the other side of the room. He raced from one side to the other, heedless of the havoc he was creating as arms and hands reached out to restrain him. His forehead was already cut and bleeding from one of his collisions. Finally three or four men were able to gain control of him, and they stretched him out on his back on one of the tables where his hysterical sobbing eventually subsided into a pathetic whimpering.

As the years wore on, the amount of overt anger and aggression as well as much of the heavy drinking diminished. But for some, unable to work out their grief effectively, heavy drinking became self-destructive. Things got worse and worse for Leo Ruiz. He no longer drank beer with the rest of his friends. He drank cane alcohol alone. He chain-smoked harsh black Inca cigarettes and rarely ate. He went for long periods without washing or changing his clothes until his appearance had totally changed. His friends informed his relatives in Lima, who took Leo back to live with them. He stayed for a week the first time before he escaped and returned to Yungay to resume his destructive drinking and increasing degeneration.

The suddenness and completeness of Yungay's tragedy left the survivors with a great deal more than ordinary grief. For one thing, under normal conditions, the death of an individual brings community support to the bereaved. Rituals of bereavement, funerals, wakes, condolence observances, modes of dress, and other mourning rites afford the survivor meaningful support. These culturally defined acts provide crucial guidelines for behavior and sentiment for survivors, particularly in the passage of the deceased from the society of the living to the realm of the dead as well as the passage of the survivor from mourner to nonmourner and renewed participation in normal life. Rituals of mourning permit the bereaved to integrate the loss into their lives, to come to terms with it, and through the grieving process, resolve the conflicts inherent in loss between allegiance to the past and healthy reintegration into life.

In Yungay the entire community had been wiped out, and for a brief time, the individual had been stripped of those basic supporting structures of the community. Not only were supporting family members all but gone, but even the familiar and comforting contexts of personal experience had been obliterated. In their stead was a barren avalanche scar and a tent camp, later replaced by an ugly barracks town, which was rapidly filling with rural migrants, increasing ever more the survivors' sense of being a beleaguered minority, punished first by nature and then by society. Compounding these miseries, the Yungaínos were faced with the singular problems confronting survivors of mass destruction. Robert Jay Lifton tells us that the survivor of major holocausts is "one who has touched, witnessed, encountered or been immersed in death in a literal or symbolic way and has himself remained alive" (1981:54). In his remarkable study of the Hiroshima survivors, Lifton presents a pattern of common problems which afflict survivors of disasters. A number of these themes have relevance for the problems of grief and mourning faced by the Yungaínos. Lifton posits that survivors are burdened by strong guilt feelings for those who died but have never been found or given a proper burial. He calls them "the homeless dead" (1967:492). The avalanche obliterated Yungay and wiped its families from the face of the earth in an instant. Reeling with shock, the survivors not unexpectedly had few supporting cultural mechanisms to cope with such cataclysm. There were no prescribed rituals for burial or mourning on such a scale. Yungay's dead were never buried, at least not in customary fashion. The importance of normal burial rituals is reflected in this Yungaína's feelings: "The avalanche was an especially terrible way to die because you can't really visit your dead because you don't really know where they are. When a person dies naturally, you know where they are and they can be visited. It is a comfort."

Her emphasis is on the avalanche as a terrible death for the survivors; it is they who suffer the consequences of the manner in which their families were killed. The thousands of bodies and fragments which Augusto Arévalo and his contingent of peasants buried in a mass grave near the base of the cemetery mound were never properly laid to rest. Few people visit the site as the final resting place of their families. While most people did not witness the ghastly procedure of the mass burial, the Yungaínos speak of it in cautiously impersonal terms, in numbers, distancing their own dead from such unspeakable visions: "Imagine. More than six thousand dead! What a horror!"

The "homeless dead" create emotional difficulties for survivors which may entail long-term psychological consequences. Lifton posits that the homeless dead haunt the survivor with the implication of negligence because they have never been given a proper burial. While the impos-

191

sibility of proper burial of the avalanche victims is recognized, such emotionally powerful attitudes are often not moderated by reason, particularly in such stressful conditions. The survivors profoundly lament the inability to bury their dead properly, to give them the full dignity normally accorded the deceased. Lifton also sees the homeless dead as involving the risk of impaired mourning for survivors. The expression of grief through customary mourning rituals allows the bereaved at once to embrace the dead, to show allegiance and fidelity, and to separate themselves, to pass the dead on, while they continue to live and function. If mourning is impaired, by whatever circumstances, this condition of ambivalance may become permanent. The impaired mourner is never able to leave the death imagery or the association with the dead, and is never able fully to work through the grief, which then becomes chronic and characterizes the survivor's entire life.

The suddenness and totality of Yungay's tragedy put survivors at the further risk of suffering from impaired mourning. However, the proximity of the camp to the avalanche, as the location of lost kin and community, played a vital role in the survivors' proper working through of grief. Even on the sunniest and warmest of days the avalanche scar is a somber and forbidding place which elicits and stimulates sentiments of grief and sorrow. When the rains came, about four months after the disaster, the avalanche acquired a cover of sparse greenery, the fruit of buried seed and natural production, somewhat softening the rough moonscape contours of the dried and crusted mud. One day in January 1971 I accompanied Rosa Martínez and Benigno Ochoa, a waiter in her restaurant, on a trip to the *playa,* the avalanche scar. Both of them carried flowers. From the camp we caught a ride with a pickup truck heading south and got off in Acobamba. I thought that hitching a ride for such a short distance was unnecessary, but as we began to walk toward the avalanche field, I noticed that Rosa was limping painfully. I asked her about it, and she told me that she still experienced considerable pain in her leg from her wounds. She also complained of severe headaches from time to time. The three of us quietly walked for a while on the road and then moved onto the avalanche surface itself. Evidence of rubble was still visible on the grey crusty surface with its sparse, wispy growth of vegetation. As we walked over the avalanche toward the crosses of Samuel del Rio Martínez and Juan Harada Martínez, I could hear Rosa murmuring to herself, "Ay vida, vida" (Ay, life, life).

The crosses of Samuel and Juan are made of wood with their names painted in black on them. Remnants of past flower offerings lay at their bases. The first thing that Benigno did was to go and get water in a can from the stream which runs along the south side of the avalanche. It was easy to forget in the midst of that desolation that I once lived by the side of that stream in Rosa's house in Yungay. While Benigno fetched the water, Rosa crossed herself and prayed silently, her lips slightly moving. She stood straight in front of the crosses of her sons. Her eyes filled with tears which soon overflowed down her cheeks, but she did not make a sound. When Benigno returned they put the flowers in the can of water and continued praying, while I stood back a little behind them, a bit lost in my own thoughts of Samuel and Rosa and the house by the stream. Rosa and Benigno, eyes downcast, prayed silently at the crosses for a few minutes more and then turned slowly, almost reluctantly, to go. As she left, Rosa looked back at Samuel's cross briefly and sighed, "Ay, papito de mi vida . . ." (Ay, little father of my life . . .). *Papito* and *mamita,* equivalents of "mummy" and "daddy" in English, are often used as terms of affection to children.

From the crosses of Rosa's sons, we moved over the avalanche to the cross of Benigno's wife, located just east of the battered palm trees approximately where the Yungay market had been. Rosa feels that she knows where her sons are buried, and has given them a "home" about fifty meters below the approximate location of her house near the stream. Benigno said that his wife was probably still at the market when the avalanche hit and thus has placed there a wooden cross with a glass-encased photograph of her in the center. While Benigno had remained relatively dry-eyed at the crosses of Rosa's sons, they both wept silently while praying at his wife's cross.

The avalanche is covered with crosses, some crude wooden ones and other more elegant creations in polished stonework. There are other monuments as well, but none are located anywhere near the site of the mass burial. Some people have chosen to place their memorials as close to their buried homes as rough calculation by existing landmarks will permit. Others have located the memorials where they think their loved ones were at the moment of death. Walking slowly back toward the camp in the fading light of the grey afternoon, we paused at the crosses of other known and dear people where Rosa and Benigno prayed briefly and silently. As we stepped off the avalanche onto the paved road in

Cochahuaín, we began to talk quietly among ourselves. Now completely dry-eyed, both Rosa and Benigno looked somewhat renewed by the experience. "Crying on the *playa* really helps," smiled Rosa. "I feel much better afterwards."

Yungaínos in general say quite openly that they go to the avalanche to cry for their families and their town. They say that crying helps them continue the arduous life they have been left with. The cathartic function of the somber atmosphere of the landslide, with its scattering of little clusters of crosses spread out over its expanse, is manifest in terms of effective working out of grief. Clearly, the proximity of the camp to the avalanche has given the Yungaínos the opportunity to give their dead a home and thus avert in most cases the continuation of the tragedy in the form of impaired mourning.

The relationship between the dead and the living, the past and the present, has always had great importance in Latin American culture in general. In Yungay this relationship with the dead always lent a special quality to the normal continuity of time. Before the disaster the intimate connections with the dead constituted a link with Yungay's tradition and history. Local poets extolled Yungay's heroes, and monuments both in the cemetery and in town commemorated outstanding citizens of the past.

However, historical time has been cleaved by the disaster. Time before the disaster is idealized, and life in old Yungay is portrayed in glowing terms as a town of honorable and educated people, a town whose progressive spirit and traditional beauty outshone anything in the Callejón de Huaylas. Yungay in "time before" is truly the "wished for former state" of disaster victims, whose daily realities had become ugly and painful with the tasks of coping with grief and rebuilding from rubble. The disaster marks time into good and bad parts. The "time before" was good, a time in which the community was perceived as unified, friendly, and healthy. "Time after" was the present, in which people lived in ugly squalor, feuding among themselves, with selfishness and egotism rampant.

However, the link with the dead also integrated time into a total continuum with shared realities and allegiances for the living. While ordinary time had been cleaved in two by the tragedy, nonordinary time—symbolic, eternal time—joined the living and the dead into a unified whole in which parallel existence is a reality which must be considered by the living in the conduct of their own lives and the life of the community. Indeed, while the disaster divided ordinary time, it had, if anything, strengthened the bond between past, present, and future in nonordinary, eternal time. Links to the past were strengthened by loss, and commitments to the future for the continued existence of the community were forged in the adversity of life.

The cemetery, which before the disaster had constituted Yungay's principle expression of its link to the past and the dead, acquired even greater importance in the aftermath of the tragedy. When the avalanche descended from Huascarán, the cemetery mound became an oasis of safety for ninety-two survivors, who watched in awe and horror from its heights as the avalanche engulfed their community. The lower tiers of burial niches were shattered by the impact of the mud, and shattered coffins and grisly remains of the long dead lay about the surface of the avalanche near the foot of the half-buried hill. The monumental statue of Christ was shaken by the earthquake, and although its base was cracked and tilted slightly, the statue still stood, arms outstretched, gazing out across the desolation.

As soon as the life of the camp had become fairly regularized, indeed within only a few months of the tragedy, Yungaínos began to turn their attention to the repair of the cemetery. While most of the disinterred bodies had been reburied with the newly dead, the disorder of the destroyed niches, the litter of coffin boards, and even the occasional ghastly remnant of a skull or other bones assaulted the survivors' sense of piety and allegiance to the dead. The repair of the cemetery became a high priority, although with the other pressing needs of the living in the camp, the job was not to be completed for almost a year.

The cemetery and the avalanche scar became known as *campo santo* or holy ground. They were imbued with an aura of the sacred. Although occasionally a few people have grumbled about the waste of good land and some have even planted crops on fields that overlap onto the scar itself, there was general appreciation and agreement when the government prohibited the use of the avalanche for any purpose beyond religious or secular rituals of commemoration. The four lone and dying palm trees in the midst of the avalanche scar have become ritually important for the renewal of the ties which every survivor maintains with his lost family. The Yungaínos constructed a small chapel of palm fronds and lashed logs using the exposed ruined tower of the church as a back wall. This little chapel together with the palm trees, symbolic of all survivors, and the cemetery became the most important ceremonial location in the disaster zone and were soon to become national monuments. Crosses by the hundreds sprang up all over the roughly four square kilometers of the Yungay lobe of the avalanche. As one survivor put it, "There should be thousands more for those families which perished entirely and therefore have no one to place their memorials." In fact, some people have placed crosses in memory of entire vanished families.

The avalanche as sacred space has acquired a supernatural aura. One never crosses that bleak devastation unmindful of what happened there and what lies under the ugly grey crust. The glaciers of Huascarán, both beautiful and terrible, compound the forbidding atmosphere with their imposing presence. Traditional beliefs of the Andean highlands have always stressed the existence of *almas* (souls), particularly those of victims, people who have met unexpected death, which are unable to go on to the afterworld and continue to inhabit this one. While this belief is more common among the Indians, more than one survivor commented to me about the number of *almas* that must pace the avalanche at night. Encounters with "spirit beings" have also taken place there.

Pablo Rios, the man who had extended such a tearful welcome to me when I first arrived in Yungay, told me of an incident in which he had accompanied a group of Peruvian tourists to the cemetery. The tourists, mostly from the coast, wanted to have their pictures taken on the avalanche and in front of the cemetery. They all climbed up to the top row of niches of the cemetery where they saw a skull, hanging in a tree not far from the base of Christ's statue. Suddenly a hail of stones flew at them from the tree. The tourists got frightened and ran, but Pablo stayed. He went to the place where he thought his son had been buried by the avalanche. He sat down and called to his son, "Antonio, Antonio, speak to me. Show yourself."

He heard the voice of a woman say to him, "Here I am." Then someone touched him on the shoulder, and he turned around but no one was there. At this point, he says, he went crazy and ran up to the cemetery where his sister found him later, curled up on the ground and weeping. She finally had to get a policeman to come and bring him down. "I was so out of my mind that she could not deal with me."

One afternoon he went up to the avalanche to pray and weep. While he was there he said he felt very much alone before the cross of his wife. The only sound was the wind faintly whistling in his ears. In his meditations he dozed off for about an hour. When he awoke, he felt the presence of someone looking at him. He turned around to find a young girl with very long hair dressed in black. When he tried to speak to her, she vanished.

Public ceremonies on the avalanche commemorating the lost city and praying for and pledging fidelity to the lost dead take place on ritually important days of the calendar year. Principal among these dates are October 28, the anniversary of the political founding of Yungay, November 2, the day of the dead, and, of course, May 31, the anniversary of the death of Yungay. My arrival in Yungay coincided by chance with the anniversary of the founding of Yungay on October 28. The first public function I witnessed in my fieldwork took place on the avalanche where I listened to a condemnation of the reconstruction authorities by Emilio Robles.

A few days later on November 2, the day of the dead, a public commemorative mass was said around midday in the little chapel on the avalanche. People of all social classes either attended the mass and psalm reading following it or visited the avalanche at some time during the day. Many placed crosses and memorial heart-shaped wreaths of purple and white flowers or black and white plastic bunting where they thought their homes were under the mud. As the hour of the mass approached, people in small clusters of five and six moved quietly across the avalanche, carrying their wreaths and crosses and tools to pierce the hard crusted surface. Their black mourning dress was stark against the light grey mud in the brilliant midday sunshine. Some carried pitchers or bottles of holy water brought from the church in Yungay to pour over the flowers and graves at the foot of the cross. No one spoke above a whisper, and the only sound heard above the soft whistle of the wind through the dying palm trees was the low, chanting drone of Padre Diaz saying mass in the little chapel. A cross about twenty feet high had been planted close to the palms, and a group of black-clad mourners clustered silently at its base, some kneelng in prayer, others standing, eyes cast upward to the cross and Huascarán beyond it.

After the mass, Padre Diaz read from the Bible to a group of thirty or forty people. He read in Latin, explaining to me later that the psalm reading was not for the people present, but for the souls of those who had died in the disaster. It was not necessary for the people to understand what he said. Their presence at the ritual was their act of devotion to the dead. By mid afternoon, the sun was beginning to drop behind the Cordillera Negra to the west, and the sky began to cloud over, hiding Huascarán's face from view. The wind picked up, adding a chill and an eerie whine to the air as it swept across the bleak terrain. People moved off, as silently as they came, in the same little groups of five and six, now dark shadows, growing smaller as they spread out in all directions across the grey rubble field toward the camp or their homes on the hillsides.

The dead came up in conversation in Yungay, almost as though they were still living. More than one anthropologist or census taker has been misled unintentionally by replies to questions as to the number of children in the family. Unless specifically instructed not to, most Yungaínos would include both the dead and the living in their families. After the disaster, some survivors counted as among the lost those who had been interred in the lower rows of niches in the cemetery which were buried by the landslide. Since the disaster, the relationship with the dead in Yungay has taken on immense importance. Those relatives who died before or during the disaster constituted one extreme in a line of continuity which most residents of Yungay Norte were determined to maintain unbroken.

One of the basic tasks, perhaps the most basic of all, that the survivor of a major cataclysm must face is the formulation of meaning for the event and its integration into some context consistent with the values and beliefs of his culture (Lifton 1967:367; Bode 1977). Among the Yungay survivors a variety of explanations for the event were current. Lower-class rural and urban survivors attributed the disaster to a punishment from God, but none were able to specify why this punishment had been visited upon Yungay. "Yungay was always a very faithful town. People gave money, went without things, so that the church and the saints were always cared for well. Yungay was a good town."

Some chose a more mechanistic explanation of the events of the disaster. Rosa Martínez felt that there had been too many foreigners (mountain climbers) up on Huascarán, "messing around," shaking up the glacier so that it was unstable. Another explanation was that a large magnet inside Huascarán attracted the "atoms let loose" by the recent French A-bomb tests in the Pacific. Apparently these "atoms" made the glacier unstable and therefore caused the disaster. Middle- and upper-class survivors saw the disaster as "an accident of nature." Some of the urban survivors blamed the authorities for not informing the community of the danger. Several years before, in the period following the Ranrahirca landslide of 1962, several teams of geologists were supposed to have completed studies of the glaciers of Huascarán. The main conclusion allegedly reached by these scientists was that the glaciers were seriously cracked and fissured and constituted a grave danger to the communities immediately below them in the valley. Some urban survivors accused department and provincial officials of hiding these conclusions from the general populace for a variety of political and economic reasons. Thus, while the earthquake and avalanche were considered accidents of nature, the death of Yungay was blamed by some people on irresponsible officials.

Notwithstanding the various explanations for the disaster by survivors, they have difficulty in finding any meaning in and for the event. Those who have been able to chalk it off simply as an accident of nature, a cruel twist of fate, have been able to avoid, at least publicly, the agonizing question of why such suffering was visited upon them. One woman, who lost a young child in the avalanche, put it in these terms: "How nice life was before the disaster. My husband had his vegetable farm and all he had to do was oversee his twelve or fifteen workers. I had a cook of my own and life was good. Now it's work, work, work every day. Dawn to past dark. [They run one of Yungay's roadside restaurants.] I never stop working. Well, I guess whatever you get in life, you have to pay for sometime and we are paying for our past happiness. Nothing good comes without a price."

For most survivors, however, the questions continue to prey upon their minds to this day. "'Why?' is the question we keep asking ourselves, over and over. And there is no answer. What had we done to deserve such punishment? We were a good town, a beautiful town. Yungay was full of good people. Why?"

Many people emerged from their experience with their faith in a divine being seriously shaken or destroyed. Rodolfo Armendariz talking with me one evening in Rosita's said that he, El Pillo, Shamu, Miguel, all of the Chupamaros, no longer believe in God. "God doesn't exist. How could God exist when He let the disaster happen? If there were a God, He wouldn't have let it happen or at least He would have warned us. No, it is very difficult to get a Yungaíno to believe in 'the God question' now."

Rosa, overhearing the conversation, came and sat down with us. "When I woke up in the hospital, there were some people praying by my bed. They asked me to pray also and I said, 'What for? If there were a God, he would not have taken away my sons.'" Rosa said that she now believes in God, but she doesn't believe in the saints anymore. "All those prayers and all those candles and all those fine images and my sons were still killed."

Pablo Mendoza, who lived in Aura before the disaster, told us that he became violently antireligious after the disaster. His wife had a large collection of saints' images, and he took them all out and threw them into the cornfield behind his ruined home. As he was doing this, his wife begged him to save her statue of the Virgin Mary. Brushing her aside, he grabbed the statue and yelled, *"Otra puta de mierda"* (another shitty whore) and hurled it into the field.

If the Yungaínos could derive little meaning from either science or religion for their tragedy, they did formulate and restore meaning to their battered existence in the aftermath. Meaning can be imposed on such suffering only if some acceptable purpose is served by the ordeal. There was little meaning to be found in Yungay's destruction, but there were modes of creating a sense of significance for the misery and instability of the aftermath.

A characteristic pattern among survivors is the need to speak of their ordeal to others and make their suffering known to the world. This is not merely the indulgence of self-pity, but rather the need to restore meaning to an existence whose bases have been destroyed. Yungaínos spoke freely to everyone, even when it caused them great distress. They wanted their story to be known. They exhorted me to tell the whole story of Yungay's tragedy to the world. This need to bear witness is part of the formulation process. By making their experience known and significant to others, they regain a sense of their own eroded significance. Part of the way to restore meaning is to become meaningful to others. The process of bearing witness involves being recognized again as significant by others, which helps to restore the survivor's assaulted personal and social identity. By speaking to others of their suffering and their struggle to survive as a community, the Yungaínos were imposing a meaning for themselves and for others on their bitter experience. Their misery in the aftermath acquired a purpose, and they could affirm themselves in making it known to the world.

The continued existence of the tradition and community of Yungay was the only thing they could affirm, in which they could invest meaning and from which they could derive a larger sense of purpose from life. When the plan to relocate the provincial capital to Tingua was unveiled, it unleashed a conflict with CRYRZA that was to have important psychological consequences as well as practical impact. With the announcement of relocation intentions, loss and grief were transformed into conflicts of interest between Yungaínos and the CRYRZA. The Yungaínos were determined to resist both the forces of nature and the efforts of society to destroy their community. As the lines of battle were drawn, the opposing interests became institutionalized in groups and strategies, which ultimately became the expression of reconstituted identities and relationships. The conflict between Yungay and CRYRZA over the relocation issue created a politics of identity formation for the beleaguered survivors.

In proposing relocation, CRYRZA became a new adversary, another disaster in the perception of the community. In effect, the crisis of the disaster had been extended into the rehabilitation period by the new threat to the integrity of the community. The threat of relocation by CRYRZA stimulated the formulation of unity, purpose, cooperation, and meaning among the survivors. In the struggle to resist relocation the Yungaínos were forging a continuity for their community and molding new meaningful identities and purposes for themselves. The living and the dead of Yungay were linked in the new purpose of resisting relocation. Betrayal of the relocation of the provincial capital in Yungay was tantamount to betraying one's dead family. On numerous occasions, survivors echoed the determination of Rosa Martínez's fidelity to the dead and Yungay when she said, "I would rather die than leave here. My life is worth nothing to me. What would it matter if another avalanche came and carried me off? We are not going to abandon our dead. I will die here close to my sons in the avalanche."

Chapter 8

Relocation, Resistance, and Ritual

Within a few months of the disaster, the possibility that the Yungaínos would indeed be forced to abandon their dead became very real with the disclosure of government plans to relocate the camp to the Tingua site. The camp in Pashulpampa solved the immediate problem of where to put the survivors temporarily, but the survivors quickly began to think of Pashulpampa, soon to be called Yungay, as a permanent location. However, after studies were undertaken to determine areas safe from future landslides, CRYRZA decided late in 1970 that Yungay, Mancos, and Ranrahirca would be moved to Tingua for greater safety from future avalanches. CRYRZA based the decision on the fact that although Yungay's location offered avalanche protection from both Huandoy and Huascarán in the form of 4,000-meter Atma Hill, the triangular safe area between the two peaks' alluvial fans was relatively small. CRYRZA officials speculated that if the provincial capital were relocated in Yungay, normal population growth would spill over into dangerous areas (Oliver-Smith 1982).

At the same time, traditional rivalries began to generate an internal threat to Yungay's continued existence as the provincial capital. Disasters often provide opportunities for preexisting conflicts to surface in the aftermath as forces for change. In predisaster times, an intense rivalry had existed between Yungay and Mancos. Although relations were friendly between the two cities, a local Yungay saying for something akin to "when hell freezes over" was "when Mancos becomes a province."

Initially, the disaster seemed to alter this relationship. The day after the avalanche, the province's only city was Mancos, which, although severely damaged and with many dead and wounded, was still essentially an intact urban settlement. As the new year began, the Mancos leaders started campaigning in the other districts for support to relocate the provincial capital in Tingua, located in Mancos district. They argued that Yungay was too far from the center of the province, too distant from the other districts. Yungay had always been the northernmost district, and the Yungay relocation site was almost a kilometer farther north. The additional distance, although only some 800 meters, provided the straw that broke the camel's back.

In the meantime the Yungaínos had become totally occupied with their struggle with the external threat of the CRYRZA to relocate their capital to Tingua. So absorbed were they with this external threat that they had done no politicking for support in the rest of the province. It was not until the other districts pledged their support for the Tingua relocation that the Yungaínos became aware of the new, internal threat to their existence. When they discovered "this treachery," they counteracted it by denouncing all the district mayors as communists and *apristas.* The departmental authorities fired the mayors immediately and reinstated them almost as quickly when they understood the nature of the dispute between the two interprovincial factions. With the "coup d'état of mayors," the battle for structural supremacy in the province had been joined. Although the Yungaínos saw the primary front in this battle in Lima, the city leaders began some conciliatory efforts toward the other districts. They invited district mayors to province-wide meetings with CRYRZA officials, listening to their opinions, taking interest in their proposals for reconstruction projects, and entertaining a generally more cordial attitude toward their "coprovincianos." While this attitude decreased the level of tension in the province, it changed few minds.

The Yungaínos considered the proponents of Tingua to be traitors. The Tingua faction of survivors was led by Andres Sarmiento, whom the Yungaínos viewed as a "Judas." Traditionally in old Yungay during Carnaval week several scarecrow-style Judas figures were made to look like the most disliked person in town, and after being paraded through the streets, were burned. During the 1971 Carnaval week, the Yungaínos produced a Judas figure with the face of Andres Sarmiento. Pinned to his shirtfront was a sign saying, "Alas, my destiny, I left my beautiful Tingua. Let them give me shelter and food here or I will hang myself." After parading the figure through the streets where it was insulted and mistreated by everyone, he was duly hanged. The next day, after donations from everyone for kerosene and beer, the Yungaínos gleefully incinerated the Judas figure of Tingua's leading citizen on the main street of Yungay.

The Yungaínos' dogged resistance to the threats to their community was deeply rooted in the necessities of the grief and mourning processes, traditional pride in community, and a practical, rational understanding of the basic requirements for urban growth. Rosa Martínez's defiant statement "I will not abandon my dead" was eloquent evidence of the emotional commitment. However, in addition to the strong emotional ties which held them to the location closest to the site of the old city, Yungaíno leaders compiled an impressive list of practical reasons to oppose the move to Tingua, illustrating a sophisticated appreciation of the importance of sociological and economic factors in the life of their community. The leaders, as well as many members of the community, reasoned that Yungay would thrive because it was centrally located in the network of peasant villages of the district. These peasant villages were the life-force of a town because they provided food for the urban population as well as a market for the commercial life of the town. As Epifano Bellido put it, "All the forty-three villages unite here. They bring the food. They all live from what they take out of the market. They bring their provisions and take away their necessities."

The Yungaínos maintained that even if the capital were relocated in Tingua, Yungay would also have to be populated for commercial reasons or the province would lose large amounts of capital to Caraz, which was closer than Tingua. The Caraz market, it was reasoned, would draw all Yungay's farm products while Tingua, with its smaller peasant population, and the province in general would decline for lack of agricultural and commercial activity. It was also claimed that the "people of the interior" would cease to trade with the rest of the province if the capital were removed to Tingua. "In other words, a political center is nothing, if it is not a commercial center," as Epicho Bellido declared.

The peasantry on the whole was considered by the urban survivors to be "human capital." The city would depend on their labor for reconstruction and maintenance. Bellido explained, "All the peasantry has always done public works for the town because the government has never done anything. And they have said that if the capital goes to Tingua, they will not do anything for Tingua. The authorities may go to Tingua, but they will remain here and will make a town here. They won't move."

205

My conversations with and surveys of peasants from Huambo barrio substantiated this claim. On the whole, peasants said they would contribute their labor to Yungay, but they would not make the journey to Tingua. They also said that the trip to Tingua would be uneconomical for them for marketing. The amount of merchandise marketed by many Indian peasants does not always exceed in value the fare they would have to pay to get to Tingua.

Yungaínos also claimed that tourism would continue to be one of Yungay's chief industries. Yungay was now world famous since the disaster, and people would come to see the site of the landslide and the famous surviving palm trees that had appeared in all the newspapers and magazines of the world. Nobody would go to Tingua because, according to Bellido, it did not have "Huascarán, the beautiful countryside, the glacial lakes, and the avalanche; the cemetery there is incomparable to anything in the callejón. Who won't go to where a whole town has disappeared? In other words, in losing, in the long run, Yungay may win because it will become even more of a tourist attraction—but it has to be done pretty."

Finally, the Yungaínos claimed that the Yungay Norte location offered more land than Tingua, which was highly debatable. Tingua offered greater safety, although this was often denied by Yungaínos. A fact conspicuous in its absence in the debate, particularly when middle- and upper-class survivors argued for Yungay, was that certain individual economic interests in the form of landholdings in the Yungay area were held by urban survivors. Proponents of the Tingua location would often criticize those in favor of Yungay for having only economic interests at heart.

Epifanio Bellido and other Yungaíno leaders were speaking from a profound understanding of their society when they emphasized the importance of the 11,000 peasants of the province to their struggle. In their view, without the peasant labor force, the peasant agricultural produce, and the market they represented for goods and services, a traditional provincial capital was clearly impossible. These peasants represented a life-force for any urban center, regardless of their lack of formal political power. The new capital of Yungay would have to be located within the village network of the bulk of the peasant population.

Cities are the "centers" of regions and share dependent relations with their regions. In Yungay, agriculture and markets, the two basic elements of production and distribution, were basic to this mutual dependency. As in many transitional societies, poor or nonexistent roads made transportation both time- and energy-consuming. Consequently, the old city was located near fertile land with a high population for easy access to productive farming. A large population practicing labor-intensive agriculture found it convenient for marketing and other purposes to be close to the city (Trigger 1972:580).

However, peasant support for Yungay was not unanimous nor entirely unconditional. When the avalanche careened down the canyon, it obliterated nine peasant villages and created a sinister barrier between six others and their new district capital in the Yungay camp. The petty mayor of Mitma barrio was killed as were many of his staff bearers and other assistants. The traditional dual village system, then, was reduced almost by half. Nine communities of Mitma no longer existed, and those that remained were now separated from Yungay by two immense landslides.

When the Yungay authorities attempted to appoint a replacement for the dead petty mayor, all the potential candidates refused on the grounds that they did not want the responsibility for only half a year. By late December of 1971 still no willing candidate could be found to fill the post. This refusal by the remaining Mitma communities to reintegrate themselves into the traditional dual authority system of Yungay's peasantry was an alarming departure from traditional peasant obedience to urban authority. While the more populous, traditional Huambo barrio rallied to the support of the city quickly, the more cholo barrio of Mitma, with greater connections to the outside system, was less willing to commit its support to the city.

The people of Mitma barrio used the disaster as a means of passively resisting the imposition of authority from Yungay. By refusing to have a petty mayor appointed by Yungay, Mitma barrio effectively limited its forced participation in the unpaid labor contributions to the city. Mitma communities then began to elect their own authorities and send their names in to Yungay for ratification only. Some Mitma communities even severed their economic relations with Yungay, preferring to market in Mancos. There seemed to be some reluctance as well in crossing the two landslides which separated some Mitma communities from the camp.

In addition, the surviving population of Mitma refused to participate in the fiestas of Santa Rosa and Santo Domingo. Since everyone had refused the responsibility of the Indian mayor's post, the entire barrio had, in effect, refused to make the financial and labor contributions normally required of them for the success of the fiesta system, which was the major ritual expression of Indian allegiance to the city. The people of Mitma said that the disaster had given them more important things to spend their money on. At heart they said they had always considered their participation in the fiesta system to be a financial burden not worth the money, time, and effort spent.

Enforcement of the traditional authority system was based largely on continuing personal relationships of prestige and power. When the system was disrupted by disaster, the time it took to reestablish all the links in the chain of communications allowed for the possibility of change. By the time attempts were made to restructure the lines of power and communication, dissidents in Mitma had already exploited the temporary power vacuum and disruption to rid themselves of a system to which they had little commitment and from which they derived few advantages. Dissatisfaction had existed within the system, and it is evident that the disaster exacerbated the situation, precipitating real structural change in the traditional political organization of Yungay.

Thus, the fiestas of Santo Domingo and Santa Rosa in Yungay Norte were considerably changed, representing in essence a change in the support resources the Yungaínos could count on in their struggle against relocation. The Huambo contingent seemed to participate with considerable gusto, but in slightly reduced numbers. There was no traditional band rivalry, and the ceremonial gift giving diminished markedly. One difficulty certainly was that Yungay was still an encampment, at best a barracks city, with no traditional plaza de armas. The solemn mass procession of images and people around the beautiful plaza de armas in Yungay lent majesty and solemnity to the events. In Yungay camp the celebrants had to be content with marching from the road to the church around the market and back to the road again several times. The setting of Yungay camp with its dusty, crowded module dwellings did little to add to the dignity of the event.

As one peasant traditionalist put it,

The fiesta this year has changed much. It's not like it was before because of this matter of the earthquake. Those people that were interested in the staff [the symbol of traditional authority] are dead. The interest is not so strong for the hill people either. The people before, the older ones, believed more in the staff, the matter of the patron, Catholic action, but now the youth is changing . . . there has been a rupture with the past, and they do not wish to continue with these traditions. They have become more egotistical, more "decent" and say that the question of the staffs is for the Indians and they are no longer Indians. They say that they are people of the town although they live in the country.

Thus, although Yungay lost the support of some of its peasantry from Mitma barrio after the disaster, the city could count on the more populous Huambo barrio with a changed but somewhat enhanced identification with the community. Armed with that support and their convictions, the Yungaínos were determined to convince CRYRZA and the government that Yungay was the only logical place for the new capital. However, when the avalanche buried Yungay, it buried the majority of the province's leadership. Most of the ruling-class members who were not killed soon left the province for less arduous surroundings, leaving only a very small and disorganized group of people with the experience and capability to lead the fight against the relocation threat.

As the formal political institutions and community organizations reorganized in the camp, the positions and roles of political importance began to cluster around this relatively reduced number of people. Indeed, it took very little time for a political elite to develop and begin to direct the activities of the community. Basically a core of thirty-one people directed the majority of Yungay's political and community organizations. These people, almost without exception, were of urban origin, more than half with some higher education, of middle- and upper-class background and, for the most part, male. In addition to those who occupied formal positions, there were also a number of individuals who were politically influential but held no offices. These people had social and economic power in old Yungay and were able to exert political influence in the camp; they became important informal leaders of the resistance. Their opinions were listened to with great respect, and they were active participants in town meetings.

The town meeting, or *cabildo abierto,* is an institution with a long tradition in Hispanic history, and it was used with great frequency in Yungay. It was essentially an open meeting of the populace with its leaders, usually in Yungay, for the expression of public opinion or support for a decision taken. On occasion the meeting was formally called by the leaders of the town, but in the continually unstable atmosphere of the relocation threat, meetings were often quickly organized and announced over the new public address system when the situation demanded swift action. When town meetings were called, a general cross-section of the population would appear, but it was always implicitly understood that participation in discussion was the realm of the "nobles" and other urban survivors. There seemed to be a tacit understanding that people who were not "nobles," people of rural origin in general and people of minimal education, were present only as spectators or ratifiers by acclaim of decisions made by the political elites. The cholo entrepreneurs, the most economically powerful class emerging in Yungay, were usually politically silent.

As in many countries, politics in Peru on any scale are often dealt with in highly personal terms. Personal influence is often considered to be the better tactic for achieving goals than formal institutions. Since the relatively flexible military dictatorship had eliminated formal channels anyway, Yungaíno leaders employed the politics of personal relationships and influence.

Members of the commissions sent to represent Yungay's cause in Lima were chosen very carefully for their personal resources as well as political skills. Emilio Robles, president of the Civic Committee, the liaison group to CRYRZA, and perhaps the town's most articulate speaker, was invariably a member of these commissions. Padre Diaz was chosen as a member as much for his stand against relocation as for the fact that he had once been a professor of ethics to the president of Peru. A local teacher, who moonlighted as a provincial stringer for a Lima tabloid, was chosen for his connections to the media. Epicho Bellido, part owner of the Expreso Serrano, added energy, capital, and free transportation to Lima. In general, people of wealth with important social and political contacts in Lima were also chosen for the commissions.

These commissions, armed with their letters of appeal, made the rounds of ministries and presidential offices, seeking the personal contacts necessary to affect decisions which would otherwise be made impersonally. Important or official friends and relatives were enlisted in the cause. The regional clubs and associations, which tied province, district, and community to the national capital and its largesse, were called on to exert their influence. In short, since the decision to relocate Yungay had been made outside of and without consultation with the community, it was clear that outside allies and support had to buttress the internal efforts to resist relocation. And they succeeded in generating considerable support for their cause among the regional associations and clubs, as well as among influential people of Yungaíno origin. These contacts later proved to be very important in the foundation and growth of the new Yungay.

Yungay's leadership also marshaled both urban and rural popular support for the resistance. In the community's frantic early months, the hundreds and soon thousands of bewildered but hopeful rural refugees would have followed the promise of assistance almost anywhere. But as the modules were constructed and a new year began in Yungay, the migrants began to sense some allegiance to the site. While proximity to the avalanche was less important to them, the Yungay site was many kilometers closer to the communities they had left in which many still had family and resources. Some migrants lived in Yungay module homes and walked to their fields in the countryside every day. Ultimately, as the relocation battle intensified, the urban poor lent their support to Yungay's cause.

In October of 1970, when the CRYRZA announced its initial relocation decision, a town meeting in Yungay was called, and the urban populace began to voice its opposition. Signs were erected and buildings were painted with "Yungay Stays Here!" in large white letters. Largely encouraged by the urban survivors, the town meeting quickly took on a threatening, disruptive tone, and the subprefect called in troops to dissolve the crowds. From that point on, an atmosphere of tension, hostility toward the CRYRZA, and determination to resist reigned in the community.

Although a number of small public meetings on resistance strategy were held in the ensuing months, a *cabildo abierto* for the whole town was not held until the middle of February in 1971. The meeting was ostensibly held to ask the populace their feelings about relocation. In effect, their feelings were well known, but a public manifestation of that will was considered necessary by the leadership. When the meeting began, several hundred people of all classes and ethnic groups had jammed into the narrow module church building. The "nobles" were all seated in front, while the rest of the populace stood, filling the back of

211

the church. Shouts of "Yungay stays here!" reflected the spirit of the group, as the meeting was brought to order.

The first of four points to be discussed was the relocation issue. One of the ex-provisional mayors, a teacher-merchant, stood to speak:

Yungay is like a sick person who has fallen from his bed. To become well again, he must return to his bed, to his roots to heal himself psychologically with all his moral values intact. History will judge us harshly if Yungay is not reconstructed in its homeland (bed), and if we allow this to happen, we will not be Yungaínos, but Ranrahirquinos or Mancosinos or Tinguinos, not Yungaínos. We must defend our afflicted mother [*madre dolorida*]. We are the true sons of Yungay and one does not abandon an afflicted mother. We must defend our land!

There were shouts of "Viva!" and enthusiastic applause as he finished. Next came the president of the women's committee who asked, in the name of all Yungaíno women, that the city be located there. A student, a boy in his early teens, stood next and said that he spoke for Yungaíno youth. Modest and self-effacing, but obviously warming to his rhetorical task, he proclaimed, "Judge me, a youth, from the perspective of your age, but hear what I have to say. The bad Yungaínos who have abandoned this place will come back like prodigal sons. Yungay will stay here!"

The mayor then rose to speak, and quiet fell on the crowd. In a low voice, he said that he simply wanted to know the will of the people on the relocation question. In response, Epifanio Bellido responded that to know the will of the people, both Spanish and Quechua should be spoken in the meeting because people were there from the villages. "We should not forget our villages. After the tragedy, many Yungaínos left as quickly as they could, but they came down from the villages to bury our dead. Now we should embrace them. We owe it to them that Yungay remains here. Yungay is their livelihood."

The mayor repeated his request to know the will of the people. The crowd roared back, "Yungay Stays Here!" People applauded wildly, stamping on the dirt floor of the church and pounding the walls. "And what will the name be? We have to decide on a name." This was answered by loud boos and "No's." At this point El Pillo said, "When a man dies, they don't just put his name up on a headstone and let it die. His name lives on. The name Yungay has not died. It lives. It lives!" More loud cheers.

With a small smile, the mayor relented and said, "The encampment Yungay Norte is now officially to be called Yungay. Agreed?"

Amidst even louder and more sustained cheers and applause, Bellido again stood and declared, "Now that this is truly decided by the people, we should all work together, united!"

At this point Emilio Robles suggested that a commission go to Lima to the Palace of Government and to the CRYRZA with a signed memorial to say that the people are unanimous in their decision to stay in Yungay. As the people crowded forward to affix their signatures or marks to the sheets of paper at the secretary's desk, the meeting dissolved in more boisterous applause and cheers, the other items on the agenda totally forgotten.

While the leaders of Yungay were marshaling support from the urban and the greater part of the rural populations for the resistance to relocation, the community's organizational life was rapidly taking shape, and specific institutions, rituals, and symbols coalesced generally. The important effect of the renewal of these organizations and activities was a sense of continuity, of consistency, and a resistance to the further alteration of the environment and society. Life had been changed so much for the worst by the disaster; the spirit that moved the camp now was to improve the present to resemble the past.

The fiesta cycle and the saints' images became a focus of this basic controversy of tradition over change. The traditional pattern of the religious fiesta cycle observances called for the celebration of a mass in the community celebrating its patron saint's day and for much ritual feasting and drinking. In Yungay on Santa Rosa's Day and Santo Domingo's Day, the Indians of the two barrios began the fiestas with ritual obligations to the town and church, followed by solemn processions of the saints' images embellished by bands and fireworks, and ended with ritual gifts, feasting, drinking, and dancing in houses on the outskirts of the town. The fireworks, bands, feasting, drinking, and dancing on these occasions are ritual prerequisites. Extreme inebriation during the celebrations was part of the ritual and was tolerated. However, in 1971 the Bishop of Huaráz issued a decree condemning all activities associated with religious festivals which were not of a specifically religious nature. The parish priest began to take steps to eliminate the "profane" aspects of religious celebrations in the district. He admonished his flock against drinking, dancing, and music during the fiesta. The people, Indian and

213

townsman alike, were dumbstruck. "No bands? How could he think such a thing? A procession without bands and rockets will lack solemnity. A fiesta without dancing and music is not a fiesta. These are our customs. Who can deny us our customs?"

Townspeople were in basic agreement with the Indians. Townspeople valued the fiesta for two reasons. The celebration of an Indian fiesta in town brought thousands of people into the city for the day, which meant many customers for the stores and market. The fiesta cycle was also symbolically important to the townpeople for the city's relationship with the peasantry. The celebration of the fiesta cycle was symbolic of Indian allegiance to Yungay and an expression of district integration. To both Indian and townsmen, then, the fiesta cycle conveyed a variety of important meanings. It had already suffered considerable alterations through the nonattendance of the dissident remains of Mitma barrio, and both sectors were determined to resist any further changes. The processions of 1971 were deprived of many of their profane aspects, much to the dismay of everyone, and with much bitterness toward the priest. By the end of 1971 he was replaced by a priest from the region who "understood" local customs and permitted their expression.

The central focus of each fiesta is the image of a saint. Repair and replacement of damaged chapels and saints' images in the aftermath was considered very important. Almost 90 percent of Yungay's communities listed chapel reconstruction as one of their three most important projects. This was certainly true in Yungay, although images of Santo Domingo and Santa Rosa had to be borrowed for the 1970 fiestas since they followed so closely in August after the destruction of the city. The fiestas of 1970 were devoted to requiem masses and solemn processions with none of the secular activities included. By fiesta time in 1971, however, new images and vestments had been purchased, and, despite the priest's prohibition, brass bands accompanied the images in the processions through the camp. Most of the secular activities of the fiesta, including dancing, feasting, and drinking, were carried on as well.

Although church attendance by townspeople was not greatly stimulated by the disaster, the church itself continued to be an important community symbol. Despite their differences with the parish priest over the fiesta issue, his refusal to consider another site for his church won him grudging admiration. The priest often declared that regardless of where they relocated the capital, he would build his new church in

Yungay because most of the people were there, meaning, specifically, the Indians, the most faithful parishioners. While some urban Yungaínos may not be among the most devout parishioners, they did recognize that the church was a central institution of their community, particularly for its relationship with the peasantry. Its location and the support of the priest for resistance to relocation were considered crucial.

The church as an institution has also provided a focus for the reorganization of community organizations in the barracks city. Two of the nine church-affiliated organizations of old Yungay regrouped in the aftermath but discarded religious functions for the secular community goals of aid acquisition and distribution to orphans, widows, and the poor. Both organizations, in acquiring different functions, have changed their role in society. Before the disaster, both groups were involved in activities that were important only in the limited context of the local ceremonial and local prestige systems. Now, both organizations were directly involved in matters vital to the physical survival of the majority of the population. While still affiliated with the church by their religious identities, both groups focused on a problem very close to the issue of Yungay survival.

Secular organizations began regrouping around issues related to the survival of the community very quickly after the disaster. When a threat to reorganize the beloved high school, Santa Ines de Yungay, in Mancos appeared, the survivors of the urban area and rural migrants immediately pitched in to turn back the threat. From these efforts to resist the loss of its high school came the impetus to reorganize the Parents' Association. School equipment was almost nonexistent, and the teachers called upon the parents to contribute for materials and furniture. Ultimately, equipping the camp's schools became the responsibility of the community and the Parents' Association. Items such as desks, chairs, blackboards, chalk, and other teaching supplies were not being supplied by the Ministry of Education. As Yungay began its second year, its children were still sitting on rocks and writing on their knees in the alternately sweltering or freezing corrugated tin structures erected by the CRYRZA. The P.A. organized scavenging expeditions to a surviving Ministry of Education warehouse in the departmental capital of Huaráz and returned triumphant with a truckload of second-hand desks for the primary schools and high school. The P.A. also organized effective fund-raising activities such as kermesses for specific school needs.

The P.A. coalesced around the need of Yungay for private assistance for its national educational institutions. Education had always played an extremely important role in Yungaíno life and was still considered one of the pillars of the city's central position in provincial life. One of the important real and symbolic attributes of Yungay identity was to be a "Santa Inesino," and loyalty to the community entailed loyalty to its school. This concept quickly reappeared as an important value among the refugees, and the Parents' Association became the principal voice for its expression.

Another, more general stimulus of organizational activity on behalf of the Yungay's survival came from regional social clubs and centers in Lima, which act to maintain the ties migrants to the city have with their homeland, as well as helping them to adjust to urban life (Doughty 1970:30). The Association for the Rehabilitation and Reconstruction of the Province of Yungay (ARRPY) was formed from a schism in the Centro Union Yungay (CUY), which favored the Tingua relocation site. Those members of CUY who disagreed split and formed ARRPY, which emphasized aid and rehabilitation for the Yungay camp. ARRPY took charge of coordinating the political campaign to keep the capital in Yungay, to distribute aid from private sources, and to coordinate activities such as the annual commemoration of the anniversary of the disaster.

Unlike the conflict-ridden regional clubs, Yungay's highly competitive sports clubs rallied the interest and participation of the population for their activities. Around January of 1971, the five original clubs began to reform the soccer league to play soccer in the Peru Cup games.

Despite their traditional intense rivalries, the clubs worked together to reorganize the soccer league and to form an "all-star" team of Yungay's best players for the valley sectional tournament. Yungaínos were proud that their league became even larger than before the disaster while neighboring Carhuaz and Caraz had not even reorganized their leagues. The clubs campaigned for funds to buy uniforms and equipment, and the league charged admission to games to pay for renting playing fields. The healthy existence of the soccer league was a symbol to many that Yungay was determined not only to survive, but to prosper.

Indeed, the community as a whole was knit together, despite their feuding and factionalism, by a dense web of symbolic and ritual enactments which expressed the underlying commitment to the tradition of Yungay. The constant flow between consensus and conflict in Yungay community life reflects what Victor Turner has called "a type of dialectical social process that involves successive experience of ... homogeneity and differentiation, equality and inequality" (1961:97). Following Durkheim, Turner posits that social life entails a continual if not consistent alternation between two contrasting forms of human interaction. Society may be seen and human relationships may be structured as a network of specific and concrete statuses and roles, networks of differentiated political, legal, and economic positions assigning value to individuals. This form of human interaction is contrasted with the vision of society as an unstructured community of equal individuals bound together, not by an organized system of status and role obligations and rights, but rather by a communion "between concrete, historical, and idiosyncratic individuals" confronting one another as human beings with whom something is shared, forming a spontaneous consciousness of "we." This model of society or social interaction is known as "communitas," usually emerging in a period, or a time (and place) separated from normal modes of structured social action. Such separate or "liminal" periods constitute an important stage in the universal rituals of passage or transition, in which individuals are separated from an earlier status or condition, enter into a marginal or ambiguous (liminal) state stripped of their normal structural characteristics, and ultimately pass on to another status or condition, whereupon they rejoin society with new or altered identities. During the liminal period in which the initiates lack both their previous status or condition and those they will ultimately assume, their social interaction with fellow initiates is a structureless, shared consciousness of common identity, without rank, property or insignia—in short, a condition of communitas. Such liminal periods are most often evoked in rituals and expressed by symbols. While these concepts of liminality and communitas refer primarily to rituals activated by human beings in specific contexts and for specific purposes, they can also help us to understand and explain behavior in conditions forced upon people by circumstance. Indeed, the way human beings structure their experience of crisis events often makes us wonder whether this cognitive structuring imitates ritual, or if ritual emerged from the tendency of humans to structure crisis events in this fashion. The similarity between the cognitive structuring of crises and rituals is striking. In the immediate postimpact stage, crises and catastrophes, such as natural disasters, seem to evoke a kind of liminal state, in which victims have been violently

217

separated from their previous social, economic, and political identities and cast into a common, relatively unstructured consciousness, involving a general reduction of status or at least a decreased recognition of rank and property. This common consciousness, perhaps "a community of suffering," arises spontaneously from the "transformative experience" (the disaster), which goes "to the root of each person's being and finds in that root something (misery, pain, confusion, being a victim) profoundly communal and shared" (Turner 1961:138). The liminal period and its spirit of communitas persist for varying amounts of time but ultimately will succumb to the need to mobilize resources and organize people for structured goals such as aid and assistance to victims.

In Yungay almost all the survivors record that the predominant characteristic of the immediate aftermath was a spirit of commonality. "We are all brothers, all without anything [*sin nada*]" was the phrase most used to describe the spirit and condition of the beleaguered survivors that afternoon on the hills of Pashulpampa. They comforted the terrified children, nursed the wounded, sought food and blankets to feed and warm themselves, without regard for status or wealth. Resources were appropriated for the use of all with little attention to property rights. A spirit of communitas, or unstructured, egalitarian sharing, bonded people during those early days of misery and confusion. The avalanche had obliterated the context and bases of status and prejudice. In the aftermath, the community, confronting different challenges, through successive phases of communitas and structure has forged a new physical identity centered around the tradition of Yungay.

These alternating phases of structure and communitas in Yungay have shown, on the one hand, a strong reappearance of differentially valued status and a marked hierarchical social structure and, on the other, a varied system of symbols and rituals evoking the commonality of experience and tradition of all Yungaínos. While not erasing social differences, the sense of commonality temporarily diminishes social distance for the organization and mobilization of resources on behalf of community. While some are more drawn into the symbolic and ritual expression of communitas than others, few Yungaínos, old or new, do not share these symbol systems or partake in the ritual enactments of Yungay communitas.

Of course, many symbols cluster around the theme of survival. The four palm trees, grey with the dust of the windswept avalanche, are the only surviving remnants of Yungay's once proud and beautiful plaza de armas. They are now weather-beaten, their trunks angled and still spattered with the crusted mud of the avalanche. The palms are evoked often as symbolic of the survivors of Yungay, and the palm generically has become an important symbol, not only of survival but of regeneration as well. On May 31, 1971, the first anniversary of the disaster, the major ritual of resistance to relocation was planting of the first palm tree for the new plaza de armas of Yungay, just up the hill from the last module row. When Emilio Robles and other survivors, surrounded by the people of Yungay and their visitors, broke the ground with a shovel and planted a tiny palm, barely eighteen inches high, just visible even above the trampled yellowed grass of the hillside field, they were making a statement with the most eloquent symbol available to Yungaínos that the new city would be "reborn." They had made their intentions clear that nothing in the ugly module city would be part of new Yungay. New Yungay would be built higher up on Atma Hill, safe from future avalanches, secure from relocation, close to its tragically lost dead and truly embedded in the environment which had given it the sobriquet "Yungay Hermosura." The little palm tree was both a symbol of their determination to rebuild and the first step in that direction.

The cemetery, crowned with the statue of Christ, arms outstretched and gazing out over the avalanche toward Huascarán, is an extraordinarily potent and important symbol for Yungaínos. It is truly a major symbolic and physical link with their past, with the dead not only of the avalanche but of old Yungay, a symbolic bridge between the old and the new.

Rosa Martínez, a tragic figure among tragic figures, also became for a time a living symbol of survival. Although born in the eastern province of Chacas, Rosa often referred to herself as having been "born in the avalanche." No one can or ever will dispute that. Despite her illiteracy, Rosa's preeminence as the first survivor catapulted her to a position of political prominence in a number of women's organizations almost immediately upon her return to Yungay. Indeed, among the entire leadership core of Yungay, Rosa was the only nonmiddle- or upper-class person and the only illiterate. Her symbolic importance to the cause of relocation, as well as her native intelligence and forceful personality, made her indispensable to community affairs. In the first year she also became an important ritual and symbolic presence, much like the palm trees on the avalanche and the cemetery. People returning to Yungay after many

219

months' absence or Yungaínos who had resided in other cities at the time of the avalanche, many she had barely known or not known at all, stopped in at the Restaurante Rosita to greet her, to exchange an embrace and an expression of sympathy and best wishes for her continued recuperation.

The barracks city itself, soon after its construction, displayed a variety of symbolic expressions of survival and perdurance. The first Yungay place symbol was the poster-paint depiction of Huascarán on the adobe altar of the makeshift church. It was not long before small businesses and artisan workshops were opened in the barracks city with names like the Bazar Huascarán, La Suiza Peruana, Restaurante New Yungay, and La Merced (a Yungay neighborhood) juice bar. One of the few Yungay-owned vehicles, a well-worn truck, previously called the Little Virgin of Chapi, was proudly renamed the Survivor of Yungay by its owner. The multiple references to Huascarán, La Suiza Peruana, the use of old Yungay's street names for the narrow alleys between barracks buildings all constituted a symbolic expression of an unwillingness to let the tradition and identity of old Yungay die. Huascarán in particular was a most frequently used symbol for stores, bars, or restaurants. Although Huascarán was feared and cursed as an "assassin" and a "vile traitor," Yungay without it was clearly unthinkable. Just as the Yungaínos would not be separated from their dead, neither would they distance themselves from Huascarán, as threatening as its presence might be. It was clearly inseparable on a symbolic level from the image and identity which the Yungaíno survivors had of their old city and their city to be.

Although Huascarán was conceded to be a potential danger, Yungaínos thought the rest of their environment a healthy place to live. The beauty of their environment was symbolic of the potential high quality of life, which for them was possible only in Yungay. Images of the brilliant sun, the clean air, the fertility of the earth, and the beautiful countryside were consistently evoked as symbols of Yungay life. The curmudgeonly priest, although often at odds with his flock, expressed the views of survivors:

Although I know all the Western Hemisphere, from California to Tierra del Fuego, there is no place in the world like the callejón, where the air is fresh and clean, washed by the rain. In Lima one suffers a horrible heat, or in June or July with the cold, your nose is always running. So if you are not sweating so much from the heat that you have to bathe every two hours so you don't stink, you have a cold from the chilly fog. No, there is no place like the callejón. That's why I have come back here. I will build my church for my faithful here, and I will die here.

So involved were many urban survivors in the resistance to relocation that often much of their day was spent working for that cause or in ritual expressions of the goal. Relocation of the capital in Yungay was the most frequent topic of conversation when survivors met, and people continually restated in intensely committed terms their allegiance to Yungay in these encounters. The *cabildos abiertos,* particularly those on questions pertaining to relocation and the future of Yungay, were often ritual expressions of profound sentiment for old Yungay and the obligation to be faithful to its tradition. Indeed, it was virtually obligatory to open or close an opinion, a suggestion, or a proposal for action with an expression of fidelity to "our martyred city," "our infirm mother," or "the cradle of our tradition." Public meetings were opened and closed with testaments of allegiance to Yungay, and private gatherings, particularly formal ones, were often punctuated with statements of fidelity to the lost city. Such expressions were important in the survivors' working through their grief, but they were also crucial in the equally therapeutic process of expression of communitas, bonding survivor and *damnificado* not only to concrete goals, but also for fleeting and fragile, but nonetheless crucial moments, in spiritual community.

This sense of spiritual union or communitas was often evoked by circumstances. The *huayco* of February 26, 1971, provided an instance in which the latent spirit of communitas emerged clearly and most usefully for the benefit of the entire society. The *huayco,* which had terrified us all, proved to have been very destructive. Early the following morning, on my way to breakfast at Rosita's, I ran into a large group of men about to head off in a truck. As the truck started up, Miguel Giraldo, who was in the group, called to me, and I caught up with it and hopped on. They explained that the bridge over the river had been destroyed, and they were going to cut logs to make a *waru* (foot bridge) across the river. We crossed the Yungay lobe of the avalanche in the brilliant morning sunshine and proceeded to Aura where, in a roadside field, a group of men were already at work, hacking away with axes at the bases of four large eucalyptus trees. Several cars full of Yungaínos pulled up behind our truck, and we all tumbled out and set to work. All the "nobles" were there among the forty to fifty people, and the air was full of excitement and commitment. Most of us, "nobles" included, took turns with the three axes, and we felled two forty-foot trees and two sixty-foot ones. The branches were trimmed and the tops cut off before we all struggled to lift the logs into the back of the huge Scania Vabis truck. The logs were very heavy; lifting them into the back of the truck took the strength of almost all the men there. After the logs were loaded, we all rode to the river in caravan, the truck leading.

There was nothing where the bridge should have been. Downstream about thirty meters there were some loose two-by-eight planks and some wire netting from the bridge's cement foundation which had been totally shattered. The water, mud, and rocks overflowed the banks of the river by about thirty meters on either side at the point of the bridge. (Later on, we discovered the twisted metal structure of the bridge more than two hundred yards downstream.) When we arrived, a small group of people had gathered on the opposite bank. Emilio Robles yelled at them to bring some rope to help pull the logs across. They went to fetch rope, and we unloaded the logs and carried them to the highest ridge of the riverbank. When the rope arrived, one end was tossed across the forty-foot span of the river and tied to the lightest and smallest of the logs, which, with much pushing from our side and hauling from the Mancos side, was passed over the river. The ends of the log were secured by embedding them in the sloping bank and piling rocks around them. Once the first log was secured, the same process was repeated with each of the logs, requiring ten or fifteen men on the Yungay side to maneuver the heavy ends and five or six on the Mancos side to deal with the lighter ends. When all the logs were across, they were secured by stones and tied together with lengths of wire from the netting of the shattered foundation. Two of the longer planks from the wrecked bridge were tied on and made a kind of walkway in between the two big logs, with the two smaller logs slightly higher on each side for steadying one's balance above the roaring river.

The noteworthy aspect of this project was that the people of Yungay, including the "nobles," got together that morning and decided that they were going to put a *waru* across the river. There was little organization in the effort. A few men fetched their axes, and everybody piled into Alfredo Torres's truck. Everyone worked, "noble" and poor alike, and there was a spirit in the air of doing something important, something necessary. People took themselves and their roles as well as the work very seriously, despite the fact that the atmosphere was cheerful. The sense was that Yungay was doing something for itself. They were serious men doing a serious job for the public good. The feeling of communitas, of everybody being Yungaínos, working together, each lugging and sweating over those heavy logs, permeated the atmosphere, lending a certain drama to the event. We must not deceive ourselves into interpreting the "nobles'" labor as anything more than symbolic, but the building of the *waru* was clearly one of those "innumerable instants of spontaneous communitas" arising at a moment of minor crisis, of relative isolation from the rest of the callejón. The separation caused by the *huayco* placed everybody in the same condition of isolation, stimulating a spirit of spontaneous communitas. The momentarily undifferentiated group of men were able to work together, in a sense, in a form of ritual homage to Yungay. They bridged the gap, ended the relative isolation, and returned the group to the alternative social organization of structural hierarchy. As with most forms of communitas, the event was short-lived but nonetheless vital for the creation and ultimate survival of the forming community.

People coalesce and disperse in terms of social solidarity because of the conditions and problems facing them, not for the sake of pure ideology. Structure and communitas describe the two poles of this process, but where a community and its members are found on the continuum is a function of what challenges it as a corporate body and them as individuals. The nature of their responses is a function of the interaction between a concrete, actual problem, a perception of the problem, and the resources available for dealing with the problem. In the case of Yungay's *waru* over the Ranrahirca River, we can point to an actual concrete problem, a concrete behavioral response, and the ideological expressions of that reality as perceived by individuals in the process of behaving. Structure and communitas accurately describe forms of human behavior; they do not explain them.

In addition to the spontaneous moments of communitas that occurred in Yungay, the community formulated a number of ritual events which were consecrated to the twin causes of commemorating the dead and the lost community and ensuring the survival and continuance of the new community. In contrast to the subdued quality of the essentially private observance of the day of the dead, the anniversary of the disaster, May 31, 1971, was characterized by an intensity of activity. Although serious in tone, it carried with it the excitement of a public event of political and social consequence as well as religious and mourning functions. The preparations for the commemorations of the tragedy's first anniversary began more than a month before the actual event. Initial preparations were often stymied by the climate of instability and indecision of the relocation question. At the first meeting of the planning committee, Davíd Obregón, a forceful older man who had been a provisional mayor, claimed that any discussion of the anniversary ceremonies was pointless because there still had been no official word on the relocation. He advocated sending groups to pressure the Lima authorities for official relocation of the city at the campsite, and if they did not acquiesce immediately, then he said "we should all go out on the avalanche and occupy the areas where we lived before the disaster!"

While subsequent meetings attended to anniversary projects, plans also included political strategies designed to present visiting dignitaries with the *fait accompli* of a "people's" relocation of the town to a site just up Atma Hill. Plans were made to celebrate the founding of a new Yungay regardless of the CRYRZA decision. A commission was appointed to find the best place for new Yungay's plaza de armas. Twenty-four palm tree seedlings were to be planted there in a public ceremony of foundation.

An especially bitter debate on the relocation issue occurred when one of the formal meetings was attended by a CRYRZA architect, whom the Yungaínos thought was there to help them trace out the new plaza. The mayor called the meeting of town notables to order and declared in a voice full of emotion that they were there to decide on the location of the plaza de armas of new Yungay. Emilio Robles immediately suggested that such an important function be recorded in the book of proceedings and signed by all those present, an obvious ploy to coerce a form of official recognition from the CRYRZA functionaries present. The CRYRZA architect asserted that he could not trace out the new plaza because no decision had been reached on the relocation site, but that he had come to plan a central park for the camp. He spoke of the need to humanize the dreary encampment because it would continue to exist for at least two years more, and it was important to improve the environment of the camp. At this point, the mayor, in a somewhat pleading tone, lamented, "For one whole year now the people of Yungay had been waiting patiently, paralyzed by a lack of decision of the authorities, never knowing where they were going or whether it was safe to go to sleep at night. Wasn't there anything they could say to relieve this stressful situation?"

The CRYRZA men sadly said no, and their sympathy was evident. Emilio Robles was in no mood for expressions of sympathy. "All this time has passed, and it is now up to the people themselves, along with their brother Yungaínos in Lima, to found their new city without the help of the government. The first founders of Yungay could do it and so can we!"

Emilio's dramatic statement was greeted by loud applause from inside as well as outside the hall where schoolchildren brought by their teachers stood in orderly rows. Then old Demetrio Pardo spoke, his voice trembling, "It is now up to the people to take the decision in our own hands after all the disrespect we have been shown, being housed in stables with only a little bit of plywood between us, our human dignity ignored. We should go armed with picks and shovels and plant our own palms and trace our own plaza de armas."

After the applause subsided, Emilio Robles again spoke, suggesting that the tracing of the plaza and the palm planting be carried out on the anniversary so that all those Yungaínos coming from Lima could participate and labor on behalf of Yungay. Returning to the now-silent CRYRZA representatives, he suggested that they help them plan a sports area for the camp for football and other games. It was then agreed by acclamation that the sports area would be a compromise project. The government was given until the weekend of the anniversary to come up with an urban plan or the Yungaínos were going to go ahead and plan their own city.

Although the week preceding the anniversary had been declared a *semana espiritual* (spiritual week) to be spent in contemplation, in Yungay it was a time of intense organizational and political activity in preparation for the weekend's rituals. The committee named months earlier was finishing up its preparations for feeding and lodging the hundreds of visitors from the coast. It was decided that as many visitors as possible were to be housed with families "in order to experience our realities." The migrant associations and Yungay clubs of Lima and other coastal cities had made elaborate plans for a caravan of vehicles several kilometers long to journey en masse up the Pativilca road to arrive at the avalanche early on the morning of May 29. They were not only to demonstrate their mourning and allegiance to Yungay, but also to present material and capital donations for the rebuilding effort. One of Yungay's most illustrious sons, Monseñor Luis Bambarén, the assistant archbishop of Lima famous for his championing the cause of the squatter settlements, was coming up to say the memorial mass. On the avalanche itself, the chapel was enlarged and reroofed with fresh palm fronds, and concrete crosses and headstones, many with glassed-in photographs, were being constructed all over the avalanche. An elaborate program detailing the many activities of the three-day (May 29, 30, 31) commemoration of the tragedy, including the inauguration of the new medical post, a province-wide meeting of political authorities, the planting of the first palm, a cultural program in the high school, several requiem masses, a pilgrimage to the cemetery, and numerous speeches, was printed and distributed.

A crisis was touched off by the publication of the program of the week's activities. When a copy reached the desk of the prefect in Huaráz, he declared it unacceptable. The national government had declared May 31 to be a day of "national mourning" but also a working day, and no special activities were to be planned. The prefect admonished the Yungaínos for their elaborate schedule of activities and said that the anniversary program was more apt for the celebration of "independence day holidays," a phrase which cruelly stung the Yungaínos.

The hostility of the Yungaínos to all outside authorities at this point prompted the departmental prefect and CRYRZA authorities to convoke yet another meeting with the Yungaíno leaders on May 28, the day the anniversary activities were to begin. The anniversary of the tragedy was expected to attract national and international attention, and CRYRZA was anxious to avoid any public demonstrations of dissatisfaction, particularly from Yungay. As everyone filed into the meeting room of the barracks building town hall, the prefect and chief engineer at the front of the room were subjected to the baleful glares and smoldering hostility of all the Yungaínos present, who knew that they would hear the Tingua relocation announcement; they had come to do battle.

As the first item of business, the CRYRZA engineer read and explained the relocation decision. It had been resolved that Yungay would be built in the general area of Pashulpampa, but on the higher slopes. The administrative capital of the province would be relocated to Tingua at a future time "when it is convenient and necessary." A storm of protest interrupted him.

As the shouting gradually diminished, the voice of Emilio Robles emerged from the rumble of protest as he began a long harangue, accusing CRYRZA of neglect, incompetence, and a variety of other more colorful sins. He cited the work of the Yungaínos themselves on the water system and the irrigation canals, accusing the CRYRZA of being not only "johnny-come-latelies," but incompetent to boot. He punctuated his diatribe with grudging praise for the chief engineer, who had managed to get an electrical generator for the camp's meager street lights, but continued to condemn the general efforts of CRYRZA for the basically nonfunctioning shower and latrine system, the lack of water, the late efforts for anniversary projects, the lack of equipment for the medical post, the rejection of the anniversary program, and the lack of psychological and social assistance to help the Yungaínos cope with the trauma of the aftermath.

Through this blistering attack, the chief engineer, in general a man of considerable energy and sincerity, stared stonily into space. When Emilio had finished, he rose and began to speak, slowly addressing himself to each point. It would have been easy, he maintained, to settle Yungay here, but they wanted to do things right. They were thinking of the dangers possible in the years to come. He stressed the fact that to do things right, they had to take time, to collect information. But the capital relocation had been decided by the fact that six of eight district mayors had voted for Tingua. The CRYRZA engineer chose not to address the question of the legitimacy of the decision, but rather to stress the phrase in the text of the decision, "when necessary and convenient." This phrase was crucial in the interpretation of the statement, and he urged the Yungaínos to examine its meaning coolly. What it really means, he maintained, was that the town will be built here and the capital will be moved to Tingua only when it's "convenient and necessary." He said that it was within the realm of possibility that it would never be "convenient or necessary" for the capital to be moved from the present location. Someone asked about the relative amounts of aid for reconstruction for Yungay as against Tingua, and the engineer responded that at the moment, all the planning and aid were for Yungay and little for Tingua. This revelation was greeted by enthusiastic applause.

227

He also stated that the CRYRZA welcomed criticism and that they were "only men," and men make mistakes. "But," he said, "the criticism should be just. I welcome and need the dialogue with the people. Yungay has been a problem to us, and I realize that not much has been done here, but that is because we did not want to waste effort and money in constructions which might have to be moved the next day." Again, however, he reassured them that their town would be located close by and that in regard to the location of the capital, the crucial phrase in the CRYRZA document was "when convenient and necessary."

The moment the meeting was adjourned, the Yungaínos rapidly conferred and, faces alight with enthusiasm and happiness, began to walk and some even to jog up the hill toward the schoolyard. There had been a plan, regardless of the outcome of the meeting, to plant a flagpole and raise a Peruvian flag in the plaza of the primary school. It was to be an act either of defiance or of celebration. Although the CRYRZA document was at best equivocal, the Yungaínos sensed a victory in the phrase, "when necessary and convenient." They approached the site chosen for the flagpole and began to deepen the pit which had been started earlier in the day. The flagpole, a eucalyptus trunk about forty feet tall, with a small pulley at the top, was brought, and with no little tugging and hauling by everyone, it was put in place to cheers and shouts. There was a brief moment of quiet when the flag was raised, but soon enthusiasm reigned again.

The raising of the flagpole was an unscheduled opening to the very structured series of organized events which began that afternoon. From the schoolyard on the hill, the crowd began to move down and across the dusty camp to the medical post for the formal inauguration ceremonies, including speeches by the prefect, the chief engineer, the departmental public health officials, and the new doctor. As we strode down the hill toward the medical post, Shamu Mendez, his face wreathed in a smile of triumph and well-being, seized my arm with one hand and threw his other arm around my shoulder as we walked. "We have a real town now, Antuco. How about that?"

At dawn the following morning the caravan of Yungaínos from Lima arrived in Aura, just south of the avalanche. Shortly before nine in the morning, the leaders of the caravan, now walking the last few kilometers in front of the line of vehicles, were met by the Yungaínos in the main street of Aura with heartfelt embraces.

There were no speeches, no pronouncements, no formal ceremonies. The encounter was manifestly symbolic to everyone of the solidarity of Yungaínos, resident and nonresident, united in grief for the survival of their tradition and community. Together the two groups, now arm in arm, crested the hill above Aura and looked out over the bleakness of the avalanche scar, now strangely softened by a sparse fringe of vegetation.

By noon the avalanche scar was alive with probably close to 3,000 people, including the many hundreds who had journeyed from the coast, the camp residents, visitors from other areas of the valley, and a great portion of the Indian population from the hills. The event itself was covered by all the major newspapers of Peru and a number of international ones, including the *New York Times*. The most important act of the first day of activities was to be the ceremony of foundation for new Yungay, the planting of the first palm for the new plaza.

When the midday heat of May had diminished somewhat toward the end of the afternoon, a procession of several hundred people, led by Yungay notables from both the camp and the coast, made its way up the rough hillside. They carried with them tools and six small palms in square cans. The spot they had chosen for the new plaza was a small plot of ground in a peasant hamlet called Acobamba. Although the plot itself was at that time unseeded, it was surrounded on all sides by rows of live oak and eucalyptus trees, which separated it from fields of corn and wheat, flourishing from plentiful summer rains. The afternoon sun bathed the spot in a softly burnished glow, and a light breeze stirred the stands of wheat as the procession solemnly approached. The leaders headed for the middle of the plot with the palms, and the crowd moved to the edges of the fields to witness the ceremony. Children climbed the trees for a better look, and the crowd, which was trampling the corn and wheat fields, edged closer.

The mayor of Yungay began the proceedings. Seizing a pickaxe, he stepped forward. Taking an oath of honor, in his and in the names of all present, "for the firm and sacred purpose of founding and building the new city of Yungay" in that spot, he sunk the pickaxe into the ground, to wild applause and shouts of "viva Yungay!" The mayor was followed by the president of ARRPY, Dr. Rafael Hidalgo, who declared that the day, May 29, 1971, constituted "a date of historical transcendence." He also buried the pickaxe in the ground before passing it to Emilio Robles.

Before taking his turn with the axe, in a voice filled with determination, Emilio declared, "What was destroyed with snow and rock and mud on May 31, 1970, we now today found again with blood and sweat and bravery; what the government through CRYRZA could not do in a year, we, as a symbol of our memory of our entombed Yungay, do in this moment." As each dignitary took the pickaxe, each intoned a statement of purpose or emotion fitting to the occasion. Following the notables of the camp and the coast came Don Augusto Arévalo of the Guardia Civil, and Nora Quispe Granados, representing Yungay women, followed by a peasant and then a child. Finally, each person present took a turn with the axe to loosen the earth for the new palms, which were planted and blessed by the padre. After the ceremony, the procession returned to the camp for the official signing of the document of the foundation of new Yungay, leaving the tiny palm trees in place among the trampled corn and wheat fields of Acobamba.

The next afternoon, aid was to be distributed among the migrants in the camp. The lines began to form early in the morning. After a cultural program at the high school, the dignitaries, "nobles," and survivors marched solemnly up the road to the avalanche, where Bishop Bambaren said mass, assisted by two priests from the valley. Although normally in Yungay there were no dry laws, for this occasion the mayor had prohibited the sale of alcohol on Sunday and Monday, May 30 and 31. Nonetheless, a few people managed to get very drunk even for the morning's activities, among them Leo Ruiz, who had wandered into the fringes of the crowd gathered outside the chapel. Since most of the men, following traditional patterns of quiet external observance rather than participation, were outside the chapel, they managed to divert Leo from creating a scandal.

In the afternoon, after still another meeting, which had now fallen into a ritualized pattern of demands by Yungay authorities and counter offers by CRYRZA officials, people began drifting toward the open field to the side of the municipal barracks building where men, women, and children awaited aid in long, separate lines stretching clear off the field and into the rows of module homes. The people, mostly peasant and urban poor, waited patiently for the ARRPY and local leaders to begin the distribution process. The ARRPY trucks which arrived with the caravan from Lima carried large cargos of crates of canned milk and meat, used clothes, material for school uniforms, bags of beans and noodles, and ponchos made of charcoal grey blanketing material. The ponchos were very short, barely reaching most peoples' waists and soon earned the name *miniponchos*. The distribution of these articles began at 3:00 in the afternoon and at 6:30 still had not abated. The lines stretched on and on, and more people joined them as dusk fell. The ARRPY distributors attempted to control the distribution by taking each individual's name and documents, but complete control of the process was impossible. It was clear that, in this distribution as in all the others, many people managed to receive double quantities, and many others whose own resources were more than ample received donations as well. Like the Cuban sweatshirts just after the disaster, the miniponchos brought by the ARRPY enjoyed a brief vogue among the middle and upper classes of Yungay. Ultimately, as in all the other distributions, there were more people than there were donations, and some had to be turned away, leading as always to claims of fraud, protests, and complaints. However, most people by nightfall did carry home a modest portion of material goods. For the urban poor and the urbanizing peasant, both largely without work, any aid at all was important in the daily struggle to keep life and household together.

The following day, May 31, 1971, dawned bright and clear, just as it had one year before. Throughout the nation, it had been declared a national day of mourning, with flags at half-mast at all public offices. In Yungay the flag of Peru was raised to half-mast on the newly erected flagpole in the early morning, after which everybody began the walk from town up to the avalanche for the commemorative events of the day. While the black-clad procession of townspeople and visitors walked solemnly up the road toward the avalanche, they were passed by cars and trucks full of people coming from other parts of the valley for the ceremony at Yungay, and soon the previous day's crowd was surpassed by many hundreds. It was to be a day of public commemoration of the tragedy and private mourning for people all over the callejón, and many were drawn by affection for Yungay and lost friends and relatives as well as by sheer curiosity for the ceremonies to take place on the grotesque avalanche scar. One particularly large group of about a hundred persons with a ten-piece brass band had come from the neighboring province of Caraz for the unveiling of a large concrete memorial donated by the province in memory of the lost city. As the band played the mournful dirge-like melodies so typical of Peruvian religious processions, the huge crowd began to cluster around the notables next to the Caraz memorial, a massive concrete oblong, its sides angled in toward the base of the cross at its top. After the priest's blessing, the Caraz mayor read the inscription from its polished face. "From the Provincial Council of Huaylas to its brother people of Yungay with profound sentiments of fraternity on their first anniversary of the tragic earthquake and avalanche which interred the city on May 31, 1970."

From there the dignitaries and crowd moved on to the other memorials, each to be blessed by the priest and dedicated by the donors. Next to the chapel and palm trees were large wreaths of flowers, one with the flag of Peru and a black-rimmed condolence card from "the revolutionary government of the armed forces" and one of red and white flowers, whose card indicated its donor to be CRYRZA. After the dedications, the dignitaries, led by the priest, filed into the palm-thatched chapel and lined up behind the altar. The rest of the crowd, which by this time numbered between two and three thousand people, crowded in and around the chapel and the protruding ruins of the old church tower, which formed the back wall of the chapel. The Indian mayors stood to the left of the altar. During the mass, the crowd stood or sat quietly shading themselves under the palms and next to the ruined church tower. Although most townpeople wore black, many of the Indian women wore their customary garb of brilliantly colored blouses and sweaters. The sermon preached by Padre Diaz that day was subdued in tone. He spoke, as many did that day, of the earthquake, of Huascarán, of old Yungay, and, most of all, of new Yungay, of the founding of a new city, with saintly, good people.

After the mass there was still another short speech by Emilio Robles as head of the Yungay Civic Committee, who this time managed to curb his criticisms of CRYRZA and limited himself to an exhortation to unity and struggle for a new Yungay. His brief presentation was followed by a "pilgrimage," led by the mayor to the cemetery mound where many people placed floral offerings at those niches undestroyed by the avalanche. After the pilgrimage, people quietly moved off alone or in small groups, spreading out over the vastness of the avalanche scar to their own, private rituals of commemoration and mourning. It was a day in which many individual memorials were blessed. People wandered over the devastation now sown with crosses and memorials, quietly conversing with friends and relatives encountered in their own mourning rituals.

Toward the end of the afternoon, I too climbed the broken stone steps of the cemetery mound, treading carefully over the rocks and rubble still strewn about, and sat, my back against the base of Christ Redemptor. I noticed that the base of the huge white statue, close to the feet, had been cracked by the earthquake and that the thick internal supporting rods were slightly bent, tilting the statue a little. But he still faced Huascarán, and the spread of his arms still seemed to encompass that which had been Yungay. I looked up at Huascarán, its glaciers glistening in the bright afternoon sun against that startling blue sky and then down over the avalanche scar, from the distance and height of the mound. Tiny black figures moved slowly and silently about, clustering here and there around crosses and monuments, or moving off in uneven, broken black lines toward Aura, Pampac, Acobamba, or new Yungay. Like everyone else there that afternoon, I thought about the day, almost that very hour, a year before, about the crushing power of mud and rock, about the chaos of violence and destruction, of trapped people in a doomed town, of Rosa Martínez's sons, or Roberto Falcón's wife and children, of his brother Nelson, of El Pillo's wife and daughter, and of too many others. I looked around me at the cemetery mound and was assaulted by images of horror. I thought of the mud and the dust of that day and of the year which had just passed with all its pain and hardship. And then my gaze wandered down again to the avalanche scar and all the people. I wondered how many of them would continue to live here. Then I realized that it really didn't matter if some never return or others leave, because the Yungaínos, new and old, opposing both natural and human forces, had taken their stand against death, and in a sense, they had won. As a tradition and as a people, Yungay had not succumbed to death. There will be other earthquakes and maybe other avalanches, and other governments as well, and Yungay may or may not survive them all. I think it will. Yungaínos have had to learn better than most the art of survival.

Chapter 9
Ten Years After:
The Lessons of Tragedy

The disaster was the greatest force for change to hit Yungay in the 1970s, but it was not the only one. The earthquake struck on the eve of what proved to be a decade of tumult for all Peru. Peru's "revolutionary" military government seized power in 1968 and soon after initiated a broad spectrum of programs designed to alter the structure of Peruvian economy and society. While many of the government programs for Yungay were temporarily postponed due to the earthquake, the government eventually integrated the disaster and the enormous influx of material and economic aid which followed it into its broader plans for the region's economic and social development. In effect, the disaster gave the government an opportunity to experiment with a pilot regional development program.* The new government implemented agrarian reform in the region within three years of the disaster. Thus, over the decade of the 1970s, rural and urban Yungaínos faced the disaster and its personal and communal tragedies and hardships, the major structural alteration of the agrarian reform, and the social and economic changes of a general region-wide program of infrastructural and economic development.

Within a year of the disaster Yungay had reestablished all but one of the major institutions and functions of the destroyed provincial capital. In one year Yungay had become a city of approximately 1,800 people, with a fully functioning local and provincial government, an active

---

*The evolution of this perspective is reflected in the changes in the directing agency's official name. CRYRZA (Committee for the Reconstruction and Rehabilitation of the Affected Zone) became ORDEZA (Organism for the Reconstruction and Development of the Affected Zone) in 1974 and subsequently ORDENOR (Organism for the Development of the North) in 1978.

economic life, renewed linkages with its peasant hinterland, a ceremonial center for two faiths, primary and secondary schools, and a marked sense of purpose and community. This rapid growth and reconstruction can be attributed at least in part to the threat posed by resettlement. This threat of relocation by the government stimulated a remarkable sense of common purpose which was demonstrated time and time again in cooperation on projects relating to reconstruction and institutionalization of the provincial capital in Yungay.

Although the battle for Yungay's permanence was won less than two years after the total destruction of the old capital, the problems of the rapidly growing settlement were far from over. The reconstruction authorities had prohibited major construction in the camp and had done little planning for the new city since its permanence was in doubt for the first two years. Essentially a whole new city had to be built for an already resident and growing population. The module housing had been built to last two years, but people were still living in the deteriorating structures four years after the disaster.

Before any planning or design could be undertaken, the reconstruction authority carried out a number of short-term studies of the population. While admittedly necessary, these questionnaire-based studies sorely tested the patience of the Yungaínos; they felt overstudied. By the time the urban development plan for Yungay was delivered, the skepticism of Yungaínos had become profound. "Look at us, look at how we are living still, after four years!" lamented a survivor to me on my return visit in 1974.

The urban development plan which the reconstruction authority finally put together called for a highly ordered zoning system with distinct sectors for specific activities. The main plaza, located somewhat below where the Yungaínos had planted the first palm, would be the hub of activities in the community. The entire urban area was to be completely electrified and have potable water and underground sewage systems, facilities which the old city had not fully enjoyed. The new city was to have a series of distinct sectors for economic activities, educational institutions, public administration, industry, health care, and residence. Never happy with the Yungaínos' determination to remain in Pashulpampa, the reconstruction authority located the residential sector high on the hillside as far from harm's way as possible in the event of another landslide.

This ambitious plan was greeted by Yungaínos with public enthusiasm and private skepticism. The Peruvian newspapers had been filled for more than a year with news of aid for Yungay: a Cuban prefabricated hospital, one hundred wooden chalet-style prefabricated houses donated by the USSR, a kindergarten from the Rotary Club, new schools, a new market. The list was all too well known to the Yungaínos who struggled along miserably in the deteriorating modules. Most of the urban development plan was completed by 1975, although work on some projects still continued as of July 1979. By September of 1973 construction was finished on the famous Russian houses, but because of a lack of vital parts for both water and electricity systems the houses were still not occupied in August of 1974. The disgust of the Yungaínos with the situation was vocal. Not only was life miserable in the modules, but the system devised for distributing the houses and the houses themselves were considered far from satisfactory.

The Russian houses were available to people on a system of priorities established by the reconstruction authority. Those with first priority were the landowners whose property had been expropriated for the construction of the community. People with second priority were, first, landowning disaster victims and, second, disaster victims who had rented homes in the old city. Migrants were in third place. These priorities were cross-cut by a system of mitigating variables such as income, family size, and disaster identity. A system of points was conceived, and each individual was given a certain number of points in accordance with his priority and the other variables. One's points or lack of them had to be defended or debated in public, a requirement which created ill feeling among everyone. Finally, the houses had different prices, although they were all of the same design of three rooms, kitchen, bathroom, and glassed-in porch. The most expensive houses, costing 90,000 soles (approximately $600.00), were closest to the new plaza. Those costing 80,000 soles and 70,000 soles were proportionately distant from the plaza and farther up the hill.

The priorities, the prices, and finally the houses themselves were all causes of dissatisfaction. The wooden construction of the houses made people extremely nervous about fires, and the small size of the rooms was also complained about. The price system offended all but the most wealthy. It was considered unjust that people who had lost everything should be required to pay so much for housing. In fact, the price of the houses with interest amounted to a monthly payment of as much as 1,000 soles ($6.60) a month for ten years. While a seemingly miniscule amount by standards of industrialized nations, such a payment forms an effective barrier to decent housing for the poor in a country whose average per capita income is approximately $200.00 a year. Thus, the pride and joy of Yungay's housing development, the Russian houses, became a primary factor in the reappearance and solidification of socio-economic class distinctions. Finally in late 1974, all the Russian houses were occupied, as were the new market and municipal building.

The majority of the population remained in the module buildings. For them a program known as *auto-construcción* was developed. Under this program, the remaining land in the residential zone was divided into lots, which were assigned to people again on the basis of priorities similar to the ones used for distributing the Russian houses. Migrants again had the last preference. The *auto-construcción* program grouped together anywhere from ten to fifty families to obtain block loans for materials and for cooperation in home construction. The reconstruction authority provided electrical and water hook-ups and technical expertise in the construction. Each family was offered the choice of five designs. The advantage of this program was that it provided a less expensive alternative and less uniformity than the identical Russian chalets. The disadvantage was that it often grouped together people of widely differing capabilities to perform cooperative tasks, resulting once more in social difficulties and hampered construction. As of July 1980 many people were still building their homes.

A few module homes persist in the community occupied by those who didn't get into the *auto-construcción* program. As one moves farther up the hill, the buildings become more makeshift and public services increasingly rudimentary and sporadic. Continued migration from the rural areas, attracted in the mid-1970s by high construction authority wages, and return migration from the coast caused by rampant inflation and shortages have created a kind of urban sprawl up the steep hillside.

In some senses, the town conveys the impression in microcosm of Peru's larger cities. The center of town is dominated by the plaza and the large and impressive municipal and market buildings. The plaza has lovely rose gardens, and the palms are now almost four feet tall. Around the plaza are the municipal and market buildings, shops, restaurants, and offices. All of the town's paved streets are around or below the plaza. The wall of the municipal building is decorated with a large and brilliantly colored painting of Huascarán overlooking the old Yungay plaza before the disaster. Huascarán is no longer visible from the plaza, but the top of Huandoy can be seen from the lower barrios of the new city.

Down the hill from the elegant new plaza is the "industrial" district, now occupied by adobe and quincha stores and dwellings. Since much of this area developed without regard for the formalized urban plan, order is only approximate among the dusty streets and passageways that lead to the many small buildings of Yungay's less favored merchants and artisans. Nonetheless, some small structures there have been given electricity, and the city fairly bristles with electrical posts, ranging from shiny bright modernistic shafts in the plaza to the knotty and bent eucalyptus poles in the industrial sector and the makeshift residential areas.

As one ascends the hill from the plaza, one sees row upon row of the prefabricated Russian chalets, arranged neatly in tiers upon the hillside. The open front yard design of the Russian houses has made the traditional walled-in compound housing pattern of the Andes impossible. Consequently the *casa rusa* owners have embellished their homes with cinder block or brick walls and gardens of flowers and shrubbery in the open front yard in order to maintain privacy as well as to lend some aesthetic quality and individuality to the drab uniformity of the chalets. Walking up the dusty streets between the double rows of Russian houses, one finds little shops, restaurants, and neighborhood bars installed in the glassed front porches of many homes. Some people have built adobe additions onto the backs or fronts of their houses, sometimes almost doubling them in size. Because they are located on tiers, each long double row of houses with its entrance road constitutes a small neighborhood, a kind of elongated city block.

Above and to the south of the Russian houses begin the neighborhoods of houses built in the *auto-construcción* program. Here Yungay is still a city very much in the process of reconstruction. It is dusty, and there are open dirt lots with piles of brick and rock strewn about. Since the city was cut in tiers out of the hillside, little vegetation relieves either the dust or the drab reddish coloration of the settlement's upper areas. Most of Yungay's homes have only one story, but as in Lima's squatter settlements, the second stories have already been started. The first floors are lived in, while the second floors are being built little by little. As soon as the second floor is finished, the family will move up there and open a small store or bar on the first floor.

Above the *auto-construcción* neighborhoods, still higher on Atma Hill, are Yungay's poorer settlements. The outskirts of town, as in most of the Third World's cities, are a collection of buildings of makeshift materials. Although this area has a semblance of streets and an urban plan, the dirt roads soon disappear into trails which cut higher into the steep slope. Up here the swirling dust of the city diminishes and the air seems clearer, but Yungay's poorest and most recent migrants can take only momentary pleasure from these things as they live their hardscrabble lives in shacks and lean-tos of mostly scrap material. Although some people are attempting to construct adobe and even brick dwellings, most have scavenged the old tents, tin roofing sheets, and the Mapresa wallboard from the modules. Here and there a whole module segment survives as a family dwelling. The reconstruction authority has provided public spigots for water, and electrical wires strung on eucalyptus posts provide lights for those who can afford the service. The view from Yungay's poorer barrios is spectacular, encompassing the entire new city nestled in its sanctuary between the two canyons of recent and ancient avalanches.

Ironically, to the north of the poorer barrios sits a cluster of large traditional two-story adobe buildings where a small number of Yungay's traditional elite, haughtily refusing the Russian houses, have constructed their homes. They live just under the ridge which separates the new city from the path of the Ancash avalanche of 1725. From their vantage point, encompassing the city and its surrounding countryside, Yungay seems in large part to have conformed to the ORDEZA urban plan. Fan-like, Yungay starts high on the hill with small, makeshift housing settlements and descends, widening on both sides to include the grey concrete or white stuccoed *auto-construcción* dwellings and then the many tiers of Russian houses, their tin roofs gleaming in regular rows, all the way down to the plaza, where the eye is detained by the open square surrounded by the large municipality, markets, and the school complex. The density of the small adobe and *quincha* workshops and stores diminishes as the eye continues its descent down the hill until, reaching the old road, the houses suddenly become much more sparse. They appear only sporadically amidst the green corn and alfalfa fields and waving groves of eucalyptus of Piguip and Pampac hills.

Plainly, Yungay is no longer the provisional refugee camp of the early years of the 1970s. It is the established capital of its province and one of the major cities of the region. The government's infrastructural development program has also carried out important changes in the region which affect the city. Probably the most far-reaching project has been the widening and paving of the road from the coast to Caraz, facilitating transportation of all sorts and shortening the trip from twelve or fifteen hours to roughly six. The new airport in Huaráz accommodates small jets easily, and flights now place the valley a mere half an hour from Lima. By 1980 tourism from Lima was growing, stimulating the growth of hotels, restaurants, and other service industries in the entire valley. All of the region's cities now enjoy full-time electric power for home and industrial use from the Huallanca hydroelectric plant at the northern end of the valley. The result of these basic improvements is that the callejón now is a much smaller and busier place than before the disaster. While Yungay is still a relatively small place and the pace of life there is noticeably less intense than in larger cities, it is now much more integrated into the life of the region and the nation.

The lives of the people of Yungay have undergone as many changes as the physical appearance of the town. The large-scale demographic shifts stimulated by forces in the political economy of the nation have affected many individual lives. The disaster almost eliminated the top of the social pyramid in Yungay but did not seriously affect the modes of production or the ideologies that buttressed them. Within two years of the disaster, however, government policies began instituting major structural changes, particularly in property ownership, social welfare, and education. Increased government spending, initially stimulated in part by the enormous international donation of capital for disaster aid, as well as the stresses of reform and reorganization, exacerbated the already strained capabilities of an economy hamstrung by a heritage of exploitation, dependency, and indebtedness. The results were severe inflation and the devaluation of currency by almost 200 percent over the decade. These powerful forces set the Peruvian population, historically a mobile one, in even greater motion.

By decapitating the social pyramid and accelerating the coastward migration of Yungay's traditional elites, the disaster created space at the top for new players in the old game. It also gave rural people a long-awaited chance to urbanize, and they repopulated the renascent city of Yungay. Consequently, Yungay suffers from many of the problems common to larger cities burdened by intense migration. The attractions of the city pull in so many migrants as to overwhelm the city's abilities to provide adequate services. In the immediate postdisaster period, Yungay migrants were attracted by material aid; as more aid arrived, more migrants were attracted, and still more aid had to be supplied. Aid-induced migration, in fact, created a city where three months before none had existed. The reconstruction authority was consequently faced with a situation very similar to that faced by urban authorities after squatter land invasions. However, because socioeconomic parameters carried over from the traditional system, the most significant result of Yungay's urban development program is that despite the temporary social leveling of the cataclysmic disaster and the avowed revolutionary posture of Peru's military government of the time, the new city has conformed largely to urban social patterns which are nationwide.

After more than ten years rural migrants have not broken class lines in significant numbers. Those that have, principally the cholo entrepreneurs, have achieved only grudging social acceptance and secondary positions of political power from the surviving remnants of old Yungay's elite. Whether the numerical inferiority of this elite will result in greater access to the benefits of society for more people in the long run remains to be seen. What is clear at present, however, is that the urban development program conformed far more to the social dictates of the traditional system in its planning and delivery and is at least partially responsible for the reinstallation of the old system and its endemic problems.

Nevertheless, in the ten years since the disaster, there have been important changes. While social revolution did not come to Yungay in an act of God, as many seemed to have expected, a number of the immediate adaptations and changes brought about in that first dreadful year have become permanent parts of Yungay life. Indeed, in many ways, many of the changes wrought by the disaster were later institutionalized by the policies of Peru's revolutionary government of the 1970s. Probably the most important change has taken place in the nature of rural-urban relations, both interpersonally and institutionally. Although the social structure was not turned upside down by the disaster, the patron-client relations which tied rural, Indian individuals in subservient relations to urban dwellers were shattered by the high mortality among Yungay's elite. The new relationships, primarily of godparenthood, do not have the same character of servile personal dependency of the old. In addition, the artificially created reconstruction economy placed a premium on manual labor and allowed rural people the opportunity to choose in the disposition of their labor. Their labor was no longer a quantity to be delivered on demand to townspeople. While their position in the social hierarchy remains the same, clearly significant changes in Indian role behavior have taken place. Indian refusal to deliver labor at traditional menial rates was a clear indication that something very basic in the relationship between Indian and townsman altered after the earthquake. The fact that two years after the earthquake the Peruvian agrarian reform divested surviving hacendados in Yungay of their lands and power over the people on the lands ultimately ratified and institutionalized the changes which the disaster had brought to interpersonal rural-urban relations.

The passing of the landlords, however, did not usher in an era of immediate prosperity for the peasants and small sharecroppers. Unbalanced in the favor of the landlords as the reciprocity was, the arrangement often provided peasants and small farmers with fertilizer and the larger tools. Rampant inflation coupled with severe drought in the late seventies curtailed abilities of some peasants to keep land in production because of this loss of capital. Although some urban people claimed that peasants had sought out their former masters to renew old relationships clandestinely, this is highly unlikely since the major concern among Yungay's peasants after the election of the centrist Belaunde in 1980 was that he would reverse the agrarian reform. Life is still difficult for Yungay's peasants, but the disaster and the reform have enabled them to achieve a degree of control over their means of production which they are far from ready to relinquish.

Although great social mobility has not been achieved by rural people in Yungay, they have achieved greater independence since the disaster. Endemic poverty still oppresses them, but certain basic institutional changes have altered aspects of the peasants' social life, if not their position. Arturo Cantaro lives and works his land with his fellow community members. He no longer "belongs" to César Morales nor to his heirs. Arturo and others like him, while still careful and on the defensive with urban people, have more flexibility and freedom over their own actions since the agrarian reform institutionalized the changes in land-tenure patterns. They are, however, still dependent, not on the landlords but on agricultural brokers. The lines of dependency and exploitation between peasant and town have not been broken, but they have changed from traditional servile forms to more modern, less personal, economic forms, which has intensified the interaction between the rural and urban sectors of Yungay society. In particular, the rural cholo agricultural brokers are emerging as the major channels of interaction between rural and urban Yungay.

From an institutional standpoint, changes in the rural-urban political relationship have also taken place. The postdisaster resistance by the inhabitants of Mitma, one of Yungay's two Indian barrios, to reintegration into the traditional political-religious authority structure has continued, shrinking the city's hinterland. The people of Mitma successfully separated themselves from a system to which they had little commitment and from which they derived few advantages. All efforts to reintegrate the wayward barrio have failed, and now, ten years later, the urban authorities appear to have resigned themselves to the situation. While people from Mitma occasionally market, attend church, or use the administrative offices in Yungay, they no longer participate in the fiestas, and they are no longer subject to the traditional labor draft imposed by the city on peasant communities. However, the people of Huambo, the more traditional barrio to Yungay's north, remain fully integrated in the system and carry out their fiesta obligations religiously. They are, as well, still contributing their labor to the new city of Yungay. The new church, designed by an architect from Lima, will be constructed primarily by donated peasant labor from Huambo.

In Yungay the disaster anticipated a number of changes in the country at large. All of Peru, in particular the urban areas, is involved at present in a process of integration of marginal peoples—a process that has been referred to as "cholification." While the process had been long under way prior to the disaster, the disaster utterly transformed the city of Yungay from a bastion of power of the traditional elite into a predominantly cholo town. This transition became perhaps most evident in the recruitment of socioeconomic and political leadership. Because of the high mortality among Yungay's traditional elites, new individuals for leadership positions were drawn from the ranks of people previously

considered ineligible for political power because of humble origins—
people like Augusto Angeles who was once a small-scale agricultural
middleman and now is becoming an economically important citizen.
Prior to the disaster these marginal people were only beginning their
difficult ascent in the socioeconomic hierarchy; they rushed into the
vacuum left by the elite who perished in the avalanche and in ten years
have become more visible in city political and economic life.

Equally important are the personal developments of the life cycles of
individuals. A decade has passed. Children born after the disaster are
brought up with a legacy of Yungay's tradition and tragedy. Children
who survived the disaster are now in the work force, many of them
married with children of their own. Time and history have both given
their gifts and taken their toll on the survivors of Yungay. People have
coped, for the most part effectively, with both the major forces of a
tumultuous decade and the passages and crises of their own lives.

Although the surviving traditional elites of Yungay, both resident and
nonresident, were divested of their landholdings by the agrarian reform
in 1974, many of them continue to maintain links .with the growing
city. The Yungay associations of migrants in Lima continue to support
the city with material donations and to lobby on its behalf in the national
capital. One of the most active supporters of Yungay's nonresident elites,
the orthopedic surgeon, Dr. Carrillo Guevara, has been elected a senator
for the Department of Ancash in the recent return to civilian rule in
April of 1980. Yungaínos are hopeful that having a Yungaíno in the
senate will bring them added benefits.

The agrarian reform that expropriated most elite lands in Yungay was
in a sense culminating a process that had been under way for some
time. Even before the disaster, many of Yungay's elites had abandoned
agriculture as a way of life. Many of those still engaged in agricultural
pursuits perished in the disaster; those who survived constituted a very
small group of people. When the agrarian reform came, there was
considerable expropriation in the province, but it was in some measure
a ratification of a largely de facto situation. César Morales's hacienda,
Timbrac, had been totally ignored by his wife and other surviving relatives, most of whom had moved to Lima. After the disaster they had
no interest in maintaining the hacienda, and with the agrarian reform
on the horizon, they were convinced that any investment of labor or
capital in the land would be wasted. Thus, César Morales's serfs, among

them Arturo Cántaro, the *teniente* of Timbrac, are now, as in effect they were the day after the disaster, both the de facto and the *de jure* owners of the land they work.

A few of Yungay's elites still own and manage small agricultural enterprises. Although Rafael Moreno Alba, new Yungay's first official mayor and the province's largest agriculturalist, still has a house in the city, he lives on a small piece of property he owns near the peasant community of Arhuay, high above the valley and ominously close to the avalanche scar. He owns a small herd of dairy cattle. His wife died in the disaster, and his children all live in Lima. He lives alone in a small house among the peasants who were once his serfs, now a rather retiring figure, not exactly fallen, but somehow displaced from a social structure which is rapidly changing.

Roberto Falcón no longer lives in Yungay and rarely visits. His life is now in Lima. He went there shortly before the first anniversary of the disaster and returned to the university. He has remarried and has obtained a teaching position in one of the city's better high schools. Juan Beltrán, the old city's mayor, has also left the province and lives and works in Casma on the coast. El Pillo, who almost succumbed to his grief in his self-described "three-year drunk," finally consented to the will of his relatives in Ica and left Yungay for reasons of both physical and mental health. While in Ica he met a woman from Santiago whom he married, and he now lives and works in Chile, apparently totally recuperated from his ordeals after the tragedy. His friends in Yungay say he writes them occasionally. Lucho Benitez, the son of one of Yungay's ex-mayors who married the Peace Corps volunteer, now lives in Illinois and teaches math in a local high school. Both he and his wife return to Yungay as often as they can. We have seen each other there several times during the summer months.

The stream of upper-class Yungay migrants has not been exclusively coastward. Some middle- and upper-sector family networks have worked out systems in which they have small businesses in Yungay, stores, vehicles, professional offices, and similar interests and activities in Lima, and individuals flow between the highland city and the national capital. Some students and young professionals will return to Yungay every weekend, particularly in winter to play in the soccer league. In effect, there are few upper- or middle-sector people in Yungay who do not have networks of social and economic support in Lima. Some upper-sector people have returned to Yungay after many years, in some cases decades or a generation, on the coast. The present mayor of Yungay, Manuel Juarez Solís, a vigorous man in his late fifties, operated a large chicken farm on the coast for over thirty years. Having achieved a certain financial independence from his enterprise, he sold it and, in his later years, has returned "to work for my town."

Middle-sector people have also been very mobile, and in the decade since the tragedy have made long-term adjustments to difficult and changing circumstances by moving between coast and highlands, between city and country. Antonio Flores and his brother Javier were the first secretary and treasurer of the reconstituted municipal government. A young man of energy and ambition, Antonio had great plans. He wanted to establish a good hotel and restaurant in new Yungay. The initial step in this enterprise was the purchase of a used pool table, which he installed in a *quincha* building down on the highway before the new city was occupied. When Antonio and Javier resigned their jobs with the municipality, Antonio left Javier in charge of the pool hall and migrated to Lima, where he and his wife and two children lived with his brother-in-law in Breña, in a lower-middle-class neighborhood. He found a job at Sears Roebuck selling men's clothing. They would hire him for two months, and at the end of two months offer him another two-month contract. The lack of job security and the small salary worried him, particularly with three sons now to support. Soon Javier, who had stayed in Yungay, became ill. Antonio explained that Javier was sick from *soledad* (solitude) since the two of them had been through so much together in the disaster. He eventually sold Antonio's billiard tables and joined him in Lima, but Javier was miserable there. City life oppressed him with its noise and dirt and masses of people.

Meanwhile, Antonio, tired of being strung along by Sears, told them to make him permanent or he would leave. They offered him a permanent job in their warehouse, but he considered that a step down and refused it. Both brothers and their families returned to Yungay. Antonio opened up a small dry-goods store in the Yungay market and has installed another pool hall that serves drinks and sandwiches. Both brothers are now permanent residents of Yungay. Although Antonio had decided to build a life for his family in Lima, the lack of employment, the skyrocketing inflation, and general insecurity of urban living convinced him that despite the attractions of cosmopolitan Lima, Yungay offered greater stability for the two brothers and their families. Today, Antonio operates the pool hall–sandwich shop, and his wife teaches primary school in one of the nearby peasant communities. Together they manage to earn enough to furnish their *casa rusa* in one of the first rows next to the plaza and to feed and clothe their four sons. Both Antonio and Maria have become deeply involved in one of the local protestant sects, and most of their social life revolves around church-oriented activities. Javier has returned to a job in the municipality and is building a new house at the edge of the Russian-house barrio.

With the growth of Yungay and the general return to relatively stable, economic activities, Rodolfo Armendariz and Rosa Martínez were able to improve the restaurant over the first half-decade. By pooling the earnings from the restaurant and Rodolfo's salary as a bus driver, they were also able to buy four hectares of land and begin building a house for themselves in the neighboring village of Punyan, just to the north of the Quebrada Ancash.

The agrarian reform rule that in order to own land in the country one had to live on that land and work it was applied in Yungay in 1973. Neither Rosa nor Rodolfo cared much for the Russian houses, and the restaurant faced an uncertain future in its location at the edge of the new city. Consequently Rosa gave the restaurant to Luisa, her surviving daughter, who had recently returned from Lima, and she and Rodolfo went to live on their land. Luisa ran the restaurant for a few more years until her marriage.

Both Rosa and Rodolfo liked living in the country. Rosa looked after the farm while Rodolfo drove his routes for the bus company. He would be home every other day for a whole day before taking the return trip to Lima. Rosa and the day laborers from the community whom she hires planted their land in wheat, corn, potatoes, and alfalfa. Slowly but surely over seven years of working and saving, Rosa and Rodolfo finally completed their house, which sits at the edge of the Quebrada Ancash. The view from their home is both beautiful and awesome. They look directly up the canyon into the icy face of Huandoy. The site of Ancash, the city obliterated by an avalanche from Huandoy in 1725, is but a few hundred yards up the canyon from them.

Tragedy struck Rosa and Rodolfo again. Late in 1977 Rodolfo developed cancer of the kidney. Rosa took him to Lima where he underwent surgery, but these measures were taken too late. He died in March of

An Indian survivor wears one of the prestigious Cuban sweatshirts on a visit to Yungay.

Building the *waru* (footbridge)—a moment of spontaneous comunitas.

The lower logs of the *waru* are extended across the rain-swollen Ranrahirca River.

One of the many shipments of aid that were to sustain the inhabitants of Yungay in the year following the disaster.

People waited many hours in long lines for their share of aid distribution.

The sign "Yungay Is Reborn Here" greeted visitors to the city on May 31, 1971, the anniversary of the disaster.

Archbishop Bambaren, a native Yungaíno, signs the official act of foundation of the new city of Yungay.

Survivors and visitors gather at the palms on the avalanche scar for a requiem mass on the anniversary of the disaster.

The first officially recognized town council of Yungay, all of them survivors.

The plaza, market area, and municipal offices of the new city, July 1980.

Auto-construcción houses, old-style adobe dwellings, and module buildings in new Yungay ten years after the disaster.

Chapter 9

1979 at the age of forty-two, consumed by the cancer which had spread throughout his body, his once-robust frame shrunken to a child's weight. Rodolfo's death shook the community of Yungay profoundly. It was Rodolfo's indomitable spirit after the disaster that had kept many people from succumbing altogether to their grief and despair. His rough, "cowboy of the road" spirit and his warmth and good humor, especially about himself (*"Soy como el oso, feo pero cariñoso"*; I'm like the bear, ugly but affectionate), endeared him to all in the community. He was a bastion of rough, good-natured strength to his fellow survivors.

With Rodolfo's death, Rosa had once again been stripped of her loved one and left alone, this time deeply in debt for Rodolfo's surgery. With characteristic willpower, Rosa resumed her life and her work and by 1980 had paid off all the medical bills. She lives alone in her house in Punyan, not too far from a younger couple, whose large and still growing family visit her often. Everyone calls her "Mama Rosa." Luisa and her husband live in Yungay and visit her often with her first grandson. Despite the tragedies that have afflicted her life, Rosa has changed very little. A decade that would have defeated many has not dimmed the spark in her eyes nor her good humor. Rosa is anything but defeated. The strength of her spirit has drawn new people to her, and her gifts to them come as fully and as freely as to those in the past. She is a survivor.

Since the disaster the fortunes of Augusto and Meche Angeles have continued to improve. He is now Yungay's largest retail storeowner and also one of its major wholesalers. In 1978 he was declared a "notable citizen." With the considerable economic power behind him, he was naturally granted one of the large stores built by the reconstruction authority in the market, and soon he began construction of a second floor to the building for a warehouse. The inside of his store is as jammed and cluttered as it was in the market module, and he and Meche continue to work from dawn to dusk with the same good humor and courtesy. They decided not to buy a Russian house and have built a large two-story adobe home in the community of Pampac close to their land. Their home is just visible from the entrance of their store. Many of the cholo entrepreneurs have enjoyed considerable success in the new community, although none have achieved Augusto's level. Nonetheless, the success of individuals like Augusto is a measure of the degree to which the disaster made mobility possible for people who had been preparing for such change for a long time. When the opportunity came, they seized it, and their increasing status and well-being in today's Yungay demonstrate how well they have succeeded.

The quality of life has improved somewhat for most people since the construction of the new city. The pace of life, the nature of social interaction, and the general pattern of existence generally conform, as would be expected, to those of highland towns in general. Dusty and sprawling, Yungay lacks the picturesque charm of its northern neighbor, Caraz, although life in the two cities follows much the same pattern. What distinguishes Yungay from its neighbors is the fact that physically it is not a product of the people or their culture. They chose the location but very little else. For this reason Yungaíno attitudes about the physical appearance of their town are mixed at best. "How do you see us?" they ask. "A little better, no?" they say, but without much enthusiasm, surrounded by their municipality, their new market, their new schools, their new Russian or *auto-construcción* houses, very few of which have conformed to traditional patterns or needs. The new municipality, for example, is an impressive structure with its large glassed front and its high vaulted ceilings, but once inside, one immediately realizes that it was not designed with any knowledge of highland conditions. Although the sun may burn brightly in the Andes, in the shade it is always cool. On the hottest of days in Yungay, the public employees and officials must wear sweaters or jackets in the high-ceilinged rooms of the municipality. Its glass front and high ceilings do not conserve warmth at all and are complained about by everyone who enters the building. The market's high ceilings produce the same effect, and it is only rarely that all the stalls are rented. People would rather sit on the ground in the sun to sell their goods than freeze in the frigid market building.

Perhaps symbolic of the relationship of Yungaínos to their new city is the plaza with its beautiful rose gardens and acoustic shell. The roses are arranged in seven trapezoidal-shaped gardens with the narrow ends pointing toward the acoustic shell in the plaza's center. The different colors of roses each represent a different region, nation, or continent: red and white for Peru, bright pink for Yungay, black for Africa, yellow for Asia, light purple for Oceania, copper-orange for Europe, and pink for the Americas. The rose gardens, surrounded by brilliant green hedges, are the pride of Yungay. But the gardens are marred by the centerpiece of the plaza, the acoustic shell, a large concrete, vaguely modernistic shape resembling upended bat wings. The Yungaínos detest the acoustic shell. The architects who designed Yungay did not consult with them when they planned it and, presumably unaware of the symbolic importance of a town plaza, blithely put the shell where the traditional plaza fountain should be. When it was first built Yungaíno men joked and commented bitterly about the *concha acoustica*. "Concha" meaning shell in Peruvian Spanish is also a slang term for female genitals. There were many threats to dynamite the huge cement shell, but since there was nothing to replace it, the reconstruction was still incomplete, and the authorities were still an active presence in the town, nothing was done, although the discontent with the shell did not diminish. The shell demonstrates the ambivalent relationship of Yungaínos to their new town. They fought hard to have their town relocated in its present site, but its actual construction was out of their hands. They are in the difficult position of being torn between gratitude for aid and resentment at the loss of autonomy and responsibility. From the very first Yungaínos needed and requested help, but they also requested that they be given a role, a voice in the structuring of that aid and its delivery. For a brief time, they were given major roles in the distribution of emergency aid. Yungaínos often complained that they would have preferred to build their own city, according to their own standards, with only economic assistance.

By the time plans were being made for the construction of the new city, the architects and engineers did little consulting with the people of Yungay and tended to present them with schemes and plans which were in fact already under way. In fairness, it must be said that the reconstruction authority was limited in its design by the forms of structures that had been donated to Yungay. For example, the wooden Russian houses with their glassed-in porches, windows on all sides, and compact design make the construction of traditional Andean housing and streets virtually impossible. However, the design of the municipality and the market also make it evident that the architects were unaware of shifts of temperature from sunlight to shade in the Andean region.

Now that construction of all public structures but the new church, which is being financed by donations from the West German Catholic church, is completed, the Yungaínos are making plans to remove the acoustic shell and replace it with a fountain. A fountain is being designed by a Yungaíno in Lima, and donations to finance its construction are being sought both in Yungay and in the community of Yungaínos in Lima. The Yungaínos grin maliciously when they speak of the party they are going to have when they finally dynamite the acoustic shell.

As the construction of the new city is a constant issue in daily life, the destruction of the old city is never far from consciousness either. Although life there approximates normalcy, Yungay is not a normal Andean city, and the comparison of their new, strange settlement with what they once knew often evokes thoughts of their tragedy, although few of them now dwell on it at length. There are some losses from which it is difficult ever to recover fully. For many Yungaínos the shadows of their loss remain even though they are now fully engaged in new lives. Some prefer not to speak of the disaster, at least to strangers. Jaime Villón, who now makes his living driving tourists to the glacial Llanganuco lagoons high between Huascarán and Huandoy, says that when he is asked about the day of the tragedy, he tells the tourists that he was in Lima that day in order not to talk about it. Some people speak about their ordeal in general terms without ever going into detail. When Yungaínos who live elsewhere return home after extended absences, they may feel "traumatized" briefly again. One young woman, recently returned from Lima to live in Yungay, was just sixteen when the disaster hit. She told how she saw people enveloped by the avalanche and just stood there and waited for her own death. She was standing next to her house, which was buried, one of the few in Cochahuaín to be destroyed, but the avalanche missed her. She was taken to Lima in the first wave of orphans and placed in a private boarding school run by nuns, one of whom was the sister of Aurea Terry de Fernandez, who paid for the rest of her education. She becomes visibly affected when she talks of the disaster and Yungay. Her eyes become filled with tears and redden and her glance darts around the room. The memories are terribly painful for her still, as they are for others, but they do not hesitate to speak of them among themselves.

Some people make jokes, albeit grim ones, about the tragedy. When I returned in the summer of 1980, I ran into an old friend, Alvaro Colón, and asked how he was. Putting on a mournful face, he replied that he was just about ready to go and "make skulls and bones" with his Yungay friends in heaven. Later on that week, a group of us climbed into Jaime Villón's truck for a trip up to Llanganuco. The road to Llanganuco more or less follows the path of the avalanche and ultimately winds right past the awesome north face of Huascarán. As we wound our way laboriously up the steep road, taking hairpin turn after hairpin turn, the avalanche always on our right and Huascarán looming above us, Alvaro kept making jokes about another avalanche which would finish us off for good. When we reached the pass with its ominous overhanging cliffs, there were a few jokes, nervous ones to be sure, about not wanting to die just yet, especially there. When we drove across the upper part of the avalanche, directly in the face of Huascarán, people spoke about the power of the avalanche and the danger of Huascarán. In effect, the disaster is far from a taboo topic in Yungay. Talking and joking about Huascarán and the disaster are ways of defusing the anxiety, which all Yungaínos have about their environment.

The first year of misery after the disaster is also recalled, by some even with a certain bittersweet nostalgia, as one would reflect on a difficult experience in which one found strength and good friends. During that same summer of 1980, I was working in the municipality, copying birth statistics one afternoon, when Shamu Mendez, one of the famous Chupamaros, came in, slightly inebriated. Since I had arrived only a few days before, we had not yet seen each other, and he threw his arms around me in a warm *abrazo* of greeting. For some reason, perhaps seeing me again after some time, he began to speak of the year I spent in Yungay after the tragedy.

After the disaster, what a life! Brother what a life! Everything had ended for us and we just said the hell with everything. Brother, did we drink! Remember all those nights we got drunk? You should write all those memories, all those things that happened to us that year. How we suffered! How we all suffered together! How beautiful that life! How beautiful that life of suffering! of brotherhood! We suffered together, even though it was terrible, it was also beautiful!

Some Yungaínos seem to look at the disaster as a kind of supreme test, the thing which on one level at least ties the survivors into one body. This is the transforming experience almost in a ritual sense. To speak of that year after the disaster as beautiful is to recognize the value of the bonds, of the relationships which were formed in that liminal period of isolation during which the encampment of Yungay was separated from the world by the uniqueness of its tragedy and suffering. Shamu is not the only person to look back on that year in terms of friendship and strength in suffering. Many see it as terrible, but they exalt in having survived it. No survivors are glad that the tragedy occurred, and would reverse history if they could, but many feel they have passed through a trial which few have had to suffer and have survived, transformed, both stronger for it and perhaps more vulnerable in certain ways, but different, elevated by a realm of experience which tested them in ways few have been tested. Yungaínos are proud they are survivors.

Some broader questions remain. Why is Yungay significant? Why should we take the time to consider this disaster and reconstruction process more than any other? In a general sense the Yungaínos do not display any marked differences from other people in the midst of a catastrophic event. Most people did not panic. Flight in this instance was a rational response. The immediate postimpact period was characterized by shock followed relatively soon by rescue and initial aid activities. Somewhat later as aid began to arrive, old schisms reappeared in exaggerated form, and social conflicts broke out as individuals and groups began to compete for scarce assistance resources. Later, some of the conflicts became submerged as people closed ranks against outside aid agencies who were felt to be unfeeling, insincere, and inefficient. People and groups in many disasters around the world conform in a general way to this pattern and sequence of behavior.

The real significance of Yungay lies in what it reveals about the importance of community and its ritual and symbolic expressions for survival in a time characterized by massive, dislocating changes, caused not just by disasters, but by political upheaval and the projects of powerful interests in the name of development. As Thayer Scudder has proposed, communities undergoing severe stress, particularly the stress of resettlement, tend to draw inward and adopt a security orientation, emphasizing increased solidarity and adherence to cultural tradition (1973). Despite total destruction and its severe emotional consequences, the Yungaínos were able to weather their individual and collective traumas. They reconstructed their community and lives largely through the choice of secure, known solutions to problems in their new community through a unified social movement motivated largely by adherence to a complex of material solutions and cultural traditions.

What we have seen develop in Yungay in that first year of aftermath and in the succeeding decade I believe demonstrates some basic and

261

important elements of human life and the response of human beings to certain increasingly common forms of change. What we have seen is the development of an essentially conservative pattern of interrelated adaptations to a force of overwhelming destruction and change. This conservatism has nothing to do with politics. Rather it is directed at maintaining a basic continuity of understanding of one's surroundings in the midst of chaos and confusion. By maintaining this line of continuity one can begin to understand, cope with, and even embrace change.

The problems facing the Yungay survivors on that apocalyptic afternoon in May more than a decade ago involved virtually every aspect of their lives. The disaster was an all-encompassing, total immersion event for every Yungaíno and tested to the utmost the coping skills of individuals and the adaptive capacities of what was left of the community. The basic problems of immediate individual material survival in most cases were solved fairly rapidly by donations. What was more crucial was the rebuilding and continued existence of a system of material provisioning of society. Urban Yungaínos knew that their community could not be materially sustained by aid for very long and immediately set to work to restore the links between their growing tent encampment and the network of traditional peasant agricultural communities, which had fed their lost community. This system of material sustenance, essentially a complex of articulated modes of production, was threatened by the government relocation plans to an area of lower peasant population density. The preservation of this system became one of the primary rationales for resisting relocation and remaining in an area with less security from future geologic accidents. For urban Yungaínos, the system of peasant agriculture tied to the local market worked, providing the food and labor that the nonproducing urban population needed to survive. Relocation threatened the material survival of an urban center as envisioned by urban survivors. Even the peasants, traditionally exploited in their economic relationships with the town, collaborated in the resistance, since relocation of the town simply increased the distance they would have had to travel to another market, which held little promise of either better prices or decreased exploitation.

The strategies adopted by the individuals and the community in the social sphere displayed an equally conservative defensive tendency. In the hours and days following the avalanche, people recognized the need for unity and cooperation of all people if they were to solve their problems. Each individual faced problems which he could not solve alone. Since virtually all individuals faced the problems of shelter, warmth, clothing, and food, they became community-wide problems. When aid arrived, constituting a scarce resource in a desperately needy community, it reawakened the sharp lines of social and ethnic differentiation between Indian peasants and the middle- and upper-class urban survivors. In a stratified society such as highland Peru, aid that is perceived to be distributed along egalitarian lines runs against the goal of the middle and upper classes, which is ultimately the maintenance of relative class position. Essentially the problem in the emergency aid period was first to make sure that one's own needs were properly taken care of and second to see that the interests of one's social group were secured. Conflicts tended to be first individual and then class oriented as groups began to defend their traditional rights under the old system. With the threat of relocation, the social conflicts did not disappear but were temporarily submerged in the new cohesion stimulated by the resistance. Once the battle against relocation was won and community survival guaranteed, the focus of interests and identifications returned again to the individual and his specific group in the social hierarchy as he reconstituted and rebuilt his own personal community and future. In short, once the community was assured of survival, people could attend to individual interests again. The social behavior of Yungaínos corresponded throughout with certain difficult-to-demarcate time phases in the disaster; the patterns of allegiance and identification altered in relation to the problems facing both individuals and society during the lengthy processes of recovery and reconstruction. The population of Yungay fragmented and coalesced a number of times around specific problems crucial to the survival of both the individual and society. The separation and coincidence of individual and societal concerns at different times became crucial to the survival of both in traditional terms.

From a social psychological standpoint, the essentially conservative strategies of Yungay, in particular the resistance to further resettlement, proved to be highly adaptive in that the survivors were able to regain a sense of participation in and control over their own lives and society, as well as to combat changes which would have meant further dislocation and stress. Overwhelming force, such as that of a disaster, has a way of demonstrating to human beings the puniness of their greatest efforts and constitutes a very real threat to sociocultural identity and social integrity and stability. The resistance to resettlement was important in that it enabled survivors to begin reestablishing a positive image of themselves as important, significant actors in their own lives. In this context, a culture, to be optimally effective psychologically as an adaptive mechanism, must "provide means by which the individual ego can be sustained, by which the individual may preserve at least a minimally satisfactory image of his self" (Goldschmidt 1974:28). As I mentioned previously, a natural disaster, particularly an overwhelming one, tends to demonstrate to survivors the relative weakness of human effort. When disaster's impact is compounded by disaster aid, which, coming from metropolitan centers or more developed nations, may be distributed in ways that diminish the sense of worth of both individuals and communities, the overall effect can be devastating. In Yungay, the avalanche demolished their city, their homes, and their families. Then the reconstruction authorities attempted to relocate them. Yungaínos felt abused and diminished by both nature and man. The conservative stance embodied primarily in the refusal to relocate, constituted a stand not only for their city, but also for themselves as people worthy of consideration.

This same conservative stance of refusal to relocate and the fervent adherence to Yungaíno identity proved to be key elements in the reestablishment of emotional equilibrium and in psychological survival for most people. We have spoken of the survivor community's allegiance to its past history and people. There was also an allegiance to a formally defined community as well as a material bond to a complex of modes of production and a socioeconomic order. In Yungay the urban resident was proud of himself, of his personal dignity and individuality, regardless of his place in the highly stratified social order, and great care was taken to maintain certain external evidence of this dignity. But the individual was also proud of being a Yungaíno, an identity which for ideological and material reasons bonded him to a wider collectivity. In Yungay the word *community* included a broader context, signifying relationships among individuals and relationships between individuals and a totality. The totality had a complex social, political, economic, and cultural identity with an overarching ideology enacted frequently in rituals of community identity and solidarity, as seen in the rites of political commemoration, the Indian fiesta cycle, and the numerous social and religious organizations dedicated to the various community functions and purposes.

Consequently, when disaster struck and disorganization and potential dissolution of the community followed, Yungaínos had a rich public, symbolic, and ritual fund to draw on in defense not only of those aspects of individual identity, but of the way of life itself, including an economy, a social hierarchy, and an ideological structure. Even some of those people traditionally most exploited by that threatened system rallied to its cause. Yungaínos could and did reactivate their community again in concrete ritual actions involving recognized public symbols, which helped restore the lost sense of community and actively gave it new life, in turn becoming a resource the survivors could draw on to infuse their shattered lives with meanings rooted in family and community tradition.

After the disaster, certain aspects of the environment assumed enormous importance for both individuals and the community as a whole. Proximity to the avalanche scar constituted loyalty to and solidarity with one's tradition and one's dead. Close to the site of destruction, people experienced profoundly the grief from their losses and fully recognized the therapeutic nature of their grieving and individual and communal rituals of mourning on the avalanche, thus minimizing the potential pathology recognized as impaired mourning. It has been suggested that remaining in the general proximity of the avalanche scar could have proved important in the mastery of the trauma of the disaster event through the experience of the context in less threatening circumstances. Finally, it was in Yungay that survivors were able to undertake the formulation process as they fought through the relocation conflict with the reconstruction authority, revitalizing their lives by finding meaning in a cause, a conflict, rather than in the despair of cataclysmic destruction.

The strategies employed consciously and unconsciously by Yungaínos in their struggle to survive reveal an essentially conservative tendency characteristic of many people caught up in many instances of rapid social change. The conservatism was predominantly a defensive stance against the incursion of further stress. In choosing to remain close to the site of their buried city and in resisting other changes, the survivors were enhancing in their perceptions the material well-being of their growing community and reducing the amount of cognitive restructuring which adapting to a new environment would have necessitated. Relocation meant further change, further disruption, further risk. Yungaínos wanted to rebuild, to return to things as they were, to return to normalcy. Their strategies of resistance to change constituted an adherence to the known, the proven, the secure and ultimately became an affirmation of their identity and a defense against cultural collapse. The conservative posture of their strategies emerges from two basic features of human life and cognition, namely the ability to organize the world and our experience of it into categories and to predict with some approximation future events on the basis of knowledge accumulated through personal experience or the experience of others.

The categories emerge from our experience of the real conditions of existence which are concrete and objective. Our categories, however, are ephemeral. They are composed of culturally idiosyncratic symbols and concepts. Thus, an empty feeling in the stomach becomes a concept—hunger—with a variety of impacts, meanings, and solutions attached to it. Recall once again Handwerker's useful phrase, we are in "a dialectic of meaning and materiality," moving constantly between our understandings and the objects of our understandings, both of which guide, structure, and otherwise affect our behavior (1980).

As social creatures, living together and dependent upon each other in a variety of ways, we experience the real conditions of existence in similar ways, resulting in shared patterns of understandings about life, essentially a common conceptual order requiring a degree of consistency or stability over time. This common constellation of ideas, understandings, and concepts constitutes a culture, and the individual's state of awareness of the systemic qualities of his culture, society, roles, and relationships has been variously termed a mazeway, a true society, or one's individual perceptual order. However it is labeled, the basic concept refers to the way each individual deals with the total physical and sociocultural environment. That is, we all have to solve a series of problems in life—nutrition, shelter, work, social, and sexual relationships—and we accomplish these largely through our own adaptations within the institutionalized forms of our culture. Because we are able to satisfy needs and wants through our culture's institutionalized forms, we grow to associate our ways with the benefits of existence. They not only supply us with solutions to problems, they lend order, stability, and predictability to life.

The second major feature of human cognition is precisely that predictability, the fact that we are able to predict within certain limitations future events on the basis of our common conceptual order, which is largely composed of accepted understandings, knowledge, and past experience. This indispensable ability to predict enables us to move forward, to take purposeful action in life based on the probabilities of success (or failure) understood from what is known from past knowledge and experience. The ideas, concepts, and assumptions people share about themselves, each other, and the world in general not only allow for mutual intelligibility, but enable them to make sense out of what has gone on, what is going on, and what may go on around them. In short, our culture in general and our "mazeways" in particular are mental structures of understandings about the conditions of existence which not only help us to solve the basic material problems, but also give us the means to reduce raw experience of life to some form of comprehensible order. It is little wonder that when that order is threatened, we hasten to defend it.

When the pattern of life has been radically and, in particular, suddenly altered, the usual response of people is to attempt to assimilate the events into existing structures in order to preserve the continuity of understanding which enables us to predict events reliably and respond effectively to them. Our ability to deal with change, then, depends upon the capacity of our basic conceptual order to integrate new events or concepts without major disruption. If, however, new events or concepts threaten the basic assumptions of our culture, we risk the loss or invalidation of that fundamental sense of order. As Peter Marris puts it:

When a pattern of relationships is disrupted in any way for which we are not fully prepared, the thread of continuity in the interpretation of life becomes attenuated or altogether lost. The loss may threaten the integrity of the structure of meanings on which the continuity rests and cannot be acknowledged without distress. But if life is to go on, the continuity must somehow be restored. When the loss is irretrievable, there must be a reinterpretation of what we have learned about our purposes and our attachments and the principles which underlie the regularity of experience—radical enough to trace out the thread again. To do this, the loss must be first accepted as something we have to understand, not just as an event that has happened, but as a series of events that we must now expect to happen and a retrospect of earlier events whose familiar meaning has now been shadowed by our changed circumstances (1975:24).

If a society's abilities to respond to the needs of its members are threatened by either internal disintegration or external force, the capacity

267

of its members to order their experience and generate the predictions which make purposeful behavior possible will be similarly endangered. When these conditions occur we can see from the historical and ethnographic record an interesting spectrum of responses. In some cases, such as the Buffalo Creek flood of 1972, the response of victims takes the form of apathy and decay, and if the predictions hold true, a tragic further disintegration of that community will continue (Erikson 1976). Catastrophe and crisis often stimulate the appearance of millennialism as "a deliberate, organized, conscious effort by members of a society to construct a more satisfying culture" (Wallace 1956b:265). Millennarian movements replete with prophets, promises of destruction of enemies, and unending well-being appear among such widely diverse cultures undergoing severe stress as European peasantries of the Middle Ages, nineteenth-century American Plains Indians, and contemporary urban Iranians. Other groups respond to particularly protracted stress by insulating themselves in defensively structured communities from external threats to which no accommodation is possible. The Mormons, the Amish, shtetl Jews, and various American Indian groups have responded in this fashion to permit the continuance of traditional patterns of behavior and belief in the enclosed community (Barkun 1974:78). The "negotiated traditionalism" of Yungay, representing an essentially conservative posture of adhering as much as possible to traditional forms while accepting certain inevitable changes, constitutes still another behavioral alternative in the face of radical change.

The strategies in Yungay were aimed at restoring the regularity of experience to all realms of life. Having been forcibly torn from their community, homes, and families by the avalanche, the Yungaínos were striving to reestablish a sense of continuity with what they had lost. Their conservative strategies did not constitute a fantasized millennialism of returning to a lost, golden age, but rather a rational attempt to retrieve what was both materially viable as well as culturally and psychologically valuable and necessary for use as a new foundation for a new community. Their strategies, both intentionally and unintentionally, developed in an effective and functional fashion to reestablish the links of continuity with the lost community on every front, from the complex of modes of production through the social structure to the individual and societal patterns of mourning. By electing to remain close to the site of their buried city, Yungaínos were reestablishing a number of continuities—the continuity of an assured means of provisioning their society, the continuity of experience, and the consistency of conceptual order—which would enable them to face future changes. Their adherence to a traditional location constituted a declaration that they would take their chances with the known dangers of the mountain rather than risk virtually everything, the entire order of their lives in every aspect, with an impersonal institution of a society in essentially strange hands.

Indeed, Yungay demonstrates the high social, economic, and psychological stakes that are at issue from the perspective of people caught up in all forms of rapid planned and unplanned change. During my research one afternoon in Yungay, I stopped to speak to a farmer working his small plot of land in Aura, the island between the two lobes of the avalanche. In the course of our conversation, I asked him why he would not consider moving since he was so close to the path of the avalanche. Sweeping his arm over the panorama of Huascarán, gleaming brilliantly in the afternoon sunshine, the fields scarred by the avalanche and the settlements of provisional housing, he exclaimed, "Here there is life!" The implications of any other alternative were obvious in his eyes.

Bibliography

Agency for International Development. 1970. *Peru Earthquake, May 31, 1970,* reprint from *Tenth Report, Fiscal Year 1970,* issued by Disaster Relief Coordinator, Agency for International Development.

Angeles, Artemio. 1963. *Yungay, Tierra Mia,* Lima: "El Ferrocarril."

Arteaga Losza, Walter, and Losza Mendez, Ricardo. n.d. *Yungay Ciudad: Martir y Bella,* unpublished ms.

Barkun, Michael. 1974. *Disaster and the Millennium,* New Haven: Yale University Press.

Barth, Fredrik. 1969. *Ethnic Groups and Boundaries,* Boston: Little Brown.

Barton, Allen H. 1970. *Communities in Disaster,* Garden City, N.Y.: Anchor Books, Doubleday and Company.

Bates, F. L., C. W. Fogleman, V. J. Parenton, R. H. Pittman, and G. S. Tracy. 1963. *The Social and Psychological Consequences of a Natural Disaster: A Longitudinal Study of Hurricane Audrey,* Disaster Study No. 18, Washington, D.C.: National Academy of Sciences, National Research Council.

Bell, Daniel. 1979. *The Cultural Contradictions of Capitalism,* New York: Basic Books.

Belshaw, Cyril. 1965. *Traditional Exchange and Modern Markets,* Englewood Cliffs, N.J.: Prentice-Hall.

Bettleheim, Bruno. 1960. *The Informed Heart,* Glencoe, Ill.: The Free Press.

Bode, Barbara. 1977. "Disaster, Social Structure, and Myth in the Peruvian Andes: The Genesis of an Explanation," *Annals of the New York Academy of Sciences* 293:246–74.

Bohannan, Paul. 1963. *Social Anthropology,* New York: Holt, Rinehart and Winston.

Carrasco, Juan, Joel Ramírez, and Delina León. 1962. "Historia de Yungay," in *Libro de Oro de Yungay,* edited by Alberto Carrión Vergara, Lima: Editorial Juridica, S.A.

Carrión Vergara, Alberto (ed.). 1962. *Libro de Oro de Yungay,* Lima: Editorial Juridica, S.A.

Bibliography

Dobyns, Henry, and Paul L. Doughty. 1976. *Peru: A Cultural History,* New York: Oxford University Press.

Doughty, Paul L. 1968. *Huaylas,* Ithaca: Cornell University Press.

———. 1970. "What Will We Do When the Rains Come?," unpublished report of the Peru Earthquake Relief Committee.

Dworkin, Judith. n.d. *Major Natural Disasters, 1957–1977,* Boulder: Natural Hazards Research and Applications Information Center.

Erickson, George E., George Plafker, and Jaime Fernandez Concha. 1970. *Preliminary Report on the Geologic Events Associated with the May 31, 1970 Earthquake,* Washington, D.C.: U.S. Department of the Interior.

Erikson, Kai. 1976. *Everything in Its Path,* New York: Simon and Schuster.

Fritz, Charles. 1968. "Disasters," in *International Encyclopedia of the Social Sciences,* edited by Davíd L. Sills, vol. 4, The MacMillen Company and the Free Press.

Gillin, John. 1965. "Ethos Components in Modern Latin American Culture," in *Contemporary Cultures and Societies of Latin America,* edited by Dwight B. Heath and Richard N. Adams, New York: Random House.

Glantz, Michael. 1976. *The Politics of Natural Disaster,* New York: Praeger.

Goldschmidt, Walter. 1974. "Ethology, Ecology and Ethnological Realities," in *Coping and Adaptations,* edited by G. V. Coelho, D. Hamburg, and J. E. Adams, New York: Basic Books.

Gridilla, Alberto. 1937. *Ancahs y sus antiguos corregimientos,* Arequipa: Editorial La Colmena.

Handwerker, W. Penn. 1980. "Anthropology, Economics and Ecology," unpublished paper.

Heath, Dwight B., and Richard N. Adams (eds.). 1965. *Contemporary Cultures and Societies of Latin America,* New York: Random House.

Honigmann, John. 1976. "The Personal Approach in Cultural Anthropological Research," *Current Anthropology* 17(2): 243–62.

Lifton, Robert J. 1967. *Death in Life, Survivors of Hiroshima,* New York: Random House.

———, 1981. "Advocacy and Corruption in the Healing Professions," in *Nourishing the Humanistic: Essays in the Dialogue Between the Social Sciences and Medical Education,* edited by William R. Rogers and David Barnard, Pittsburgh: University of Pittsburgh Press.

Mangin, William. 1967. *Las Comunidades Alteñas de America Latina.* Mexico, D.F.: Instituto Indigenista Interamericano.

Marris, Peter. 1975. *Loss and Change,* Garden City, N.Y.: Anchor Books, Doubleday and Company.

Montoya, Rodrigo. 1970. *Informe DESCO sobre el sismo,* Lima: Cuadernos DESCO.

Oliver-Smith, Anthony. 1977a. "Traditional Agriculture, Central Places and

Bibliography

Post-Disaster Urban Relocation in Peru," *American Ethnologist* 4(1): 102–16.

————. 1977b. "Disaster Rehabilitation and Social Change in Yungay, Peru," *Human Organization* 6(3):491–509.

————. 1979. "The Crisis Dyad: Meaning and Culture in Anthropology and Medicine," in *Nourishing the Humanistic in Medicine,* edited by William R. Rogers and David Barnard, Pittsburgh: University of Pittsburgh Press.

————. 1982. "Here There is Life: The Social and Cultural Dynamics of Successful Resistance to Resettlement in Postdisaster Peru," in *Involuntary Migration and Resettlement: The Problems and Responses of Dislocated People,* edited by Art Hansen and Anthony Oliver-Smith, Boulder: Westview Press.

Orlove, Benjamin. 1977. *Alpacas, Sheep and Men,* New York: Academic Press.

Patch, Richard. 1970. *The Peruvian Earthquake of 1970, Part IV: Yungay,* American Universities Field Staff Report, West Coast South America Series no. 9.

Peretz, David. 1970. "Development, Object-Relationships and Loss," in *Loss and Grief: Psychological Management in Medical Practice,* edited by B. Schoenberg, A. C. Carr, D. Peretz, and A. H. Kutscher, New York: Columbia University Press.

————. 1970. "Reaction to Loss," in *Loss and Grief: Psychological Management in Medical Practice,* edited by B. Schoenberg, A. C. Carr, D. Peretz, and A. H. Kutscher, New York: Columbia University Press.

Prince, Samuel H. 1920. *Catastrophe and Social Change,* New York: Columbia University Press.

Schwimmer, Eric G. 1969. *Cultural Consequences of a Volcanic Eruption Experienced by the Mount Lamington Orokaiva,* Eugene: Department of Anthropology, University of Oregon.

Scudder, Thayer. 1973. "The Impact of Human Activities on the Physical and Social Environments: New Directions in Anthropological Ecology: Manmade Dams and Resettlement," *Annual Review of Anthropology* 2:27–61.

Stein, William. 1961. *Hualcan: Life in the Highlands of Peru,* Ithaca: Cornell University Press.

Trigger, Bruce. 1972. Determinants of Urban Growth in Pre-Industrial Societies," in *Man, Settlement and Urbanism,* edited by P. Ucko, R. Tringham, and G. W. Dimbleby, London and Cambridge, Mass.: Gerald Duckworth and Schenkman.

Turner, Victor. 1961. *The Ritual Process,* Chicago: Aldine Publishing Co.

Urdang, Laurence. 1968. *The Random House Dictionary of the English Language.* New York: Random House.

van den Berghe, Pierre, and George Primov. 1977. *Inequality in the Peruvian Andes.* Columbia: University of Missouri Press.

Bibliography

Wallace, Anthony F. C. 1956a. "Mazeway Resynthesis: A Biocultural Theory of Religius Inspiration," *Transactions of the New York Academy of Sciences* 18 (7):626–38.

———. 1956b. "Revitalization Movements," *American Anthropologist* 58:264–81.

———. 1957. "Mazeway Disintegration: The Individual's Perception of Sociocultural Disorganization," *Human Organization* 16 (2):23–27.

Walton, Nyle. 1974. "Human Spatial Organization in an Andean Valley: The Callejón de Huaylas, Peru," Ph.D. dissertation, Department of Geography, University of Georgia.

Zavaleta Figueroa, Isaías. 1970. *El Callejón de Huaylas Antes y Despues del Terremoto,* vols. I, II, and III (vols. II and III published in 1971), Caraz: Ediciones Paron.

Index

275

Index

Index

223; responses to, 268; studies of, 20; tragedy as a condition, 27. *See also* emotions; event, the

Dobyns, Henry, and Paul L. Doughty, 37, 38

Doughty, Paul, 101, 170, 180, 216

drunkenness, 103, 123, 139, 162, 172, 178, 190

Dworkin, Judith, 13

earthquakes: Guatemalan and Nicaraguan, 75; Yungay, 4, 11, 75

economics: business conflicts, 149; buyer/seller ratio, 126; communication and transportation, 52, 57, 59, 69, 72, 73, 82; postdisaster, 110–12; resumption of marketing, 25, 110, 126, 128, 129, 132, 164, 205–7. *See also* agriculture

education, 44, 45, 53, 55, 61, 63, 65, 67; retention of the institutions of, 112, 132, 164, 215

electricity, 69, 72, 239, 240, 241

emotions: crying in public, 185–87, 194; disaster and stability of, 28, 76, 136–39, 146, 149, 157, 164, 216, 268; faith, 199; feelings of abandonment and isolation, 76, 78, 81, 83, 88, 98, 156, 163, 188, 200; grief, 28, 162, 179, 184–87, 188; mourning, 180, 184–87, 192–94; psychological impact of aid, 88, 153, 159, 261, 264; self-anger, 189; stress, 83, 88, 109, 148, 260, 261; tragedy as a condition, 27, 188, 189

encomienda, 35

Erickson, George E., George Plafker, and Jaime Fernandez Concha, 12

Erikson, Kai, 268

estancia, 65

ethnicity, 33, 49–69; displaced by needs for human contact, 76

event systems, 16

event, the, 4–5; emergency period of, 76–78, 81, 85, 88, 99, 100, 106, 147; first two weeks of, 86, 87, 100, 109, 136, 147; liminal period of, 217; meaningful integration of, 198–201; months after, one, 97, 110, 117, two, 110, 111, three, 102, 177, four, 20, six, 103, 111, 164, 189; rehabilitation and reconstruction

period of, 99, 105; studies on, 156; the year after, 148, 157, 160

experience and predictability, 15, 16, 17, 267–68

Expreso Serrano, 3, 20, 110, 122, 174, 183, 210; the owner of, 21, 174, 205, 206, 210, 212

Falcón, Roberto (pseudonym), 2, 4, 7, 55, 73, 80, 120, 135, 173, 181, 246

field hospitals, 89

fiesta cycle, 213

Flores, Antonio (pseudonym), 7, 59, 121, 154, 164, 167, 247

fountain, 47, 258

friendship, 59, 122, 171–75; los Chupamaros, 173

Fritz, Charles, 78

Fundo Concepción, 102, 105

gente decente, 59, 137; decente, 58, 60, 152

gente grande, 61

geology, 105, 199

Gillin, John, 48

Giraldo, Miguel (pseudonym), 166, 171, 186, 221

Glantz, Michael, 14

gorrero (hustler, freeloader), 106

Gran Unidad Escolar Santa Inéz de Yungay, 52, 112, 215

Gridilla, Alberto, 36

grief: for culture, 188; sharing, 28, 162, 179, 184–87; sorrow, 26, 137; tragedy and, 27, 188, 189; venting of, 153

hacendados, 139, 152

haciendas, 54, 65; the teniente, 67, 78, 117, 131, 243, 246; Timbrac, 54, 67, 117, 245

Handwerker, W. Penn, 15, 266

"Hay que trabajar para vivir," 159

health, 89, 98, 100, 106–8

hermanos, 181

Hidalgo, Rafael, 229

Hiroshima, 191

history, contrasted to social change, 16

hombre culto, 45

homeless dead, the, 191, 192

Honigmann, John, 27

277

Index

Index

Index

267; class percentages and, 118, 128; rehabilitation system and, 101, 150

social classes: class distinctions, 238, 240, 242; elite, 53–58, 119–20, 245–46; Indian, 131; lower, 60–62, 65–69, 123, 125–30, 176; middle, 58–60, 121–23, 148–50, 247; networks of, 210; terraced housing and, 109, 143

social mobility, 51, 62, 65, 117, 123, 125, 130, 243, 256–57. *See also, as examples of, for elites,* Beltrán, Juan; Falcón, Roberto; Robles, Emilio; *for lower classes,* Angeles, Augusto and Mercedes; Cantaro, Arturo; Martínez, Rosa; Tamaríz brothers; *for middle class,* Armendariz, Rodolfo; Bellido, Epifanio; Flores, Antonio

society: consensus/conflict dialectic of, 216–18, 223, 263, 266; dual village system of, 207–9; hazard management in, 13; infrastructure of, 241; land ownership and, 37, 38, 50, 54, 65; life-cycle celebrations of, 177–83, 190; living and dead in, 48, 190–98; "notable citizen" of, 256; open meetings of, 209, 211; personalization in, 142; postdisaster conflicts in, 147, 151; postdisaster utopia of, 76; refugee camp, 145, 161–68; restructuring, 263; selflessness in, 127; status-leveling effects and, 146, 147; symbols of survival of, 218–21; urban development and, 236–40, 258; urban/rural relations in, 64, 67, 68, 136–39, 146

soledad, 247

sorrow, 26, 137

Spain, 52

Stein, William, 170

Tallín (the Russian), 97

Tamaríz brothers (pseudonym), 4, 62, 117, 129

tapaco, 55

"Tengo mi modulo," 144

teniente, 246

terms of address, 67, 193

theft, 100, 137, 151

Third World cities, 106, 240

Timbrac (hacienda), 54, 67, 117, 245

time and human experience, 15–17, 27, 184–85, 194

Tingua, 21, 44, 102, 103, 105; rivalry with, 113, 189, 203–5, 216

tocayo, 154

tourism, 206, 241; mountain climbing, 69

town meeting (cabildo abierto), 209, 211, 221

Trigger, Bruce, 207

tristeza, 48

Tumpa, 164

Tupamaros, the, 172

Turner, Victor, 217, 218

United States, the, 52

Urban Guard, 40, 41

Urgang, 13

Utcush, 146

Van den Berghe, Pierre, and George Primov, 51, 273

Velasco Alvarado, Juan, 84, 160

Velasco, Consuela Gonzalez de, 158

vivo, 105

Wallace, Anthony F. C., 15, 20, 187, 268

Walton, Nyle, 35, 36

warmi-mandarán, 181

waru, 221, 250–51

water, 77, 79, 97, 107, 240

Yanama Chico, 4, 62, 129

Yaravi Ancashino, 154, 156

Yungay, centrality of, 38, 42, 43, 45, 66, 67, 205–7, 216; grid plan of old, 47; history of, 33–41; the province and, 41–46; the refugee camps for, 21, 22, 101–6, 108, 160, 161, 208; renaming places in, 220; a social sketch of old, 39, 46–73. *See also* Yungay Norte

Yungay Norte, 102, 105, 106, 112, 115; provincial council at, 110; as refounded Yungay, 213, 224, 229, 240

Yungay province, 22, 41, 103

Yungay Sur, 102, 105, 189

Zavaleta Figueroa, Isaías, 7, 9